Gospel Light's

# BIG BOOK
## OF CAPTIVATING SKITS

AGE

| 1 | REAL LIFE |
| 2 | BIBLE SKITS |
| 3 | FOR THE |
| 4 | MODERN KID |

- 100 modern Bible-based teaching skits
- Indexed by Bible verse, Bible character and topic
- Great to use any time you have kids together
- Communicates Bible truths in a fun way

**Reproducible!**

Family Face-Off

**JAKE**        **ESAU**

CD-ROM INCLUDED

Gospel Light

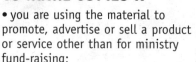
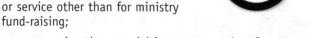
## EDITORIAL STAFF

**Founder,** Dr. Henrietta Mears • **Publisher Emeritus,** William T. Greig • **Publisher, Children's Curriculum and Resources,** Bill Greig III • **Senior Consulting Publisher,** Dr. Elmer L. Towns • **Senior Managing Editor,** Sheryl Haystead • **Senior Consulting Editor,** Wesley Haystead, M.S.Ed. • **Senior Editor, Biblical and Theological Issues,** Bayard Taylor, M.Div. • **Associate Editor,** Veronica Neal • **Contributing Editors,** Tom Boal, Noni Pendleton, Heather Kempton Wahl • **Art Directors,** Lenndy McCullough, Samantha Hsu • **Designer,** Rosanne Moreland

Some of this material was originally published in Preteen Curriculum *Planet 56* (Ventura, CA: Gospel Light, 1996, 1998), Preteen Curriculum *The Edge* (Ventura, CA: Gospel Light, 2005, 2006) and Gospel Light Vacation Bible School Curricula (Ventura, CA: Gospel Light).

Scripture quotations are taken from the *Holy Bible, New International Version®*. Copyright © 1973, 1978, 1984 by International Bible Society. Used by permission of Zondervan Publishing House. All rights reserved.

© 2006 Gospel Light, Ventura, CA 93006. All rights reserved. Printed in the U.S.A.

# Table of Contents

## Indices

# Using This Book

## Bringing Bible Stories to Life!

Drama activities in a classroom are valuable learning opportunities because of the process group members experience, not because of the quality of the final performance. Bible stories come alive when acted out, and Bible truth is seen to be relevant when applied to contemporary situations. In addition:

- Acting out a situation will push group members to think about the application of Bible truth to a real-life circumstance.

- Dramatic activities provide a unique opportunity to briefly step into another person's shoes and experience some of his or her attitudes and feelings.

## Copies of the Skits

Purchase of this book includes the right to make copies for those who will be involved in putting on the skits.

## Choosing a Skit

The skits may be used in a variety of ways:

- To **summarize** a Bible story;

- To **illustrate** a concept or topic;

- To **introduce** a Bible character;

- To **reinforce** a Bible story or life application.

The skits will be enjoyed in a variety of settings by students from **ages 8 through 12:**

- Sunday School, second hour or midweek programs;

- Camps;

- Large or small groups;

- Special events.

To help you find a skit that matches a topic or Bible story you will be studying, indexes list:

- **Bible characters** (p. 212);

- **Scripture references** (p. 209);

- **Topics** (p. 217).

## Getting Ready

After you've chosen and reproduced copies of the skit for the participants, here are some tips for preparing to lead the group:

- Familiarize yourself with the corresponding Bible story, if applicable, by reading the Scripture passage.

- Read the skit, noting any vocabulary or pronunciation help you will need to give your group.

- Adapt the script if needed by reducing or increasing the number of characters, adding a scene, etc.

## Practical Tips

One of the nicest things about skits is that they are easy to prepare. Skits are not big Broadway-type productions. They can be informal and spontaneous. They can be primped or polished to the hilt when the mood strikes. A lot or a little—it all depends on how you want to do it. Here are the basics to go on:

- Good acting is a plus, but it's not essential in order to have a positive experience. What is essential is that the lines are heard by the audience. The performers need to speak slowly and clearly with their mouths directed at the audience.

- It is not necessary for performers to memorize the script. Reading works just as well. Provide several highlighter pens for performers to mark their parts. You may give out the script ahead of time for the performer to practice. However, if you hand out the scripts ahead of time, bring extra copies on performance day, because someone will undoubtedly forget his or her copy.

- Practicing the skits ahead of time will be most important for younger groups and groups for whom English is a second language.

# Using Skits with Poor Readers

If your group includes students with poor reading skills or learning disabilities, or those for whom English is a second language, don't lose heart! With a little planning and some TLC, you can help poor readers gain badly needed confidence and liven up your classroom with Bible skits.

The following list of ideas can be adapted for use in any setting. Choose the techniques that best suit your group and resources.

## For Informal Presentations and Read-Throughs

- Highlight each character's lines on a separate copy of the script and add pronunciation pointers as needed.

- Have the entire group read through the skit in pairs or small groups before presenting the skit to the whole group.

- Give everyone in the group a script to follow as selected readers read aloud. Receiving information through more than one sense makes the drama more accessible. This technique also assists students who are better visual than aural learners. It can also ease performers' nerves by providing something other than the readers on which to focus.

- Use lots of visual aids and props.

- If a skit is particularly long or has long speeches, the teacher or leader should summarize a portion of the skit. Never feel obligated to perform a skit in its entirety; only use as much as your group can handle.

- Use a "jump-in" technique that gives readers control over how much they want to read: When a volunteer has read as much as he or she wants, another volunteer jumps in and continues reading. Or let each reader choose a helper to consult with whenever necessary. On an overhead projector or chalkboard, post a word bank or key with pronunciations and/or definitions to words the students might have trouble with. Before the group reading, review the words and locate them in the script with the group.

## For More Formal Presentations and Performances

- Assign a "drama coach" to each reader to provide one-on-one help in interpreting and learning lines. Coaches may be other students or an adult.

- The leader may read aloud all character parts before they're assigned. The leader should also discuss the tone of the skit, pronunciation and meaning of difficult words, and make suggestions for changes and word substitutions.

- To provide extra help, the leader may record each character part on a separate cassette to distribute to readers. Record each part twice, the first time speaking slowly and distinctly with no dramatic flair, the second time with dramatic flair so students hear how the lines should be delivered.

- For struggling readers, write out each sentence on a separate index card; this technique makes the job look smaller, and each job is an accomplishment.

- Hand out the script well in advance of the performance date; call and have the student read his or her part to you over the phone to practice.

- Give permission to improvise. Students who understand the sense of speech, and whose verbal skills exceed their reading skills, may communicate better if allowed to paraphrase.

# Old Testament

# Mrs. Bixby

### Characters: MRS. BIXBY; RACHEL; ANDREW

**Props:** Characters may wish to pantomime the use of props.

**Scene:** *Church classroom. RACHEL and ANDREW are helping MRS. BIXBY put candy in the gift boxes of clothing and food being donated as Christmas presents for refugees.*

**MRS. BIXBY:** *(Putting large shopping bags of candy on a table.)* Thank you both for offering to help me. This is certainly going to be a big job!

**RACHEL:** We don't mind. Besides, we get to spend time with you, our favorite teacher.

**MRS. BIXBY:** Favorite teacher, huh? Well, don't let this get out, but you are two of my favorite students.

**RACHEL:** *(Laughing.)* You say that to ALL of your students.

**MRS. BIXBY:** *(Laughs.)* I suppose I do. But I do enjoy spending time with you two. We've become very good friends.

**ANDREW:** Yeah. Hey, by the way, thanks for coming to my school play.

**MRS. BIXBY:** It was my pleasure. I was so proud of you. Well, enough chitchat. We need to get to work. It was so wonderful of Mr. Smith to donate all this candy to put in our boxes. I'm sure the children at the refugee center will really enjoy something special like this. *(She hands bags of candy to RACHEL and ANDREW.)* Now, I think we will have just enough for two in each box.

**RACHEL:** *(Opening her bag of candy.)* Ooo. Look at this! Chewy Chocolate Bars! I LOVE those!

**ANDREW:** You can't LOVE candy, Rachel. Don't you remember we learned about that?

**RACHEL:** *(Laughs.)* Oh yeah. OK. I really LIKE Chewy Chocolate Bars!

**ANDREW:** *(Opening his bag of candy.)* Well, I really like these Double Chocolate Fudge Drops. Do you have a favorite, Mrs. Bixby?

**MRS. BIXBY:** I think the Chunky Chocolate Peanut Butter Cups are my favorite.

*(MRS. BIXBY, RACHEL and ANDREW work for a while, putting candy into boxes.)*

**MRS. BIXBY:** Stuffing all this candy into the boxes is making me hungry. I've got some snacks for us in the kitchen. I'll go get them. *(She exits.)*

**ANDREW:** She's hungry! I would just love to eat a bag of these Fudge Drops!

**RACHEL:** I can hardly stand giving away all these Chewy Chocolate Bars. What would it hurt if I ate just one? I mean, who's going to notice? There's lots of candy here. No one would ever miss just one.

**ANDREW:** I don't know, Rachel. It doesn't seem right.

**RACHEL:** But what's really wrong with it? I'm just going to eat one. (RACHEL *takes a candy bar and eats it.*) Oh, this tastes so good!

**ANDREW:** Well, I suppose just one candy wouldn't hurt. (ANDREW *opens a bag of Fudge Drops and begins eating them.*) Oh yeah, these are my favorites!

**RACHEL:** (*Finished eating her candy.*) Oh, that was wonderful! Maybe just one more.

(RACHEL *and* ANDREW *eat several candy bars and bags of Fudge Drops.*)

**ANDREW:** Uh-oh.

**RACHEL:** What?

**ANDREW:** I think I ate too many. I'm feeling a little sick.

**RACHEL:** Yeah, me, too. In fact, I don't think I'll ever eat another candy bar.

**ANDREW:** Oh no! I hear Mrs. Bixby coming.

**RACHEL:** We'd better hide the evidence quick.

(RACHEL *and* ANDREW *start stuffing candy wrappers into each other's coat pockets, shoes, etc.*)

**ANDREW:** And don't say anything. Teachers can smell chocolate on your breath.

**MRS. BIXBY:** (*Entering with a plate of cookies, candy bars and small chocolate candies.*) And how are my hard workers doing?

**RACHEL:** (*Looking down at box.*) Fine.

**MRS. BIXBY:** I brought us some snacks. I even brought some of your favorite candies. Help yourself!

**ANDREW:** (*Looking down, trying to look busy.*) Um, no thanks.

**MRS. BIXBY:** Goodness. What's wrong with the two of you?

**RACHEL:** (*Covering mouth with hand.*) Nothing.

**ANDREW:** (*Turning away.*) Just working.

**MRS. BIXBY:** Do I smell chocolate? Have you been eating some of the candy?

**ANDREW:** No! (*A candy wrapper drops out of* ANDREW's *pocket.*)

**RACHEL:** (*To* ANDREW.) Oh, great! Now you've really blown it!

**MRS. BIXBY:** (*Tell what you think Mrs. Bixby said.*)

For the **real story** read Genesis 12:1-5; 15:1-7; 21:1-7

# Promised!

**Characters: ELIEZER,** a very old servant of Abe's; **ISAAC,** Abe's son, a teenager; **ABE,** God's friend, a very old man; **SARAH,** Isaac's mother, a very old woman

**Scene:** ISAAC *and* ELIEZER *are out under the stars on yet another quiet, starry night in Canaan.* ABE *and* SARAH *are in bed, listening through the wall of their tent.*

**ELIEZER:** Look at those stars, boy!

**ISAAC:** There sure are a lot of them. Look, there's that little group of seven.

**ELIEZER:** The Seven Sisters.

**ISAAC:** Why didn't I ever have any?

**ELIEZER:** What?

**ISAAC:** Sisters.

**ELIEZER:** Your parents didn't need any. Only needed you. You're the start.

**ISAAC:** Oh, right! Here I am, out here in nowhere. Nobody even knows I'm alive!

**ELIEZER:** Are you KIDDIN'? HE does!

**ISAAC:** He who?

**ELIEZER:** GOD's who! You're gonna have children and grandchildren and great-grandchildren... more of them than there are stars in the sky!

**ISAAC:** THAT'S how I'll be a star? I'm not gonna be famous?

**ELIEZER:** Sure! Everyone will know your story! Kids will be named after you!

**ISAAC:** Promise me?

**ELIEZER:** Sure!

**ABE:** *(Whispers.)* God promised ME!

**SARAH:** *(Whispers.)* Me, too. And it still makes me laugh!

**ELIEZER:** Y'know, my boy, I've been with your father a LONG time. I've seen him rescue your cousin, Lot. I've seen Sodom go up in smoke—what a cloud of dust that little city raised! I've seen him fight battles and talk to kings and shear big sheep that didn't want to be shorn—your pop's done it all! I've seen him out here under this very sky, on his face talking to God.

**ISAAC:** He stayed up past sundown just so he could talk to God? He's NEVER up that late nowadays!

**ABE:** *(Whispers.)* Who says I'm ASLEEP?

**SARAH:** *(Whispers.)* Hard to sleep when those two never stop talking!

**ELIEZER:** He wasn't all that young then either! But he did go to bed later then. I remember once when he was out here, talking to God. It was before you were born. He laughed so hard, he woke me up!

**ABE:** *(Whispers.)* Did I ever laugh! You two don't know the half of it!

**SARAH:** *(Whispers.)* I laughed, too. And Isaac STILL keeps me awake, like he did when he was a baby!

**ISAAC:** So he laughed because he didn't believe that promise about stars God made?

**ELIEZER:** Y'know, I can't rightly tell. I would never interrupt your pop when he was praying. But he sure must have thought it was funny that God was going to keep that promise!

**ABE:** *(Whispers.)* It DID seem funny at the time! Unbelievable!

**SARAH:** *(Whispers.)* But God got the last laugh. He did what He promised! Now if our "promise" would just quiet down so we could sleep.

**ISAAC:** So, when I have a wife, we're going to have lots and lots of children? Wait a minute—where AM I gonna get a wife out here in the middle of nowhere? If that's how I'm gonna be a star, I can't exactly do it all by MYSELF, y'know.

**ELIEZER:** You're willing to share your star status with a wife, eh? Now, isn't that generous of you! Well, you know what your pop would say—

**ELIEZER & ISAAC:** "God will provide."

**ISAAC:** Promise?

**ABE:** *(Whispers.)* Of COURSE it's a promise! I heard it MYSELF!

**SARAH:** *(Whispers.)* We DO need to think about this wife business, Abe. Our little Isaac is growing up!

**ELIEZER:** Sure it's a promise! God certainly wouldn't have gone to all this trouble, bringing your pop out here and sending him on all these adventures, just to forget to find you a wife! That would put a real kink in that "stars of the heavens" promise.

**ISAAC:** And He ALWAYS keeps His promises?

**ELIEZER:** You betcha!

**SARAH:** *(Whispers.)* He promised me, too! I remember.

**ABE:** *(Yells.)* Of COURSE God always keeps His promises! Now go to bed, you two! We'll talk about this "wife and stars" business in the morning!

**ISAAC:** Uh, I guess he wasn't asleep!

**ELIEZER:** I can PROMISE you that!

**For the real story read Genesis 13**

# Lot's Choice

**Characters: LUD,** one of Lot's herdsmen; **LOT,** Abraham's nephew; **ABRAHAM,** a man who followed God's instructions to move to a new land

**Scene:** *On a mountain overlooking the Jordan Valley.*

**LUD:** *(LUD enters and stomps over to* LOT.*)* I have had it!

**LOT:** What's the problem this time?

**LUD:** It's your uncle's herdsmen. They are deliberately getting their herds mixed up with ours.

**LOT:** I don't think it's deliberate. There just isn't enough space for all of us.

**LUD:** You can say that again!

**LOT:** I don't think it's deliberate?

**LUD:** No, I meant the part about there not being enough space.

**LOT:** Ah.

**LUD:** Too bad we can't just lose those herdsmen of your uncle's.

**LOT:** What do you mean?

**LUD:** I could tell them I've found a GREAT place with lots of water and food for the animals.

**LOT:** If this place is so great, why don't we ALL go there?

**LUD:** There really isn't such a place. I just tell them that. Then I take them way, way out in the desert, so far they can't get back, and then I leave them.

**LOT:** And how are you going to get back if they can't?

**LUD:** OK, bad idea.

**ABRAHAM:** *(Enters.)* Good afternoon, Lot!

**LOT:** Good afternoon, Uncle Abraham.

**ABRAHAM:** I hear from my herdsmen that our herdsmen are having some troubles.

**LUD:** Don't believe a word! It wasn't our fault!

**ABRAHAM:** I didn't say it was your fault.

**LUD:** Oh yeah! Well, they started it!

**ABRAHAM:** Started what?

**LUD:** The fight! That's what you're here about, isn't it?

**LOT:** *(To* LUD.*)* Fight? You didn't say anything about a fight.

**LUD:** It was just a little skirmish between 50 of their guys and us.

**LOT:** *(Groans.)*

**ABRAHAM:** No. I'm not talking about the fight. I'm talking about the problem that caused the fight. There just doesn't seem to be enough water and food for both our herds.

**LUD:** You can say that again.

**ABRAHAM:** I'm not talking about the fight?

**LUD:** No, the part about there not being enough water and food.

**ABRAHAM:** Ah. Well, I think I've come up with a solution.

**LUD:** Hey! That isn't fair.

**LOT:** *(To LUD.)* Silence! How do you know it isn't fair? You haven't heard his idea yet!

**ABRAHAM:** There'd be plenty of land and water if we weren't trying to use it together.

**LOT:** What?

**LUD:** You've got a lot of nerve sending us out into the desert!

**LOT:** *(To LUD.)* Silence! Or you will be an UNEMPLOYED herdsman! *(To ABRAHAM.)* What are you suggesting, Uncle?

**ABRAHAM:** I'm suggesting we split up. You go one way, and I'll go the other.

**LOT:** Split up? But you're my family! We've been together since my father died.

**ABRAHAM:** Do you have a better solution?

**LOT:** No. But where do you want me to go?

**ABRAHAM:** Lot, there is plenty of land out there. You pick where you want to go, and I'll go in the other direction.

**LOT:** Well, OK. Hm. I'll pick...

**LUD:** *(Whispers to LOT.)* Pick the good side. Pick the good side.

**LOT:** *(To LUD.)* The good side?

**LUD:** *(To LOT.)* Yeah, the land around the Jordan River. It has lots of water and grass, and it's beautiful!

**LOT:** *(To ABRAHAM.)* You're serious about this? I pick whatever I want? You won't get mad?

**ABRAHAM:** I won't get mad. You pick where you want. God will provide us both with plenty.

**LOT:** Well, then I pick the land by the Jordan River.

**LUD:** *(Shouts.)* Yes!!

**ABRAHAM:** Very well. I'll move my herds in the other direction. Good-bye Lot, and good luck! *(ABRAHAM exits.)*

**LOT:** Good-bye, Uncle!

**LUD:** *(To LOT.)* See? What did I tell you? My plan worked!

**LOT:** *(Grinning.)* No. MY plan worked.

**For the real story read Genesis 25:19-34**

# In a Stew!

**Characters: ENOCH (E-nohk)**, servant of Isaac; **JACOB (JAY-kuhb)**, son of Isaac; **ESAU (E-sahw)**, twin brother of Jacob, but he was born first!

**Props:** Characters may wish to pantomime the use of props.

**Scene:** *Cooking area of* ISAAC's *camping site.* JACOB *is stirring stew in a pot.*

**ENOCH:** *(Enters, sniffing the air.)* What is that wonderful smell?

**JACOB:** Stew. And no, you can't have any.

**ENOCH:** I didn't ask for any. What kind of stew is it?

**JACOB:** Lentil.

**ENOCH:** *(Looking in pot.)* You have quite a bit there. It wouldn't hurt you to share a little.

**JACOB:** I have important plans for it.

**ENOCH:** Like what?

**JACOB:** That's none of your business.

**ENOCH:** I see. Well, I'll just go whisper a word of this in your father's ear. *(Starts to exit.)*

**JACOB:** Hold it!

**ENOCH:** Yes?

**JACOB:** Fine. You can have a couple of bites. *(Dishes up stew from pot.)* When my father dies, you're going to find yourself unemployed, you blackmailer.

**ENOCH:** That will be up to your brother, Esau, won't it? After all, he's the one who will inherit everything. He's the one who has the birthright.

**JACOB:** Humph! That birthright rule is stupid. Why should Esau get most of everything just because he was born first? I'm his twin!

**ENOCH:** Traditions are traditions. You can't change traditions.

**JACOB:** We'll see about that.

**ENOCH:** Do I smell a plan brewing?

**JACOB:** Not that I'd tell you about.

**ENOCH:** I see. Well, I'll just be on my way to see your father.

**JACOB:** Why are you going to see him?

**ENOCH:** I know you, Jacob. You'll find a way to get that birthright from Esau. I'm just going to talk to your father to make sure I'll still have employment. Or a promotion to Most Trusted Servant would be nice.

**JACOB:** I'll think about it.

**ENOCH:** Better think fast. Here comes Esau now. I'd sure hate for your father to show up and mess up your plans.

**JACOB:** OK. Fine. You have a job. I promise.

**ENOCH:** Thank you, my master.

**ESAU:** *(Entering.)* Something smells mighty good in here, younger brother.

**JACOB:** Yes, I've made some lentil stew as a surprise for Mom.

**ESAU:** Good! I'm starving! Your lentil stew is the best in the world. Fill up my bowl to the brim.

**JACOB:** I don't think you heard me correctly. I said it's for Mom.

**ESAU:** Mom won't mind sharing.

**JACOB:** Yes, but I will.

**ESAU:** Look, Jacob, I'm tired! I've been out hunting.

**JACOB:** Catch anything?

**ESAU:** NO! And I haven't had anything to eat either! Now, what'll it take to get some food out of you?

**JACOB:** Hm, let me think about this.

**ENOCH:** *(To ESAU.)* Run fast, Esau, before you do something foolish and lose something valuable.

**ESAU:** Who are you to call me foolish? Right now there is nothing I wouldn't give for some of that stew. *(To JACOB.)* What kind of a brother are you, anyway, to make MY favorite stew and then give it to Mom?

**JACOB:** Lentil is YOUR favorite kind of stew? Oh dear, silly me, I always get so confused.

**ENOCH:** *(To self.)* I don't know which brother is worse!

**ESAU:** *(To JACOB.)* Look, Jacob, I'm starving. You've got food. I'm the eldest. So I'm ordering you to give me the food.

**JACOB:** You are no older than me!

**ESAU:** I'm the one with the birthright.

**JACOB:** Yes. You are. You have the birthright. I have the food.

**ENOCH:** I can see where this is going.

**JACOB and ESAU:** Will you be quiet!

**ESAU:** You want the birthright? Fine, you can have the birthright, and I'll take the food.

**JACOB:** Do you swear it?

**ESAU:** I give my oath. I swear. I renounce. YOU have the birthright. Now give ME some food.

**JACOB:** Gladly, dear brother, gladly. *(Hands ESAU a bowl.)*

**ENOCH:** Wait until Isaac hears about this one! *(Starts to exit.)*

**JACOB:** Wait!

**ENOCH:** Why?

**JACOB:** I couldn't have my Most Trusted Servant leaving my side, could I?

**ENOCH:** Most Trusted Servant? No, I suppose not.

**ESAU:** *(Eating.)* This is really good! Best you've ever made!

**JACOB:** *(To ENOCH.)* When do you think he'll realize what he's done?

**ENOCH:** Knowing him? Not until after he's eaten his fourth or fifth bowl of stew.

For the **real story** read Genesis 27:1-45

# Family Discussions

**Characters: SHIBAH (SHEE-bah),** Enoch's wife and Rebekah's servant; **ENOCH,** servant of Isaac; **ISAAC,** head of the family and father of Esau and Jacob; **REBEKAH,** Isaac's wife; **ESAU,** Isaac's son and Jacob's twin brother

**Props:** Characters may wish to pantomime the use of props.

**Scene:** *Cooking area.* ENOCH *is sitting, eating food.*

**SHIBAH:** *(Enters, obviously in distress.)* Oh, dear. Oh, dear.

**ENOCH:** Yes, love of my life.

**SHIBAH:** *(Turns angrily to* ENOCH.*)* YOU! You said our future was set. You said Jacob had named you his Most Trusted Servant. You said...

**ENOCH:** Yeah, so?

**SHIBAH:** Have you no idea what has happened?

**ENOCH:** Rebekah made a really great meal. Isaac's favorite, if I'm not mistaken.

**SHIBAH:** It's Isaac's favorite, all right. That's why my mistress made it for Jacob to serve to Isaac.

**ENOCH:** Well, that's just plain silly. Why would she do that? I mean, I told you that Esau was going to make a meal for Isaac. Look, there's some of it over there.

**SHIBAH:** And why was Esau making the meal?

**ENOCH:** To receive his father's blessing. *(Stops and thinks.)* Jacob's done it again, hasn't he?

**SHIBAH:** Yes, Jacob has tricked Isaac into giving him the blessing instead of to Esau.

**ENOCH:** Now Jacob has the blessing and his inheritance! As his Most Trusted Servant, I should do very well.

**SHIBAH:** And where is your master?

**ENOCH:** How would I know where he is? I don't watch him day and night.

**SHIBAH:** Well, you should!

*(*ISAAC *and* REBEKAH *enter.* REBEKAH *is leading the blind* ISAAC.*)*

**ISAAC:** Oh, what have I done? Esau, my favorite son, has nothing. No birthright, no inheritance. That scoundrel Jacob has taken off with everything! I knew that boy would amount to no good!

**REBEKAH:** At least he hasn't married local girls like Esau did. Those two women really get on my nerves.

**ISAAC:** That's true. Esau did not marry well. But at least he's no liar like his brother, Jacob.

**REBEKAH:** How can you stand up for Esau when he sold his birthright for a bowl of stew?

**ISAAC:** You always stick up for Jacob. You are always making excuses for him. Maybe if we'd been stricter with him, he wouldn't have turned out so badly!

**REBEKAH:** There's nothing wrong with Jacob!

**ISAAC:** I'm dying and he leaves town. And you say there's nothing wrong with him. *(REBEKAH and ISAAC exit.)*

**ENOCH:** *(To SHIBAH.)* He left town?

**SHIBAH:** Yes, my ambitious husband, he's left town! When Isaac dies, what do you think will happen to us?

**ENOCH:** I dread to think.

**ESAU:** *(Entering.)* How could my father have mistaken Jacob for me?

**ENOCH:** Well, your father IS blind.

**ESAU:** All he had to do was touch him. Look at me! I have hair on my arms and hands. My brother Jacob is COMPLETELY hairless on his arms and hands. He looks like a baby!

**SHIBAH:** I believe he wore goat hair on his arms and legs.

**ESAU:** Goat hair? OK. So maybe he could fool my father's touch. But couldn't my father tell it wasn't my voice?

**ENOCH:** Well, he IS pretty old.

**SHIBAH:** *(To ESAU.)* I understand your father asked several times if it was really you, or if the man before him was Esau, and Jacob told him yes.

**ESAU:** That liar! *(To SHIBAH.)* How did you know?

**SHIBAH:** Oh, I just heard rumors.

**ESAU:** Rumors! Ha! If someone heard, then someone saw! And they didn't stop it!

**ENOCH:** This is just awful, my master! Please let me help you find this person who allowed you to suffer so.

**ESAU:** I thought you were on Jacob's side.

**ENOCH:** I am your FATHER'S servant. I try to serve ALL the members of his family faithfully.

**ESAU:** Good! You can serve me! The first thing we need to do is find my brother, Jacob! He's gonna pay for this one. *(ESAU exits.)*

**ENOCH:** *(To SHIBAH.)* So how DID you know what Isaac said?

**SHIBAH:** Who do you think helped Rebekah tie the goatskins on Jacob?

**ENOCH:** You? *(SHIBAH nods her head.)* How long ago did Jacob leave?

**SHIBAH:** Not long.

**ENOCH:** Maybe if we hurry, we can catch up to him.

# A Greek Tragedy*: Joseph's Tale

**Characters: CHORUS** (In an ancient Greek drama the chorus acted as narrators and sometimes as a character's conscience.) Two or more students read in unison; **JOSEPH,** an enthusiastic, happy, seventeen-year-old Bible-times hero; **BROTHERS,** Joseph's ten bitter and jealous brothers. (Ben, the eleventh brother, loved Joseph.) Two or more students read in unison; **BIBLICAL AUTHORITY,** the one who makes sure the tragedy writer gets it right; **POTIPHAR,** a rich official for the Pharaoh (or King) of Egypt

**Scene:** *An empty stage. (The ancient Greeks didn't use scenery.)*

**CHORUS:** Today we present for you the tragedy of Joseph's life.

**JOSEPH:** Tragedy of my life? My life's not a tragedy! Just look at this great coat my dad gave me. And I had this really neat dream last night! The moon and the sun...

**BROTHERS:** ... and the stars all bowed down before him. Look at him! He thinks he's greater than we are. We've got to do something about Joseph!

**CHORUS:** Hey, you guys are skipping ahead! Our part is first! There once lived a man named Jacob, and Jacob had twelve sons, but his favorite son was the next to the youngest one.

**BROTHERS:** Oh, yeah? Well we can rhyme, too. We have thought of a devious plan to rid ourselves of this irritating young man! When he comes to see us, and he will, we'll kill him by throwing him in this well.

**CHORUS:** But instead of killing him, the brothers decided to sell Joseph as a slave.

**BROTHERS:** We make more money that way, and we won't have to break any commandments.

**BIBLICAL AUTHORITY:** Psst. Guys, the 10 Commandments haven't been written yet.

**BROTHERS:** Don't bother us with technicalities. We did something about that Joseph!

**CHORUS:** Poor, poor Joseph, who used to be free, was now tied up and bound for slavery.

**JOSEPH:** Well, this is a real bummer. I didn't even get to tell Dad good-bye. But as long as God is with me I have nothing to fear.

**CHORUS:** Joseph was sold for a good fee to an Egyptian named Potiphar.

**JOSEPH:** This is certainly a nasty development. I hardly had any chores at home—

---

* tragedy=having a sad or disastrous ending

now it's work, work, work all the time. And if I don't work, I could get beaten.

**POTIPHAR:** That's right, so quit your yapping and get to work!

**JOSEPH:** If it's work you want me to do, then I'm going to do my best job! That's what God would want!

**CHORUS:** Joseph worked very hard. In fact, Potiphar was really impressed.

**POTIPHAR:** Joseph, my boy, I've been really pleased with your work, and I'd like to give you a promotion.

**JOSEPH:** Freedom would be better, but a promotion is nice.

**POTIPHAR:** Huh? Er, yes, well... Son, I'm going to put you in charge of my entire household. That means you'll be the boss in this house, ah, except for over me...um, and my wife.

**JOSEPH:** Yes, sir. I'll do my best!

**BROTHERS:** We can't believe this! There he is, Mr. Goody-goody doing great again! We wish someone would do something about Joseph!

**BIBLICAL AUTHORITY:** Psst, guys, actually Joseph's brothers had NO idea about what had happened to Joseph.

**BROTHERS:** Oh, sorry. *(Whisper.)* But we wish someone would do something about Joseph.

**CHORUS:** Potiphar wasn't the only one who was impressed with Joseph, Potiphar's wife was also impressed!

**JOSEPH:** She must like my great work!

**BIBLICAL AUTHORITY:** Psst, it says here in the Bible she thought you were really handsome.

**JOSEPH:** Handsome? Really? Wow! That's great! Hey, wait a minute. This could be a problem.

**CHORUS:** Uh-huh.

**JOSEPH:** She's married—to my master! I've got to set her straight on this.

**CHORUS:** Poor, poor Joseph. When he refused Potiphar's wife, she got angry and told Potiphar a lie about Joseph.

**POTIPHAR:** He did WHAT?!?

**CHORUS:** Potiphar believed his wife's lie and had Joseph thrown into prison.

**BROTHERS:** Alright!!!

**BIBLICAL AUTHORITY:** Guys...

**BROTHERS:** Yeah, yeah, we aren't supposed to know. *(Whisper.)* But someone did something about Joseph. Maybe now he won't be so happy and enthusiastic. Maybe now he'll be bitter, like us!

**CHORUS:** Poor, poor Joseph!

**JOSEPH:** Well, this IS a nasty turn of events. But I know God is with me. And I'll do my best!

**BROTHERS:** *(Groan.)*

**For the real story read Genesis 43–45**

# A Greek Comedy: Joseph's Brothers

**Characters: CHORUS** (In an ancient Greek drama the chorus acted as narrators.) Two or more students read in unison; **JOSEPH**, a Bible-times hero; **BROTHERS**, Joseph's ten bitter and jealous brothers. Two or more students read in unison; **JUDAH,** one of those ten older, and hopefully wiser, brothers; **BENJAMIN,** the youngest brother—the only one who loved Joseph; **BIBLICAL AUTHORITY,** the one who makes sure the comedy writer gets it right!

**Scene:** *An empty stage. (The ancient Greeks didn't use scenery.)*

**CHORUS:** Today we present for you the comedy of the lives of Joseph's brothers.

**BROTHERS:** Comedy?!? There's nothing funny about our lives! Our father has been REALLY depressed since Joseph died.

**CHORUS:** Joseph didn't die—you sold him as a slave.

**BROTHERS:** Ssh! Dad doesn't know that! Anyway, now there's this terrible drought! If we don't get rain for our crops and animals soon, we are all going to die!

**CHORUS:** Meanwhile in Egypt, Pharaoh has a very smart governor. This guy was storing grain for seven years. So there was plenty to eat in Egypt.

**BROTHERS:** Really? Maybe we should go have a talk with this guy. A trip to Egypt! This'll be great! Let's go talk to Dad!

**BIBLICAL AUTHORITY:** Actually, the Bible says it was Jacob's idea for his sons to go to Egypt.

**BROTHERS:** Oh, right. *(Whining.)* Aw, Dad, do we really have to go?

**CHORUS:** When the brothers arrived in Egypt, Pharaoh's governor should have seemed familiar to them, but they didn't recognize him.

**BROTHERS:** OK, look—we need some food...

**BIBLICAL AUTHORITY:** Psst! Guys, the Bible says the brothers bowed down before the governor with their faces to the ground.

**BROTHERS:** You're kidding?!? *(On knees, bowing.)* Please great ruler, have pity on us and sell us food to eat.

**CHORUS:** Pharaoh's governor recognized the men bowing before him, and he remembered a dream he'd had many years before.

**BROTHERS:** This guy had a dream about us? What an honor!

**CHORUS:** Yes, it was something about the sun, moon and stars bowing down.

**BROTHERS:** Hey, that's the same as Joseph's dream!

**CHORUS:** You're SO clever. Anyway, the governor wanted to test the ten brothers to see if they had become less bitter and selfish with age.

**JOSEPH:** You're spies! You've come to find out the weak points in our defenses!

**BROTHERS:** No! No! Honest! We are just poor shepherds in need of food. Our poor old father sent us here to buy food from you. See, here's our money.

**JOSEPH:** Are you ALL of your father's sons?

**BROTHERS:** Um, no. We have a younger brother at home, with our dad. And..., well, we have a brother who died, or, at least we believe he's dead.

**JOSEPH:** Prove your story! Send someone back to get this younger brother. Or better yet, I'll keep one of you here in my prison until you return with your younger brother.

**BROTHERS:** *(Stand.)* We're in big trouble, now! Dad'll never let us take Benjamin with us!

**CHORUS:** And so, Joseph's brothers, minus one, returned home and told their father what had happened. The drought continued, and before long the family needed food again. Understandably, Jacob really didn't want to trust his precious son to his brothers...

**BROTHERS:** Hey! We've changed!

**CHORUS:** We'll see. When the brothers returned to Egypt, the governor seemed pleased. He gave them food and then sent them on their way home. But the brothers hadn't gone far when the governor's servant stopped them. He searched the food sacks and found the governor's silver cup in Benjamin's sack.

**BROTHERS:** Benjamin! What have you done?

**BENJAMIN:** I haven't done anything! I don't know how it got there!

**CHORUS:** The steward said that the rest could go, but Benjamin had to return and become a slave.

**BROTHERS:** We thought this was supposed to be a comedy. This isn't very funny!

**CHORUS:** We find it VERY funny—after what YOU did to Joseph.

**BROTHERS:** Oh, yeah. Poor Joseph.

**CHORUS:** The brothers returned to the governor's house. Judah knelt down before the governor and pleaded with him.

**JUDAH:** *(Kneeling.)* Please, take me as your slave instead and let Benjamin go.

**BIBLICAL AUTHORITY:** This is the good part, guys!

**BROTHERS:** We could use a good part.

**BIBLICAL AUTHORITY:** *(To* CHORUS.*)* Well, tell them.

**CHORUS:** Joseph, the governor, couldn't take it anymore. It appeared the brothers really HAD changed. Joseph was so happy, he started to cry.

**BROTHERS:** *(To* JOSEPH.*)* You're Joseph?

**JOSEPH:** Yes, I am your brother Joseph!

**BROTHERS:** Your dream came true about us bowing down to you. Guess the joke's on us.

**JOSEPH:** Brothers, this has been no joke. God took all the bad you did and made it work for His plans. Because of you, I was able to help you, our dad, and everyone in Egypt make it through this drought without starving.

**BROTHERS:** Wow!

**For the real story read Exodus 2:1-10**

# Boy in a Basket

**Characters: FATHER,** an Israelite father; **MOTHER,** an Israelite mother; **MIRIAM,** their daughter; **PRINCESS,** Pharaoh's daughter; **MAID 1, MAID 2, MAID 3,** three maids of Princess; **NARRATOR**

**Props:** Characters may pantomime props.

**Scene One:** *Home of* MOSES' *family.*

**NARRATOR:** Our story begins in ancient Egypt, near the banks of the Nile River. The Egyptian Pharaoh is worried that the Israelites he keeps as slaves will one day rise up and take over. So he has issued a terrible order: Kill all the Israelite baby boys! But one brave family has kept their infant son hidden for three months.

*(FATHER paces frantically; MOTHER calmly weaves a basket.)*

**FATHER:** This can't go on any longer. I can't take the stress.

**MOTHER:** The stress?

**FATHER:** Yes, the stress! Will the baby cry? Will Pharaoh's soldiers hear?

**MOTHER:** Oh, THAT stress.

**FATHER:** Yes! That stress! Hiding him here is the WORST plan ever! Something must be done!

**MOTHER:** I agree.

**FATHER:** I don't believe this. I'm going crazy and you're sitting there, calmly weaving reeds. What are you weaving?

**MOTHER:** A basket.

**FATHER:** You think a basket will keep him safe? The stress has made you even crazier than I am!

**MOTHER:** I'm not crazy. Look, we can't keep him quiet forever. Sooner or later, Pharaoh's men will hear him.

**FATHER:** And when they find we have a baby boy, they'll kill us AND him.

**MOTHER:** But what if they don't find a baby here? What if instead of trusting in our ability to hide the baby, we trust God instead?

**FATHER:** Isn't that what we've been doing?

**MOTHER:** Yes... but not fully. Here's my plan. I weave a basket.

**FATHER:** To stay busy?

**MOTHER:** Listen! I cover it with tar to make it waterproof and put the baby inside.

**FATHER:** So the baby won't get wet when it rains?

**MOTHER:** No. So it will float on the river.

**FATHER:** Float on the river! Where do you plan for it to go?

**MOTHER:** That's up to God. We simply trust that God has a plan for the baby.

**FATHER:** And I thought the OTHER plan was bad... IF the basket doesn't sink, and IF the crocodiles don't get him, it's only a matter of time before Pharaoh's men find him and kill him!

**MOTHER:** Don't you think we can trust God with our baby?

**FATHER:** *(Reluctantly.)* Okay, maybe you're right. But I'm likely to go crazy, not knowing what will happen to our son.

**MOTHER:** So would I. But I have an idea.

**FATHER:** What is it?

**MOTHER:** Our daughter Miriam can help me take the basket to the river. Then she will hide, see what happens and come home to tell us.

**FATHER:** Well, at least we'll know what happens to him. But it's so...difficult.

**Scene Two:** *Nile River.*

**NARRATOR:** Later that day, a young girl hides in the reeds, anxiously waiting to see what will happen to her baby brother.

**MIRIAM:** *(To herself.)* Miriam, keep that baby quiet! Miriam, get me some reeds! Miriam, watch over that baby in the basket! Watch him do WHAT? Get captured by Pharaoh's men, or eaten by crocodiles? *(Sees PRINCESS and MAIDS approaching.)* Oh, no! Pharaoh's daughter!

**PRINCESS:** Ooooh! I can't wait for a nice bath in the Nile! The squishy mud, the cool water...

**MAID 1:** *(Whispering.)* The snapping crocodiles.

**MAID 2:** *(Whispering.)* The swirling currents.

**MAID 3:** *(Whispering.)* The biting insects.

**PRINCESS:** What was that?

**MAIDS:** *(Together.)* Nothing, your highness!

**MIRIAM:** *(To herself.)* Maybe she won't see the basket!

**PRINCESS:** *(Pointing off stage right.)* Is that a basket floating behind those reeds? Bring it here!

**MAID 1:** *(Crosses stage right, peering offstage.)* It's just a soggy old basket. Someone as wealthy and powerful as you must have THOUSANDS of baskets nicer than that one!

**MIRIAM:** *(To herself.)* Okay, she's SEEN the basket. But maybe she won't want it!

**PRINCESS:** I said, "Bring it here!"

**MIRIAM:** *(To herself.)* Okay, so she WANTS

the basket. But maybe she won't open it? Maybe the baby won't cry?

*(MAID 1 picks up basket and brings it to the PRINCESS.)*

**PRINCESS:** *(Opening basket.)* Look! It's a baby! And he's crying! *(MIRIAM shrugs and rolls her eyes.)*

**MAID 1:** *(Sticking fingers in ears.)* He sure has a good set of lungs on him!

**PRINCESS:** Poor little guy must be hungry. *(Hands basket to MAID 1.)* Nurse him!

**MAID 1:** But I haven't had a baby. I can't nurse him! *(Hands basket to MAID 2.)* Here, YOU nurse him.

**MAID 2:** I can't nurse him, either. *(Hands basket to MAID 3.)* Here, YOU nurse him.

**MAID 3:** Well, I can't nurse him, either!

**MIRIAM:** *(To herself.)* Oh, brother! *(Stepping out of reeds.)* Um, your highness? Um... I could... if you wanted—

**PRINCESS:** Speak up, girl! What is it?

**MIRIAM:** Would you like me to find an Israelite woman to nurse the baby for you?

**PRINCESS:** Yes, go!

**NARRATOR:** A short time later, Miriam returns with her mother.

**MIRIAM:** This lady says she'd be happy to help you with the baby!

**PRINCESS:** *(Handing baby to MOTHER.)* Take this baby and nurse him for me, and I will pay you.

**MOTHER:** Yes, your highness! I will!

*(MIRIAM and MOTHER walk away, carrying the baby and the basket.)*

**MIRIAM:** Mother, that was the BEST plan!

**MOTHER:** Trusting God is ALWAYS the best plan, Miriam.

For the **real story** read Exodous 3–4:17

# A Leader for God?

**Characters: MOSES,** God's newly appointed leader of the Hebrews; **AARON,** Moses' brother

**Scene:** *The mountain of Horeb.*

**AARON:** Moses! Moses!

**MOSES:** Aaron, is that you?

**AARON:** No, it's my twin brother.

**MOSES:** Aaron, you don't have a twin. I'm the only brother you've got.

**AARON:** Such a genius. Look, I got a message to meet you here.

**MOSES:** Yes, Aaron. I've seen God! And talked with Him!

**AARON:** You SAW God and you're still alive to tell about it? R-i-i-ght.

**MOSES:** Well, actually, what I saw was a burning bush.

**AARON:** You think God is a burning bush? R-i-i-ght.

**MOSES:** God isn't a burning bush, Aaron, that's just the way He got my attention!

**AARON:** R-i-i-ght. So you talked to this burning bush...

**MOSES:** Yes, and God told me...

**AARON:** Hold it! This burning bush talked?

**MOSES:** It wasn't really a burning bush. It was God.

**AARON:** How do you know?

**MOSES:** Because, well, the bush didn't burn up, and besides, He said He was.

**AARON:** And you believed a talking bush? R-i-i-ght.

**MOSES:** He said He was the God of our father and of Abraham and of Jacob. He's the God who promised to always be with us.

**AARON:** Did you ask Him His name?

**MOSES:** He said it was "I AM WHO I AM."

**AARON:** *(Gulps.)* What did I AM WHO I AM want you to do?

**MOSES:** He wants me to go to Pharaoh and demand that he release the Hebrew slaves!

**AARON:** YOU? Who's going to believe YOU?

**MOSES:** Well, I asked Him the same question.

**AARON:** You QUESTIONED God and lived? R-i-i-ght. What did He say?

**MOSES:** He showed me three awesome ways to prove what I was doing was from God.

**AARON:** Like what?

**MOSES:** If I throw this stick on the ground, it becomes a snake.

**AARON:** A SNAKE? R-i-i-ght.

**MOSES:** Then if I pick the snake up by the tail...

**AARON:** What fool would pick up a snake by the TAIL? You'd get bitten.

**MOSES:** No, I won't, because it will become a stick again.

**AARON:** R-i-i-ght.

**MOSES:** Then if I put my hand inside my cloak it becomes leprous.

**AARON:** Why would anyone want to get leprosy*? That's a horrible disease! No one would want to be around you!

**MOSES:** Aaron! Calm down! When I put my hand back inside my cloak, it becomes healthy again.

**AARON:** Well, I guess that WOULD be pretty impressive.

**MOSES:** And He said if people still didn't believe me, I was to go to the Nile to get water in a jug and then pour the water on the ground and it'll turn into blood!

**AARON:** Blood! Yuck!

**MOSES:** Don't you see? It will prove to those Egyptians that our God is the only God and that their god of the Nile is just a fake.

**AARON:** I think it'll take more than a few miracles to get Pharaoh to give up all his slaves. But what happens next?

**MOSES:** I lead the people out of Egypt.

**AARON:** You? A leader? R-i-i-ght. YOU'VE been hiding out in the desert for 40 years!

**MOSES:** I know. I tried to tell God I wasn't much of a leader, but He insisted on me.

**AARON:** You ARGUED with God and lived? R-i-i-ght.

**MOSES:** I just pointed out I wasn't much of a speaker.

**AARON:** You've got that right! You meet a stranger and you get so nervous you forget your name.

**MOSES:** And I pointed out that I'm sort of a nobody, so who'd listen to me?

**AARON:** Right again. You've got "insecure" written all over you. Not much in the way of leadership material.

**MOSES:** Well, God came up with a plan for a way I could talk to Pharaoh.

**AARON:** So, what's the plan?

**MOSES:** You're going to speak for me.

**AARON:** ME???

**MOSES:** R-i-i-ght.

---

*Leprosy—a serious skin disease that causes loss of feeling and many deformities.

**For the real story read Exodus 6–12:42**

# Great Wise Man??

**Characters: NARRATOR; PHARAOH,** king of Egypt; **GUARD,** one of Pharaoh's bodyguards; **HIRAM,** an Israelite fleeing from Egypt; **MOSES,** a leader of the Israelites; **SERVANT,** a servant of Pharaoh

**NARRATOR:** For months, Moses had been trying to get the Pharaoh of Egypt to free the Israelite slaves. Moses warned Pharaoh that God would punish Egypt if Pharaoh did not free the Israelites. It took 10 plagues, including the death of his firstborn son, before Pharaoh finally agreed to let the Israelites go.

**ACT ONE: The Morning After**

**Scene:** PHARAOH's *palace in Egypt.*

**PHARAOH:** *(Enters sleepily.)* Guards! Where are my guards?

**GUARD:** Yes, oh Pharaoh, oh Mighty Warrior, Ray of the Sun.

**PHARAOH:** What happened to "Great Wise Man"?

**GUARD:** Um, well, sire—

**PHARAOH:** Oh, never mind. Why don't I hear the banging of hammers, the chipping of stone, the cracks of whips, the groans of slaves building my buildings?

**GUARD:** Oh Pharaoh, oh Mighty Warrior, Ray of the Sun—

**PHARAOH:** You forgot "Great Wise Man" again.

**GUARD:** Yes, well, um—

**PHARAOH:** Never mind. Answer my question!

**GUARD:** Does not my Pharaoh remember that he freed the Israelite slaves?

**PHARAOH:** Freed the slaves? Why on earth would I do that?

**GUARD:** Because of all the plagues the Israelites' God sent. Does not my Pharaoh remember the death of his firstborn son?

**PHARAOH:** Of course I remember! But how am I going to get all those buildings built without a bunch of slaves? Go get them back!

**GUARD:** Does my Pharaoh think that is truly wise, considering all the locusts that were sent during the eighth plague?

**PHARAOH:** Who are you to question my wisdom? Am I not the Great Wise Man?

**GUARD:** Well, um—

**PHARAOH:** Oh, never mind. Go get those slaves back!

**GUARD:** Yes, oh great Pharaoh, oh Mighty Warrior, oh Ray of the Sun. *(Exits.)*

**PHARAOH:** He keeps forgetting "Great Wise Man." Hm, I'd better go with them if I want this done right. *(Exits.)*

## ACT TWO: In the Desert

**Scene:** *On the shore of the Red Sea.*

**HIRAM:** *(Enters with* MOSES.*)* Moses, I think there's something I should point out to you.

**MOSES:** What's that?

**HIRAM:** WE'RE TRAPPED! LIKE RATS IN A CAGE! WE'RE GOING TO DIE!

**MOSES:** We're not trapped. Whatever made you think that?

**HIRAM:** Oh, I don't know. Maybe it's that HUGE Egyptian army racing behind us and we've got NOWHERE to go but into all this water in front of us! I don't know if you've taken a survey, but not too many of us are good swimmers. Let's face it: WE'RE GOING TO DIE! *(HIRAM grabs hold of MOSES in fear.)*

**MOSES:** Hiram, where is your faith? I know it looks scary, but we've got to believe God will take care of us.

**HIRAM:** It's going to take a mighty big miracle to get us out of this one.

**MOSES:** I think the creator of the universe can handle it. Don't be afraid, my friend. God helped us escape from Egypt. He will help us escape from this, too.

## ACT THREE: Some Time Later

**Scene:** *On the other side of the Red Sea.*

**HIRAM:** *(Enters, excitedly.)* Moses, I can't believe it! It was spectacular! I mean, when you parted the water, I mean, WOW! If I hadn't been there, I wouldn't have believed it!

**MOSES:** Thank God, not me. He provided the way of escape. All I did was raise up my staff.

**HIRAM:** Yeah… I hate to admit this, but I had some real doubts about God getting us out of there. It sure looked hopeless. But, WOW! Imagine, parting that water, just for us!

**MOSES:** Yes, Hiram. Our God is a mighty God. He promised to never leave us or forsake us.

## ACT FOUR: The Palace: A Little Later Still

**Scene:** *Back in* PHARAOH*'s palace in Egypt.*

**GUARD:** *(Enters, talking to* SERVANT.*)* And then, I couldn't believe my eyes! Somehow the water had been pushed apart so that the Israelites could escape by walking through on dry ground. The army raced across in pursuit. But they got halfway and suddenly those huge walls of water came rushing over them. It was terrible! All were drowned.

**SERVANT:** The Israelites have escaped? The entire Egyptian army drowned?

**GUARD:** Yes. It's like Moses tried to tell Pharaoh—no one is more powerful than God.

**SERVANT:** Yeah. And now we know why no one called Pharaoh "Great Wise Man."

For the **real deal** read Exodus 20:1-17

# Jeopardyland

**Characters: ALICE TRIPUP,** game show host; **PAT,** game show contestant; **SAL,** game show contestant; **DUDE,** game show contestant; **AUDIENCE**

**Props:** Characters may wish to pantomime the use of props.

**Scene:** *Game show.*

**ALICE:** I'm Alice Tripup and you're in...

**AUDIENCE:** Jeopardyland!!

**ALICE:** And welcome to our three contestants—Pat *(waves)*, Sal *(waves)*, and Dude *(nods head)*.

**ALICE:** Let's look at our categories today "That's What It Means?" "It's the Law!" and "Truly Trivial." Pat, you may select first.

**PAT:** I'll take "That's What It Means?" for one hundred.

**ALICE:** Oh, I'm sorry Pat, but you forgot to say...

**AUDIENCE:** Thank you, Alice!

**ALICE:** Sal, it's your turn.

**SAL:** Thank you, Alice. I'll take "It's the Law!" for one hundred.

**ALICE:** The eighth commandment.

**SAL:** Do not steal!

**ALICE:** Oh, I'm sorry Sal, but you forgot to...

**AUDIENCE:** Ring in!!

**ALICE:** AND you forgot to phrase your answer in the form of a question. That's 200 points against you. Pat or Dude, would you like to answer?

**PAT:** *(Rings bell.)* What is "do not steal"?

**ALICE:** Correct. You may select the next answer.

**PAT:** Thank you, Alice. I'll take "Truly Trivial" for one hundred.

**ALICE:** Rephidim!

**DUDE:** Bless you.

**ALICE:** I didn't sneeze. That is the next answer.

**DUDE:** To what?

**ALICE:** Pat or Sal, do you have an answer? *(PAT and SAL shake heads.)* Rephidim was where Moses was before he and the Hebrews went to the Desert of Sinai. Pat, you may select again.

**PAT:** Thank you, Alice. I'll take "It's the Law!" for two hundred.

**ALICE:** You shall have no other gods before Him.

**SAL:** *(Rings bell.)* Who is God?

**ALICE:** Oh, I'm sorry.

**SAL:** Hey, I KNOW the answer is God.

**ALICE:** According to Jeopardyland rules, you forgot to...

**AUDIENCE:** Turn around twice!

**ALICE:** I'm afraid we'll have to scratch that question. Pat, please select again.

**PAT:** Thank you, Alice. I'll take "That's What It Means?" for 100 points.

**ALICE:** Covet!

**DUDE:** You sure got a bad cold there, Alice.

**ALICE:** It's not a cold! It's the answer!

**DUDE:** Oh. *(Rings bell. Turns around twice.)* What is to want something somebody else has real bad?

**ALICE:** That is correct, but you don't turn around twice on the fourth question, only on questions that are a multiple of three or have a three in them. When the number is a square, such as four, you are supposed to bow first. Didn't any of you read the rule manuals sent to you?

**DUDE:** *(Holds up large, thick book.)* You mean this?

**ALICE:** Exactly. *(Contestants don't answer.)* Very well, let's continue. Dude, I believe you gave the last correct answer so you may select the next category.

**SAL:** But he didn't bow before he gave his answer!

**ALICE:** The judges have ruled an exception in this case.

**PAT:** Why?

**ALICE:** Because the rule manual says they can. Dude, your selection please.

**DUDE:** Um, okay. I'll take "That's What It Means?" for 200 points.

**ALICE:** Murder.

**PAT:** *(Rings bell, then madly flips through the pages of the rule book for several minutes.)*

**ALICE:** Oh, I'm sorry, Pat, but your time is up. Sal or Dude do you know the answer?

**SAL:** *(Under breath.)* What is going to happen when this show is over?

**ALICE:** I'm sorry, Sal, but you need to ring the bell first and speak clearly. Also, before every fifth answer you need to...

**AUDIENCE:** Bark like a dog!

**DUDE:** Bark like a DOG?

**ALICE:** I'm sorry, Dude, that is the wrong answer. The answer is to forcibly kill someone. Dude, I think you have the selection.

**DUDE:** *(Hesitantly.)* Um, are there, like, any rules I need to know now?

**ALICE:** Not to make a selection.

**PAT:** Don't forget that "thank you" rule.

**ALICE:** That rule only applies to contestants in the number one and two spots.

**PAT & SAL:** WHAT???

**ALICE:** It's all there in the manual. If you'd memorized all the rules before the show, you would know all these things.

**SAL:** *(Holds up book.)* Who can remember all these rules?

**For the real story read Leviticus 9; 22**

# Making Sacrifices

**Characters: LEVI,** a priest;
**ELIAS,** Levi's nephew and, unfortunately, a priest trainee

**Scene:** *The Temple.*

**LEVI:** Now, Elias, becoming a priest is a very important step. Are you SURE you're ready?

**ELIAS:** Oh yeah, I'm sure, Uncle Levi.

**LEVI:** Being a priest is a very important position. The priest is responsible for the ceremonies that allow people to stand in this Temple, the house of God, and worship God.

**ELIAS:** But, Uncle Levi... I mean, Your Honor the Priest, why do you have to help the people worship God?

**LEVI:** Because God is perfect and people aren't. People need to be cleansed of their sins before coming into the presence of the perfect God.

**ELIAS:** I don't get it.

**LEVI:** Perhaps you'll understand better after I've explained our duties to you. Now, here is where we receive the offerings that people have brought.

**ELIAS:** Wow! People pay ME—

**LEVI:** They are NOT paying YOU; they are bringing these offerings to GOD. Priests act as mediators between God and His people.

**ELIAS:** Meaty-eaters?

**LEVI:** "Mediators." It means people who help bring separated people back together. We help bring the people to God, and God to the people.

**ELIAS:** Oh. So what kind of stuff do the people bring?

**LEVI:** They bring their best stuff, er, offerings. They bring in their most perfect animals, their finest grain, the best of whatever they have.

**ELIAS:** So after the people give me their stuff, what do I do with it?

**LEVI:** You give it as a sacrifice to God.

**ELIAS:** Is that done through a delivery service?

**LEVI:** Haven't you ever seen a sacrifice?

**ELIAS:** Well, I usually close my eyes. I don't like blood.

**LEVI:** *(Groans.)* Why exactly did you decide to become a priest?

**ELIAS:** Well, it's the family business.

**LEVI:** *(Sighs.)* Now pay close attention to me. To offer the sacrifice to God, we burn it.

**ELIAS:** Why?

**LEVI:** Where does smoke go?

**ELIAS:** Oh. The smoke goes up in the air, reminding us we're giving the sacrifice to God.

**LEVI:** Very good.

**ELIAS:** But if we're just going to burn the offerings, why do people bring us their best?

**LEVI:** Because they are NOT bringing the offerings to US; they are bringing the offerings to GOD. Do you think it would be acceptable to offer God anything less than our best?

**ELIAS:** I guess not. So once the people have paid God to get into the Temple, what do we do?

**LEVI:** No! No! No! The people aren't paying God to get into the Temple. They are making atonement for the sins they have committed.

**ELIAS:** At home mint? We make candy here?

**LEVI:** (Groans.) "Atonement!" "Atonement" means to make up for the sins you've committed. When we sacrifice an animal, we can become "at one" with God after sin has separated us from Him.

**ELIAS:** But why do the people have to do it every time they come into the Temple?

**LEVI:** Elias, do you really believe that giving up just ONE very important thing will pay God for the sins you or anyone else has committed?

**ELIAS:** We can NEVER make ourselves good enough for God. I mean, we'll be paying for our sins forever.

**LEVI:** Exactly. But God has a plan to help us, Elias. He will send us a Savior to take away all our sins once and for all.

**ELIAS:** Oh, good! I hope He gets here soon.

**LEVI:** (Suspiciously.) Why?

**ELIAS:** You know that goat you had put aside for that sacrifice today?

**LEVI:** Yes?

**ELIAS:** I think I accidentally let him escape.

**For the real story read Numbers 13:1-15, 21–25**

# Spy Talk

**Characters:**
SHAMMUA (shah-MOO-ah);
IGAL (I-gahl); PALTI (PAHL-tee);
NAHBI (NAH-bee); JOSHUA
(JAHSH-oo-wuh); CALEB (KAY-lehb)

**Scene:** *In a field not too far from Jericho, a city in Canaan.*

**SHAMMUA:** Whoa! Did you see the size of those guys?

**IGAL:** What guys?

**PALTI:** Did you see the size of those walls?

**IGAL:** What guys? What walls?

**NAHBI:** Did you see the size of the city?

**IGAL:** What guys? What walls? What city?

**JOSHUA:** Did you see the size of the vineyards?

**CALEB:** And how about the grain? This really is the land of milk and honey!

**IGAL:** WHAT guys? WHAT walls? WHAT city?

**SHAMMUA:** Igal, what kind of a spy are you if you can't see?

**IGAL:** Moses picked me as a spy, and he must have known what he was doing.

**NAHBI:** Unless, of course, you forgot to MENTION that you can't see.

**CALEB:** Leave him alone. He's a great cover. How many spies travel with blind companions?

**IGAL:** I'm not blind!

**SHAMMUA:** You'd have to be blind not to see that huge city over there.

**PALTI:** It must hold thousands of people! And all great warriors, from the looks of it!

**JOSHUA:** Well, Igal, at least you should be able to smell. What do you smell?

**IGAL:** *(Sniffs.)* Hm. Sweet grass, ripening grain, fresh fruit, healthy animals and fragrant honey.

**PALTI:** You can't smell healthy animals!

**IGAL:** Oh yes, I can!

**SHAMMUA:** It doesn't matter. With those monsters over there, there is no way we're going to be able to move to this land.

**CALEB:** You forget, we've got God on our side.

**SHAMMUA:** What can God do about all this? If it was just one city, maybe. But they've all looked like this!

**PALTI:** Yeah. Remember those giants in Hebron? These guys make those giants look small!

IGAL: What giants?

JOSHUA: They weren't giants. They were just some very tall people.

NAHBI: They were giants, and there's no way we can defeat them!

JOSHUA: If God could help us escape from Egypt, the most powerful country in the world, can't He help us here?

SHAMMUA, PALTI, and NAHBI: Uh...no!

CALEB: Why not?

SHAMMUA: Take a real good look at the walls around that city. What's God going to do? Knock their walls down?

JOSHUA: He might.

PALTI: Get a grip, Joshua!

JOSHUA: You know, Igal can see some things better than you, and he's blind!

IGAL: I'm NOT blind!

JOSHUA: Augh! You guys aren't listening!

CALEB: C'mon, Joshua. Let's go get some fruit to take back to Moses. When the people see that, they'll know God keeps His promises. (JOSHUA and CALEB exit.)

NAHBI: Caleb's going to get us all killed!

IGAL: I don't understand.

SHAMMUA: What don't you understand?

IGAL: Well, obviously the land is wonderful! I can hear water and goats and sheep. It's just like God said it would be. The land of milk and honey.

PALTI: Yeah, it's pretty wonderful, all right.

IGAL: So what's the problem? Why can't we come here like God said?

NAHBI: You know those men and walls and cities you can't see? Well, they are EVERY-WHERE! And they don't look like they'd want to share!

IGAL: And what do Caleb and Joshua want to do?

PALTI: They want us all—including our wives and our children—to march into this land and claim it as ours!

IGAL: But, doesn't it belong to us?

SHAMMUA: Yes, but I don't think these people care about that. They'll fight to keep it.

IGAL: So Joshua and Caleb are wrong?

PALTI: Right.

IGAL: Joshua and Caleb are right?

NAHBI: No, no. Joshua and Caleb think that God is going to help us.

IGAL: And God isn't going to help us?

SHAMMUA: Look. God gave us brains to think with. And any idiot can see that there's no way we can fight off all these people!

IGAL: I see. No, I don't see...I guess.

PALTI: Let's face it, Igal. You can't see anything! It's hopeless!

For the **real story** read Joshua 3–4

# Jordan Crossing

**Characters: JOSHUA,** the leader of the Israelites; **ELIAS,** one of the priests who carried the Ark of the Covenant; **BEN,** one of the priests who carried the Ark of the Covenant; **ADAM,** one of the priests who carried the Ark of the Covenant

**Scene:** *At the edge of the Jordan River. JOSHUA is speaking to the priests.*

**JOSHUA:** Listen up, everyone! We're ready to march into the land God has promised us.

**ELIAS:** Right. And exactly HOW are we going to cross that rather full and RAGING river?

**JOSHUA:** I'm glad you asked that question, Elias. First, you priests will enter the river with the Ark of the Covenant.

**ELIAS:** OK, hold it right there, Joshua. Everyone knows military men go first in any dangerous situation. And I believe that a rather full and RAGING river could definitely be classified as dangerous.

**JOSHUA:** That's not the plan. Priests will go first, as they ALWAYS do, to show God's presence with us.

**ELIAS:** Look, this was definitely NOT in the contract! Carrying the Ark of the Covenant? Yes. Saying prayers for the people? Yes. Walking into a full and RAGING river FIRST? No!

**JOSHUA:** These are God's instructions. Are you saying you won't follow God's instructions?

**ELIAS:** Well, no. But are you SURE you heard Him right?

**JOSHUA:** Yes! Now, as I was saying, the priests will step into the river, the full and RAGING river, and then they will stop.

**ELIAS:** Stop? What for?

**JOSHUA:** Elias, it would really help me if you'd listen until I'm finished with my instructions.

**ELIAS:** Oh, fine. I'll listen.

**JOSHUA:** Thank you. Now, once the priests have stepped into the river, God will stop the water from flowing, and the rest of us may cross the river in safety.

**ELIAS:** And what are we priests doing?

**JOSHUA:** You are standing with the Ark of the Covenant.

**ELIAS:** While the entire group goes by?! That's hundreds, no, thousands of people! It'll take all day! It may even take more than a day!

**JOSHUA:** Elias!

**ELIAS:** Yeah, I know—just listen. But it isn't fair. We're going to have to stand in that full and RAGING river the WHOLE time!

**BEN:** *(To ELIAS.)* You weren't listening, Elias. He said the river would dry up.

**ELIAS:** Oh yeah, right. This I've got to see.

**JOSHUA:** Elias, I'm not sure you're exactly what we are looking for in a priest.

**ELIAS:** OK, OK. I'll be quiet. What other instructions do you have?

**JOSHUA:** That's it. Do you think you can remember it?

**ELIAS:** Yeah. We go stand in that full and RAGING river.

**BEN:** Then God will hold back the river.

**ADAM:** And all the people will cross.

**JOSHUA:** Excellent! Do any of you, except Elias, have any questions?

**BEN:** Do you want us to follow the last person across the river or wait for your signal?

**JOSHUA:** Wait for my signal. All right. Let's go!

**ELIAS:** This had better work.

**ADAM:** Elias, who provided us with food in the desert?

**ELIAS:** *(Thinks.)* Um, God.

**BEN:** And who provided us with water from rocks in the desert?

**ELIAS:** *(Thinks.)* Um, God.

**ADAM:** And who parted the Red Sea, so our parents could escape from the Egyptians?

**ELIAS:** *(Thinks.)* Um, God.

**BEN:** So if God did all those things, why can't you believe He'll help us across this river?

**ELIAS:** I kinda forgot about those other things.

**ADAM:** You forgot?! How could you forget?

**ELIAS:** I don't know. I guess because I saw the river was big and full and RAGING. It scared me and I forgot about everything else.

**BEN:** I guess that could happen.

**ADAM:** Look. Here we are at the river.

**ELIAS:** OK. Let's step in. *(ELIAS closes eyes and, with BEN and ADAM, carefully steps into the river.)*

**BEN:** Elias! Look! Open your eyes!

**ELIAS:** I'm not in the water yet.

**ADAM:** Open your eyes, Elias!

**ELIAS:** *(Opens eyes.)* Wow! Where'd that full and RAGING river go?

**BEN:** It's stopped flowing, just like Joshua said it would!

**ELIAS:** Wow! I really gotta remember this!

**ADAM:** OK. I'll ask. Why do you have to remember this?

**ELIAS:** So the next time I'm scared, I won't be!

**BEN and ADAM:** Good idea!

For the **real story** read Judges 6:1-24

# Gideon's Guest

**Characters: PURAH,** Gideon's not-necessarily faithful servant; **GIDEON,** a young man, the lowest member of the lowest tribe; **VOICE,** God

### ACT ONE

**Scene:** *In a winepress.*

**PURAH:** Five! Six! Seven! EIGHT! It's PURAH, open up the GATE!

**GIDEON:** Shhh! Do you want someone to hear you?

**PURAH:** You said to use the password, so you'd know it was me.

**GIDEON:** Yes, but not so loudly. Someone might hear you!

**PURAH:** Yeah, whatever. Isn't it going to be rather inconvenient to thresh the grain in this winepress? I mean, where's the wind that's going to blow away the chaff?

**GIDEON:** I'll have to do it without the wind.

**PURAH:** It's going to take you a long, LONG time.

**GIDEON:** I know. Just go get the rest of the wheat, will ya?

**PURAH:** OK, but I don't understand why you're threshing grain here in the winepress. This is where they make wine, you know.

**GIDEON:** I'm hiding from the Midianites. You know if they saw me threshing wheat, they'd take it away. And then what would we eat? They've already stolen most of our animals and ruined our other crops.

**PURAH:** I guess you've got a point there...

**GIDEON:** Yes, I do! Now, go!

**PURAH:** I'm going. I'm going. Relax! I was just asking a simple question. Hey, this is a nice shade tree! *(Sits down under tree.)*

**GIDEON:** Purah, if YOU don't bring me more wheat stalks to thresh, how am I supposed to get MY job done?

**PURAH:** Hmm, that's a tough question. I guess I'd have to say I don't know.

**GIDEON:** Purah, look! Is that my father over there? *(Points off in the distance.)*

**PURAH:** *(Without looking around.)* Out here? I doubt it. But, um, I'll be going now, just in case.

**GIDEON:** *(To himself.)* Now I know why my father gave Purah to ME as a servant. DAD couldn't take it any longer. I guess when you're the youngest, you get stuck with everyone's hand-me-downs! *(Sees a man standing by the tree.)* Uh-oh. Who's that?

**VOICE:** The Lord is with you, mighty man of courage!

**GIDEON:** *(To himself.)* He can't be talking to me. Mighty man! That's a good one. But there's no one else here. *(To VOICE.)* Look, if the Lord is with us, why are we in so much trouble with the Midianites? Obviously, God has abandoned us!

**VOICE:** Go save Israel from the Midianites. I'm sending you to do this.

**GIDEON:** Whoa! Me? How can I save Israel? You probably don't know this, but my family is the weakest in my tribe and I'm the youngest in my family. I'm not a leader! *(To himself.)* I can't even get Purah to do what I ask.

**VOICE:** I will be with you. You will defeat the Midianites all at once.

**GIDEON:** What? *(To himself.)* This guy must be nuts! Or a prophet. Or—I wonder if this is really an angel of God? I'd better check this out! *(To VOICE.)* If You are who You say You are, prove it by doing a miracle. *(To self.)* Wait. If this is God, that would be a pretty rude thing to say. *(To VOICE.)* Um, what I mean to say is, please wait here. I want to bring You an offering.

**VOICE:** I will wait.

**GIDEON:** *(To himself.)* No one at home is EVER going to believe this when I tell them! Imagine—me, a leader.

## ACT TWO

**Scene:** GIDEON'*s home*

**GIDEON:** Purah! Purah! Help me quick! I need some bread and meat.

**PURAH:** Why? You hungry?

**GIDEON:** No no. It's for this prophet...or angel...or maybe it's God...

**PURAH:** Threshing wheat in that winepress is getting to you! Now you're imagining things.

**GIDEON:** No, Purah, I am not imagining things. He wants ME to save Israel from the Midianites.

**PURAH:** *(Laughs uncontrollably.)* Ho! Ho! YOU? Ol' Hide-in-the-Winepress? That's a pretty good one.

**GIDEON:** Purah, I'm SERIOUS! And I want that bread and meat now!

**PURAH:** OK. OK. Here's the bread and meat. (GIDEON *leaves.*) Boy, what got into him? I wonder what he's going to do next?

For the **real story** read Judges 13

# He Said What?

### Characters: MANOAH'S WIFE; MANOAH

**WIFE:** Manoah, will you please put your paper down? I have something very important to discuss with you.

**MANOAH:** What is it, my dear?

**WIFE:** I don't know if you've noticed or not, but we don't have any children.

**MANOAH:** It would be hard not to notice. Is there a point to your comment?

**WIFE:** Yes. We are going to have a son very soon.

**MANOAH:** We're having a SON? A boy to take fishing and send to a good college?

**WIFE:** That's what I said! A son!

**MANOAH:** You sound very sure of yourself. Are you absolutely certain about this? Not the child part. I know you can be certain about that. But what makes you think it will be a boy? People have girl babies, too, you know.

**WIFE:** An angel of the Lord appeared to me and said I would have a son. I am 100 percent certain that an ANGEL would not lie to me.

**MANOAH:** Do me a favor, please. Don't tell the neighbors you were speaking to an angel. I mean, why would an angel speak to you? Or to me, for that matter? We are not famous, like Moses or Joshua or even Gideon. Angels don't speak to nobodies.

**WIFE:** But those three you just mentioned were nobodies! They are only famous because God or His angels spoke to them.

**MANOAH:** You have a point there. OK, I believe that an angel spoke to you. Did he tell you anything special about our son? Will he go to a good college?

**WIFE:** He said that our son would deliver Israel from the Philistines (FIL-ih-steens) and that he is to be a Nazirite (NAA-zer-ite).

**MANOAH:** Deliver Israel like Joshua and Gideon did? That's great! But I have a problem with that Nazirite business. We're from the tribe of Dan and we don't live anywhere NEAR Nazareth. How can our son be a Nazirite?

**WIFE:** You're thinking of NAZARENE. Our son is to take the Nazirite vow from birth. You know. The vow in the Law.

**MANOAH:** Oh, right! That vow! Maybe you could refresh my memory a little.

**WIFE:** Remember? A person devotes himself entirely to the Lord. He doesn't drink wine...

**MANOAH:** Well, at least my son won't be a drunkard.

**WIFE:** And he is not to approach any dead body...

**MANOAH:** Hm...that could be a problem. I suppose that if we want decent funerals when we die, we'd better have more children.

**WIFE:** And a razor is never to touch his hair.

**MANOAH:** Hold on, now! I don't know that I like that part. I mean, what's he going to look like in twenty years? He'll be tripping and falling over all that hair! How long is this Nazirite vow supposed to last?

**WIFE:** All of his life.

**MANOAH:** Well, this plan has some good points, but I don't know. I would like to meet this angel and make sure we've got all the instructions right. Maybe I will ask God to have the angel come again so that I could ask some questions.

For the **real story** read **Judges 16**

# Samson and Delilah

**Characters: SAMSON,** a man of God (well, at least he's SUPPOSED to be!); **DELILAH,** a beautiful but greedy woman; **PHILISTINE LEADERS,** the rulers from the five major Philistine cities; **AUDIENCE,** a group of people who sit and watch a performance, and who actually get to say something in this skit; **NARRATOR,** (hey—we ALL know what narrators do)

**Scene:** DELILAH'S *plush apartment in the Valley of Sorek.*

**SAMSON:** Thanks for a wonderful evening, Delilah!

**DELILAH:** Do you really have to go?

**SAMSON:** Gotta kill some Philistines in the morning!

**DELILAH:** Kill is such a disgusting word. Why don't you go out and just scare a few?

**SAMSON:** Huh? Oh yeah, I forgot, you like Philistines. Sorry, but it's my job and I gotta do it.

**DELILAH:** My big, strong hero. *(SAMSON exits. PHILISTINE LEADERS enter.)*

**PHILISTINE LEADERS:** Delilah, hey there, what do you know? Where did that great big moose go?

**DELILAH:** He's gone to kill some more Philistines.

**PHILISTINE LEADERS:** Bad news! Delilah, what do you say, you get his secret, we'll take him away?

**DELILAH:** The secret of his strength? How much?

**PHILISTINE LEADERS:** Delilah, we know something like this isn't cheap, say about eleven hundred shekels each?

**DELILAH:** You're slipping guys, "cheap" and "each" don't rhyme. BUT, eleven hundred shekels times five, that's, uh…

**AUDIENCE:** Fifty-five hundred shekels!

**DELILAH:** Gee, thanks. Fifty-five hundred shekels is a lot of money! I'll do it!

**AUDIENCE:** Don't do it!

**DELILAH:** I already said I would. A place like this takes a lot of money to keep up, not to mention the rent.

**PHILISTINE LEADERS:** Hey, Delilah, you're a real good friend. Just let us know what to do in the end.

**DELILAH:** Yeah, I'll be in touch.

**NARRATOR:** The next evening…

**DELILAH:** Samson, my sweet strong sap, uh…superhero, do you think we should keep secrets from each other, now that we're so involved and all?

**SAMSON:** You keeping a secret from me?

**DELILAH:** Of course not, my beloved lug. But you're keeping a secret from me.

**SAMSON:** What secret?

**DELILAH:** About your strength. Tell me, where does your superhuman strength come from?

**AUDIENCE:** Don't do it, Samson! Don't tell her!

**DELILAH:** Are you going to listen to them, people you don't even know, or me, someone you HOPE you're going to spend a lot of time with?

**SAMSON:** Hey, if it's that important to you, I'll tell you.

**AUDIENCE:** Don't do it!

**SAMSON:** All you have to do is tie me up with some new vines. That'll do it.

**DELILAH:** Really! Well, you must be tired. Why don't you take a little nap? *(Calls to PHILISTINE LEADERS.)* Oh, guys!

**NARRATOR:** Sometime later…

**PHILISTINE LEADERS:** Hey, Delilah, those vines just broke. And we got pummeled by that great big bloke!

**DELILAH:** You mean he LIED to me? The nerve of that guy!

**SAMSON:** Heh, heh, that was a pretty funny joke I played on you.

**DELILAH:** I'm not amused! I can't believe I mean so little to you that you would lie to me like that! And you said you loved me. *(Starts to cry.)*

**SAMSON:** OK, OK. I'll tell you what makes me strong.

**AUDIENCE:** Don't do it!

**DELILAH:** Mind your own business. What's your secret, my precious baboo?

**SAMSON:** If I'm tied up with brand new ropes, then I will be helpless as a kitten.

**DELILAH:** Oh, NEW ROPES. Now I know that you love me. Come and rest a while.

**NARRATOR:** Sometime later…

**PHILISTINE LEADERS:** There's no difference between new ropes or old. One twist of his wrist and neither will hold.

**DELILAH:** He LIED to me AGAIN! I thought we'd got this straightened out!

**SAMSON:** Heh, heh. I was just fooling with you.

**DELILAH:** FOOLING WITH ME? You mean MAKING A FOOL OF ME! I can't believe you'd treat someone you love like this!

**SAMSON:** It was just a joke.

**DELILAH:** I'm NOT laughing!

**SAMSON:** OK, OK. You win, I'll tell you.

**AUDIENCE:** Don't do it!

**DELILAH:** You'd better do it! And it'd better be the truth or you'll never see me again!

**AUDIENCE:** Don't do it!

**SAMSON:** Hey, I've gotta do it or I'll lose her. And what could be worse than that?

**AUDIENCE:** Don't do it!

**NARRATOR:** Sometime later…

**PHILISTINE LEADERS:** Hey, Delilah, good job cutting off his hair. He's a harmless guy, with a big blank stare.

**DELILAH:** Blank stare? I wonder what that means? Oh well. Now I'M rich, rich, rich!

**AUDIENCE:** Samson, we told you not to do it!

**SAMSON:** I guess I should have listened to you guys. Now I don't have my strength or my eyes.

**For the real story read Ruth**

# Naomi, Is that You?

**Characters: NAOMI,** a widow;
**RUTH,** Naomi's daughter-in-law;
**FRIEDA,** resident of Bethlehem;
**JOANNA,** resident of Bethlehem;
**ROBERTA,** resident of Bethlehem;
**SMITTY,** resident of Bethlehem;
**GEORGE,** friend of Boaz;
**WOMAN,** resident of Bethlehem

**Scene:** *The main street in Bethlehem, before the time of King David.* NAOMI *and* RUTH *walk past* FRIEDA.

**FRIEDA:** Naomi? Is that you? Long time, no see. How's life been treating you?

**NAOMI:** Oh, I've had my ups and downs. But one of my greatest joys is my daughter-in-law Ruth.

**FRIEDA:** *(Looks puzzled.)* Really?

**JOANNA:** *(Entering.)* Naomi! Haven't seen you in ages. How's life going?

**FRIEDA:** She's had her ups and downs.

**NAOMI:** Yes, and this is my wonderful daughter-in-law Ruth. She's been such a blessing to me. Why, when my sons died in Moab, she and Orpah were my rocks.

**ROBERTA:** *(Entering. To* JOANNA.*)* Isn't that Naomi?

**JOANNA:** Yes, and her daughter, Beth.

**FRIEDA:** No, no, it's Opa, her sister-in-law.

**NAOMI:** Um, no, this is Ruth, my daughter-in-law. My other daughter-in-law, Orpah, didn't come with us. She stayed with her family in Moab.

**ROBERTA:** And Ruth came with you? *(Quietly to* JOANNA.*)* Instead of staying with her family? But why? (JOANNA *shrugs.*)

**SMITTY:** *(Entering. To* FRIEDA.*)* Hey, is that Naomi? I haven't seen her in years. Not since she, Elimelech, and the boys moved during the Great Famine of '45, or was it '54?

**FRIEDA:** The famine was '54 through '45.

**SMITTY:** Oh yeah. So, Naomi, how's it going?

**JOANNA:** She's had her ups and downs.

**FRIEDA:** And this is her sister, Moab.

**NAOMI:** No, no, this is Ruth, my daughter-in-law, from the land of Moab.

**SMITTY:** Oh, so where are your sons?

**FRIEDA:** *(Whispers to* SMITTY.*)* They're dead.

**SMITTY:** Oh, sorry. So what are you doing now?

**NAOMI:** Well, we're preparing for Ruth's wedding.

**ALL:** What?!

**SMITTY:** Who's the lucky guy?

**NAOMI:** Ruth is going to marry Boaz.

**ROBERTA:** Boaz? How'd she meet him?

**NAOMI:** That's an interesting story, really. Ruth has saved my life. Every day she's gone out after the harvesters to gather the left-over grain. She's worked so hard to help me, her MOTHER-IN-LAW. Well, one day she came home and told me about this nice man and...well, she said Boaz was handsome.

**ALL:** Ooooh!

**NAOMI:** Oh, stop it, now. Anyway, Ruth said Boaz had told his harvesters to leave a little extra grain behind for her, and he told her to only glean in his fields.

**SMITTY:** Sounds like a proposal to me.

**ROBERTA:** Smitty, be quiet.

**NAOMI:** I knew about Boaz. He happens to be a relative of my husband, so he had a right to marry Ruth. Well, I advised Ruth to explain who she was. And Boaz decided to marry her.

**GEORGE:** *(Entering in a hurry.)* Hey, Naomi, where've you been?

**FRIEDA:** She's been in the land of Moab, where she moved during the Great Famine.

**SMITTY:** Her two sons got married there, and then they died. *(Whispers.)* But don't say anything about it.

**GEORGE:** Yes, but—

**ROBERTA:** Her daughter-in-law Orpah went back to live with her own family. But her incredible daughter-in-law Ruth came back here with her.

**JOANNA:** And one day, while Ruth was out in the fields picking up grain to feed the two of them—

**ROBERTA:** She met Boaz, and they're getting married, tonight.

**GEORGE:** Yes, I KNOW all that. I just wanted to know where she's been this afternoon! They're ready to start the wedding!

**NAOMI:** Oh, dear! Come on, Ruth. It was nice seeing you all again.

**WOMAN:** *(Entering.)* Hey, wasn't that Naomi? And who was that with her?

**ALL:** Groan.

For the **real story** read 1 Samuel 8–10; 1 Kings 2:10-12; 2 Chronicles 10:1-5

# Hall of Kings

**Characters: TISH,** a girl on the museum tour; **RODNEY,** the museum guide, a whiny talker; **MS. PRISLEY,** a Bible scholar on the museum tour; **JOSH,** a boy on the museum tour

**Scene:** *The Hall of Kings in a museum of Bible times.*

**TISH:** *(Entering with* JOSH.) Look at all those statues!

**RODNEY:** *(Stopping* JOSH *and* TISH.) Wait here, please.

**MS. PRISLEY:** *(Enters.)* Is this the tour?

**RODNEY:** The tour doesn't leave for ten minutes.

**MS. PRISLEY:** Why?

**RODNEY:** We're on break.

**JOSH:** *(To* TISH.) "We"? *(TISH shrugs shoulders.)*

**MS. PRISLEY:** *(To* RODNEY.) Young man, the sign says the next tour begins at 10:30, which is just about right now.

**RODNEY:** Oh, fine. We wouldn't want to be a

few minutes late, now would we? Our name is Rodney, and we will be your guide today. Step this way.

**TISH:** Can Josh and I go, too?

**RODNEY:** You two look a little young for THIS tour.

**MS. PRISLEY:** Of course, you children can come along. Young man, let's begin.

**RODNEY:** Oh, fine. We will begin with the statue of Samuel.

**MS. PRISLEY:** Samuel? Why is Samuel in the Hall of Kings? Samuel was NOT a king.

**RODNEY:** Ma'am, if you will just be patient, we will explain. Now, here we have a statue of Samuel. Though he was NOT a king *(glares at* MS. PRISLEY*)*, he did begin the reign of kings by anointing the first king, Saul. Moving on to Saul's statue—

**MS. PRISLEY:** Excuse me, young man, but you forgot to mention that Samuel was against the idea of a king.

**JOSH:** Why didn't Samuel want a king?

**MS. PRISLEY:** Samuel knew that God was the only King the Israelites needed.

**TISH:** So why did Samuel anoint a king?

**MS. PRISLEY:** Well, God decided to let the people have what they wanted, but He also warned them.

**RODNEY:** WE are giving the tour, if you don't mind!

**TISH:** *(To* RODNEY.) So what was the warning?

**RODNEY:** That is NOT on the tour.

**MS. PRISLEY:** God warned the Israelites that the kings would take some of their property and their sons and their daughters to be slaves.

**RODNEY:** We are ready to continue on the tour!

**JOSH:** *(To TISH.)* Why does he keep saying "we"? Is there someone we can't see? *(TISH shrugs her shoulders.)*

**RODNEY:** Here is the statue of King Saul. Saul fought many battles against the Philistines to reclaim the land of Israel!

**JOSH:** He fought them by himself?

**RODNEY:** No, no. Of course not! He led armies to battle.

**MS. PRISLEY:** And he ordered people's sons to be in the army and claimed people's food to feed the army.

**TISH:** Oh. Just like in Samuel's warning!

**RODNEY:** Shall we move on? Here is the statue of King David. King David brought all the tribes of Israel together into one nation.

**MS. PRISLEY:** Actually, with God's help, David was able to reclaim the land of Israel, so the people of Israel could be one nation. David loved God very much, and he wrote many songs worshiping God.

**TISH:** Wow! Is that right, Rodney?

**RODNEY:** I suppose. Our next king is Solomon, son of David. He brought great wealth to the kingdom of Israel.

**MS. PRISLEY:** Solomon was also given wisdom by God. And Solomon built the beautiful Temple for God. Unfortunately, Solomon forgot to obey all God's laws. So when he died, God split his kingdom between two people.

**RODNEY:** Ahem! During the reign of Solomon's son, Rehoboam, Israel was divided into two kingdoms. Rehoboam ruled the kingdom of Judah in the south, and Jeroboam took over the larger kingdom of Israel in the north.

**JOSH:** *(To TISH.)* Just like the lady said.

**RODNEY:** Silence, please! After Rehoboam came Abijah and Asa. However, the kingdom of Israel had quite a few kings during the same time ending with Ahab.

**MS. PRISLEY:** *(To JOSH and TISH.)* And Ahab married the wicked queen Jezebel who led the people to worship the false god Baal.

**RODNEY:** *(Annoyed, to MS. PRISLEY.)* Would you like to give this tour?

**MS. PRISLEY:** Thank you, young man. I'd be delighted.

**RODNEY:** Oh, fine. We'll be taking our break if you need us.

**JOSH:** *(To MS. PRISLEY.)* Why does he keep saying "we"?

**MS. PRISLEY:** In the past, that's how kings and queens referred to themselves because they thought they were better than other people. I think that young man has been in this hall too long.

**TISH:** But he hasn't learned much in all that time.

**MS. PRISLEY:** Rodney's like a lot of these kings—he's forgotten how important God is in all this history. Some of these kings loved God and followed His commands. But many of the kings became more interested in being powerful than they did in following God.

**JOSH:** That must be why God warned Samuel.

**MS. PRISLEY:** Precisely!

**TISH:** Now somebody needs to warn Rodney!

**For the real story read 1 Samuel 13:13-14; 16:1-13**

# The Right Man

**Characters: Samuel,** Human Resources Director for Israel; **MS. LEE,** Samuel's secretary, speaks in a nasal tone; **ELIAB (ee-LYE-ab),** military man, stands at attention whenever he is addressed; **ABINADAB (a-BIN-a-dab),** smooth politician, wants to shake hands a lot; **DAVID,** sincere, but inexperienced youth; **NARRATOR**

**Props:** Characters may wish to pantomime the use of props.

**Scene:** SAMUEL'S *office. SAMUEL is dictating into a cassette recorder.*

## ACT ONE

**SAMUEL:** To King Saul, the Lord's Anointed One, etc., etc. Your Majesty, I have received word from Management that you continue to ignore His policies and procedures. Therefore, I regret to inform you that Management has decided not to renew your contract as King of Israel with any of your descendants. Sincerely, Samuel, the Lord's Prophet, etc., etc. *(Speaks into intercom.)* Ms. Lee?

**MS. LEE:** Yes, Mr. Samuel?

**SAMUEL:** I have a letter for you to type. And please show in the first applicant for the position of king.

**MS. LEE:** Yes, Mr. Samuel. *(Enters with ELIAB.)* This is Mr. Eliab, Mr. Samuel.

**ELIAB:** Mr. Samuel, sir!

**SAMUEL:** Have a seat, Eliab. You have quite an impressive application here. Tall, handsome, strong—would you say those are your best qualities?

**ELIAB:** Yes, sir! And people like me, too, sir!

**SAMUEL:** Please sit down. Says here you've had military training.

**ELIAB:** Yes, sir! I've received ten medals of honor in the King's army, sir!

**SAMUEL:** Sit! I see. Well, now, suppose the army was challenged by an enemy of the Lord's army, which was twice the size of your army. As king, what would you do?

**ELIAB:** Well, sir, it would be foolish to risk my army when we couldn't win. I'd negotiate. And I wouldn't be so foolish as to challenge them first.

**SAMUEL:** I see. Well, thank you very much. We'll be in touch. *(ELIAB exits.)*

**MS. LEE:** *(Over intercom.)* Mr. Samuel, the Lord is on Line One.

**SAMUEL:** *(Picks up phone.)* My Lord, this is Samuel. Well, I thought he seemed like an excellent candidate...I see. Well, You know best. *(Hangs up.)* Ms. Lee, send in the next candidate.

**ABINADAB:** *(Enters.)* Hello, Mr. Samuel! Abinadab is my name, and leadership is my game!

**SAMUEL:** Yes, Mr. Abinadab. Have a seat.

**ABINADAB:** Certainly! And let me say, you've done a mighty fine job of decorating in here.

Your color scheme says authority, yet compassion!

**SAMUEL:** Well, thank you, Mr. Abinadab. I've read your application and all 100 letters of recommendation from your closest friends, but I'd like to ask you a question.

**ABINADAB:** Certainly! Anything at all!

**SAMUEL:** Suppose an enemy of the Lord's decided to attack Israel. This army is twice the size of your army. As king, what would you do?

**ABINADAB:** Hmm. Well, I'd send gifts from the treasury to sweeten their attitude. Then I'd use all my charm to work out an agreement.

**SAMUEL:** That sounds reasonable. Well, we'll let you know. (ABINADAB *exits.* SAMUEL *picks up the phone.*) My Lord, Samuel here...Well, I thought he was an excellent candidate...Yes, alright. You know best. (*Speaks into intercom.*) Ms. Lee, send in the next candidate.

## ACT TWO

**NARRATOR:** Samuel continued his interviews with five more candidates for the position of king, but none of them met with the Lord's approval.

**SAMUEL:** (*On phone.*) Not him, either? Yes, Lord, You know best. (*Sighs; hangs up phone. Speaks into intercom.*) Ms. Lee, send in the next candidate.

**MS. LEE:** That's it, Mr. Samuel. There's no one else out here.

**SAMUEL:** Get ahold of Jesse. He's got to have someone else!

**MS. LEE:** Right away, Mr. Samuel. Oh—King Saul is on the line for you.

**SAMUEL:** Thank you, Ms. Lee. (*Picks up phone.*) This is Samuel, Your Majesty...Yes, I sent the letter...Do you remember the Gilgal (GIL-gal) incident?...And the Amalekite (uh-MAL-eh-kite) incident?

**MS. LEE:** (*Enters; speaks quickly.*) It's five, so I'm leaving. Mr. Jesse is sending someone over, but says he's just a boy. Doesn't think you'll be too interested. Your repairman says the donkey needs new shoes. And the town council wants you to return their call. (MS. LEE *exits quickly.*)

**SAMUEL:** Hey, wait a minute! (*Into phone.*) No, Your Majesty, I wasn't talking to you... But...Your Majesty, throwing spears is no way to solve your problems! (*Hangs up phone.*) He'll never learn.

**DAVID:** (*Knocks on door.*) Hello, I'm David. My father, Jesse, said you wished to speak to me.

**SAMUEL:** Yes, son. Have a seat. Now, ah, what do you DO?

**DAVID:** I'm a shepherd. I take care of my father's sheep.

**SAMUEL:** A shepherd. I see. Do you have any, uh, hobbies?

**DAVID:** I like to sing. I've even written some of my own songs.

**SAMUEL:** (*Sighs.*) A shepherd and a songwriter.

**DAVID:** I write songs about the Lord and how He takes care of me.

**SAMUEL:** Really? OK, suppose an enemy of the Lord threatened to attack Israel. What would you do?

**DAVID:** I'd go fight them, of course.

**SAMUEL:** Of course?

**DAVID:** If they are enemies of the Lord, then He will help me defeat them, just as He helps me defeat the lions and bears that threaten my sheep!

**SAMUEL:** Hmm. (*Picks up phone.*) Yes, my Lord. I agree. He's an excellent choice. (*Hangs up.*) Kneel, son. You are to be the next king of Israel.

**For the real story read 1 Samuel 16:14-23**

# Harp and Soul

**Characters: STEWARD; SHEPHERD; SERVANT; MUSICIANS,** a group of three court musicians; **BAIRD THE BARD,** a storyteller

**Props:** Characters may wish to pantomime the use of props.

(BARD *enters.*)

**BARD:** Let me tell you a tale of a miserable king, and a talented young shepherd who knew how to sing. There's a steward who tried to make everything click, and some royal musicians who can't play a lick. Put them together and all will unfold, in a wonderful tale that we'll call "Harp and Soul".

**Scene One:** *The Castle.*

(STEWARD, SERVANT, *and* MUSICIANS *enter.*)

**STEWARD:** (*To* MUSICIANS.) OK, guys, let's take it once more from the top. And this time, please lose all that silly "doo-wop." Remember, we're trying to SOOTHE the king's soul. You KNOW what it's like when he loses control!

**MUSICIANS:** Right on, sir! Doo-wop...er, we mean, one, two, three...(MUSICIANS *play instruments horribly.*)

**STEWARD:** (*Covering his ears.*) Please STOP! I can't stand it! You're all killing me!

**SERVANT:** Now calm yourself, sir, or you're going to get ill. I've heard of a fellow with musical skill. They say he sings and is good with a harp. He IS fairly young, but I hear he's quite sharp!

**STEWARD:** (*Glares at* MUSICIANS.) Don't stand there! Go get him! It can't be too soon! Let's hope that he really can carry a tune!

(*All exit.*)

**BARD:** So off on his horse rode the servant in haste. He knew that there wasn't a moment to waste.

**Scene Two:** *The Countryside.*

(SHEPHERD *enters first, followed by* SERVANT.)

**SERVANT:** (*Panting.*) Excuse me, young man. Could you please help me out? I'm looking for someone who lives hereabout. He plays the harp well and can sing a good song. Am I in the right place? Have I got it all wrong?

**SHEPHERD:** I'm the person you want, sir. I sing and I play when I'm watching the sheep at the end of the day.

**SERVANT:** You're the one? You're the singer? It is really true! Will you come with me now? I've a GREAT job for you!

(SHEPHERD *and* SERVANT *exit.*)

**BARD:** To the castle they came where the steward was pacing, fearing the wrath of the king they were facing.

**Scene Three:** *The Castle.*

(SERVANT, SHEPHERD, STEWARD *and* MUSICIANS *enter.*)

**SERVANT:** Here he is, sir! It's TRUE! We have nothing to fear! There's NO WAY that his music will fail to bring cheer!

**STEWARD:** *(To* SERVANT.*)* Let's hope this works out. The king's all in a tizzy. *(To* SHEPHERD.*)* Are you ready to work? We have got to get busy! You see, we've a problem. Our king gets so mad, he pitches these fits that are horribly bad. He rants and he raves and explodes like a bomb. We think that your music will help him stay calm.

**SHEPHERD:** I am only a shepherd who plays and sings. Are you sure you want ME to play for the king?

**STEWARD:** *(Pointing to* MUSICIANS.*)* If you only knew what we heard, my dear lad! There's no WAY in the WORLD you could be half that bad!

**SHEPHERD:** Then I'll do it! I'll do it with all my heart! Tell me, where do I go and just when do I start?

*(Everyone exits.)*

**BARD:** Sure enough, just that evening the hills and the dales were filled with the sounds of the king's angry wails. The newly hired shepherd was put to the test but he played and he sang and he gave it his best! Then all of a sudden, to his great surprise, the king stopped his ranting, his shrieks and his cries.

*(STEWARD and* SHEPHERD *enter.)*

**STEWARD:** He's NEVER recovered in just quite that way. It was great! But please tell me, just what did you play?

**SHEPHERD:** My songs are so simple. They're really just prayers. I give God my praises and tell Him my cares. He makes me so glad—that's the very best part. I sing all my songs straight to Him from my heart.

**STEWARD:** I don't need to tell you the king is so pleased! He wants you to live here! Please say you'll agree!

**SHEPHERD:** How can I say no? To God be the praise. I'll serve with my whole heart for all of my days.

*(STEWARD and* SHEPHERD *exit.)*

**BARD:** So the shepherd stayed on and he served his king well. And that ends the tale we came here to tell. You may have heard something that's like this before. If you just can't quite place it and want to hear more, the Bible will tell you of David, the king, who once was a shepherd who knew how to sing.

**For the real deal read 1 Samuel 20**

# The Friendship Game

**Characters: T. RUTH BRAKER; AUDIENCE; JONATHAN; ABNER; JOAB (JOH-ahb); DAVID**

**Props:** Characters may wish to pantomime the use of props.

**Scene:** *Game show set with three chairs on one side of a partition and one on the other side.*

**T. RUTH:** *(Enters.)* Welcome one and all to...

**AUDIENCE:** The Friendship Game!

**T. RUTH:** Where one contestant selects one of three friends to be his or her BEST FRIEND. And I'm your host...

**AUDIENCE:** T. Ruth Braker! *(Cheers.)*

**T. RUTH:** Thank you! And now let's meet our friends. Friend #1 is the son of a king and heir to the throne. He's an excellent warrior and one of his hobbies is archery. Please welcome, Jonathan, son of Saul!

**AUDIENCE:** *(Claps and cheers.)* Yeah!

**JONATHAN:** *(Enters waving and sits in chair.)* Thank you, T. Ruth!

**T. RUTH:** Friend #2 is the commander of the army and cousin to the king. Please welcome Abner, son of Ner.

**AUDIENCE:** *(Claps and cheers.)* Yeah!

**ABNER:** *(Enters and sits in chair.)* Thank you! Thank you!

**T. RUTH:** And Friend #3 is actually a nephew of our contestant today. Please welcome the young and enthusiastic Joab.

**AUDIENCE:** *(Claps and cheers.)* Yeah!

**JOAB:** *(Enters waving wildly to the AUDIENCE.)* Hello, everybody!

**T. RUTH:** Now, let's meet our contestant. The youngest of ten children, our contestant's hobbies include writing songs, playing the harp, defeating Philistines and slaying giants. Please welcome David, son of Jesse!

**AUDIENCE:** *(Cheers wildly.)*

**DAVID:** Thank you. And thank you, T. Ruth, for that kind introduction.

**T. RUTH:** My pleasure. Now, are you ready to find that friend of your dreams?

**DAVID:** I'm ready.

**T. RUTH:** You will ask a question and each of the contestants will have an opportunity to answer. You may ask your first question.

**DAVID:** Thank you, T. Ruth. Friend #1, describe your best feature as a friend.

**JONATHAN:** Well, I guess I'm pretty loyal. And I'm not concerned about status or anything like that.

**DAVID:** Great! Friend #2?

**ABNER:** Well, I'm loyal, up to a point. I like to do what I believe is right.

**DAVID:** That's pretty good, too. Friend #3?

**JOAB:** Hey, I'm loyal, too!

**DAVID:** Okay. Friend #1, if I were in trouble, would you try to help me, or would you want to keep yourself safe?

**JONATHAN:** What kind of a friend would I be if I didn't stand by you in times of trouble? Of course I would help you.

**ABNER:** Yeah, well it would depend on what kind of trouble you were in. Now, say, if you were to make the king mad, I'd have to support the king.

**JOAB:** Hey, wrong or right, I'll stick by you. I'll even do some dirty work for you, if you want.

**DAVID:** Well, I'm not sure that's what I'm looking for. Friend #3, suppose I became king and gave an order you didn't agree with, would you follow it?

**JOAB:** A person has to think for himself.

**DAVID:** But what if it was God's will?

**JOAB:** Hey, sometimes you've gotta help God along! You know what I mean?

**DAVID:** Not exactly. Friend #2?

**ABNER:** I'll always obey the orders of whoever is in power, no matter what!

**DAVID:** I see. How about you, Friend #1?

**JONATHAN:** I always try to follow the will of God. So I would do my best to do what's right.

**DAVID:** OK. Friend #2, suppose you were close to the king, and he decided to kill me, what would you do?

**ABNER:** I AM close to the king. I would hunt you down for him.

**DAVID:** Whoa! How about you, Friend #3?

**JOAB:** Me? Close to the king? Fat chance. I'd help you hide. I'd even kill the king for you.

**DAVID:** Well, that wasn't what I was asking. Friend #1, what would you do?

**JONATHAN:** Well, if I found out the king wanted to hurt you unjustly, I would warn you and help you in whatever way I could.

**T. RUTH:** All right, David. Time is up. Which friend do you choose? Friend #1, Friend #2 or Friend #3?

**DAVID:** Well, they all have good qualities, but I think I'll pick Friend #1 because he is willing to do whatever God wants. It's hard to go wrong with a friend like that.

**T. RUTH:** Thank you to all our participants. Join us again tomorrow for...

**AUDIENCE:** The Friendship Game!

For the **real story** read 1 Samuel 21:1-3, 10-12; 22:1-5; 23—24

# The Fugitive

**Characters: NARRATOR; DAVID; SAUL; SERVANTS** and **SOLDIERS; SOLDIER 1; MAN 1; MAN 2; ECHO**

**Props:** Characters may wish to pantomime the use of props.

**NARRATOR:** Unjustly accused of treason by King Saul, David had to flee for his life. Aided by Saul's son, Jonathan, David escaped. For now, the sentence of death has been delayed. David is free. Free to jump at every shadow, free to hide from the king's men, free to roam from place to place hoping to find a haven of safety from Saul.

Free to be...THE FUGITIVE.

## ACT ONE

(SAUL *enters court filled with kneeling SER-VANTS and SOLDIERS.*)

**SAUL:** (*Screaming with rage.*) You call yourselves servants?

**SERVANTS and SOLDIERS:** (*Mumbling.*) Yes, m'lord.

**SAUL:** Can David give you promotions?

**SERVANTS and SOLDIERS:** No m'lord.

**SAUL:** Then why do you all conspire with him? (*Voice changes to whining.*) Doesn't anybody care about me? You all knew Jonathan, my own son, was helping him. And now David has 400 men with him! Everybody hates me. You're all no good. Doesn't anybody feel sorry for me? (*Buries face in hands and sobs.*)

**SOLDIER 1:** (*Enters and salutes.*) M'lord. We've just heard that David and his men were spotted—

**SAUL:** (*Interrupts.*) Good. If they've got spots, maybe they're all going to die of some horrible disease.

**SOLDIER 1:** No, m'lord. I mean, they were seen, out in the wilderness.

**SAUL:** Well, why didn't you say so in the first place? Follow me, men. We're going after him.

(SAUL *and* SOLDIER 1 *exit.* SERVANTS and SOLDIERS *sit on the floor.*)

## ACT TWO

(DAVID, MAN 1 *and* MAN 2 *enter and stand together as in a cave.*)

**DAVID:** We should be safe in this cave. There are so many caves in these hills, Saul won't know where to begin looking for us!

**MAN 1:** This cave is awesome, David. Listen! Helllllooo!

**ECHO:** Helllloo...hellloo...hello!

**MAN 2:** Let me try! Shalommm!

**ECHO:** Shalommm...shalomm...shalom.

**DAVID:** (*Thoughtfully.*) Shalom. Shalom means "peace". I sure could use a little peace right now. We ALL need a rest from Saul's constant—

**MAN 1:** (*Whispering.*) Shhhh! Someone's coming into the cave.

(DAVID, MAN 1 *and* MAN 2 *back up and crouch on the ground to hide.* SAUL *enters cave and peers around, trying to adjust his eyes.*)

**MAN 1:** (*Punches* DAVID'S *shoulder.*) Look! God has delivered Saul into your hands!

**MAN 2:** Now you can do whatever you want to him.

**MAN 1:** You could kill him!

**DAVID:** Wait here.

(SAUL *stands with his back toward* DAVID. DAVID *creeps up to* SAUL *and pretends to cut off a piece of his robe.* SAUL *is unaware.* DAVID *creeps back to* MEN.)

**MAN 1:** That's IT?

**MAN 2:** Why not cut off his whole robe? (*Draws a finger across his throat.*) Right about throat level.

**DAVID:** God forbid that I should hurt or kill His king. Let him go in peace—shalom!

(SAUL *walks out of cave.* DAVID *and* MEN *follow.*)

**DAVID:** (*Calling loudly.*) My lord and king!

**SAUL:** (*Turns around.*) Who's there?

**DAVID:** (*Bows down.*) Why do you listen to men who say "David wants to hurt you?" I could have cut your throat in this cave. Look! I cut off a piece of your robe. But I have never tried to hurt you, and I never will.

**SAUL:** (*Choking up.*) Is this the voice of David?

**DAVID:** It is.

**MAN 1:** What's wrong with Saul?

**MAN 2:** It looks like there's something wrong with his face. I've never seen it like that.

**SAUL:** Oh, how could I be so cruel and stupid? You have shown me how good you are. Now I KNOW the kingdom will be yours.

**MAN 1:** It looks like...

**MAN 2:** It can't be...

**MAN 1** and **MAN 2:** (*Together.*) He's crying!

**SAUL:** Show mercy to me, my son, and promise me one thing.

**DAVID:** You only have to ask.

**SAUL:** When the Lord makes you king, don't destroy my family. Do not blot my name out from the earth.

**DAVID:** As surely as the Lord reigns, this I promise you.

**NARRATOR:** Because David was wise, he sought to stop his conflict with Saul, not to prolong it. He knew that seeking a peaceful solution was better than getting even. So Saul went home. But David kept hiding, for he knew that Saul would never really give up the chase. This is the life of one on the run—never to rest in complete peace, always vigilant against the threat of being caught. Such is the life of...THE FUGITIVE.

For the **real story** read 1 Samuel 24

# Foe or Friend

**Characters: JEROME; SAUL; ABNER; DOEG (DOH-ehg); DAVID**

**Scene:** *Saul's camp in the Desert of En Gedi.*

**JEROME:** O great King Saul, where have you been?

**SAUL:** Oh...ah...um...

**JEROME:** I've heard some strange names before, but "Oahum" is new to me.

**SAUL:** No, I wasn't saying a name. I was just thinking.

**JEROME:** Ah, so you've been to Oahum to think. Most excellent, oh my noble king.

**SAUL:** No, I didn't go to a place called Oahum, I went to a cave to...to...

**JEROME:** Certainly the Cave TuTu must be a cave of great depth and beauty if my noble king chose to think in it.

**SAUL:** No! I wasn't. OK, yes, that's what I was doing—thinking.

**ABNER:** *(Enters and bows low before SAUL.)* Your most regal majesty.

**SAUL:** What is the news?

**ABNER:** Your soldiers have searched most diligently to the east. Your soldiers have searched most faithfully to the west. Your soldiers have searched—

**SAUL:** Enough! Did you find that low-lying, lily-livered skunk?

**ABNER:** No, my most generous king, we did not.

**JEROME:** Did you try the land of Oahum?

**ABNER:** Where?

**SAUL:** Never mind. Bring Doeg to me!

**ABNER:** As swiftly as my feet may fly, with your bidding I will comply. *(Exits.)*

**JEROME:** For whom does my noble king search?

**SAUL:** That no-good, cowardly traitor, David.

**JEROME:** Is that the same David who killed our enemy Goliath?

**SAUL:** Yes, that curse-of-the-earth, slimeball David.

**JEROME:** Is that the same David who used to sing you songs to help you feel better?

**SAUL:** Yes, that lowlife David.

**JEROME:** Is that the same David who's been successful in every battle he's led against the Philistines?

**SAUL:** Yes, that show-stealing, dastardly David.

**JEROME:** Perhaps you should have done some MORE thinking in the land of Oahum.

**SAUL:** WHAT?!?

**JEROME:** Forgive me, my most intolerant king, but David doesn't seem to be much of an enemy.

**SAUL:** That shows what you know! Do not the people love him MORE than me? Is not God MORE pleased with David than me?

**JEROME:** Well, yes, but...

**SAUL:** There you have it then. He's a low-lying, lily-livered, no-good, cowardly, show-stealing traitor, and I will not rest until I have found him and cut him down like the dog he is.

**DOEG:** *(Enters.)* You called me, my most glorious king.

**JEROME:** I believe the king would like to cut you down.

**DOEG:** *(Horrified.)* Why? What have I done?

**SAUL:** No, no. I said I wanted to cut down DAVID like a dog.

**DOEG:** As well you should, my most unobservant king.

**SAUL:** Huh? Look, are you sure your reports said David was here?

**DOEG:** I am most certain, your most magnificent majesty.

**SAUL:** Well, he doesn't seem to be—

**DAVID:** *(Shouting from hillside.)* My lord and king!

**SAUL:** Who said that?

**JEROME:** That guy standing up there on the hill waving something. Looks like David.

**SAUL:** Is that you, David?

**DAVID:** Yes, it is. Look, here is a piece of your cloak that I cut off while you were in the cave.

**JEROME:** I knew they should have looked in Oahum.

**SAUL:** *(To JEROME.)* Silence, fool!

**DAVID:** I could have just as easily killed you, but I didn't. I am NOT your enemy. I am your loyal subject and friend. So why are you trying to kill me?

**JEROME:** You know, my noble king, there is a big chunk of your robe missing. Maybe he's right—he could have killed you!

**SAUL:** Silence! I must think. It's true, he could have killed me, but he didn't. Have I been wrong? *(To DAVID.)* David, my son. You are right. I have been unfair to you. I'm so sorry! You are safe to travel about my country as you wish. *(To DOEG.)* Tell Abner to get my soldiers ready. We are leaving!

**DOEG:** Do you think that is wise? I could go up and kill him now.

**SAUL:** No, I have given my word. And that lowbred shepherd has proven that he is my friend. *(SAUL exits.)*

**JEROME:** How long do you think the friendship will last?

**DOEG:** Not long. Not long at all.

For the **real story** read 1 Samuel 25:1-42

# What Did You Say?

**Characters: DAVID; HELPER,** good-natured, but dense; **ABIGAIL,** dignified and smart; **MAID,** good-natured, but dense; **MESSENGER**

**Scene:** DAVID'S *camp headquarters.* DAVID *is dictating a letter to his helper.*

## ACT ONE

**DAVID:** Peace be to thee and to thy house and unto all that thou hast.

**HELPER:** WHAT?

**DAVID:** It's a standard greeting. It's a way of saying hello.

**HELPER:** Oh, then I'll write "hello."

**DAVID:** NO, write it as I SAID it. These matters must be handled correctly!

**HELPER:** Oh. Well, what was it you said again?

**DAVID:** *(Sighs.)* Peace be to thee and to thy house and...

**HELPER:** Hold it! I can't write that fast!

**DAVID:** I shall write the message myself!... Now, see that my men go forth with this message to Nabal.

**HELPER:** Fourth? But I thought you were sending TEN men.

**DAVID:** Go forth means to go—in this case, to go to the house of Nabal.

**HELPER:** Oh. *(Whistles loudly.)*

**MESSENGER:** Here I am!

**HELPER:** Deliver this to Nabal. David, do you think Nabal will really share his food with us?

**DAVID:** Have not we been guarding his flocks? Does not he owe his prosperity and good fortune to the benefit of our protection?

**HELPER:** Huh?

**DAVID:** We've been making sure his sheep and shepherds were safe, which has kept him from losing them, so he's richer for it. Therefore, he should give us some food when we need it.

**HELPER:** Oh. Why don't you speak in plain English?

**DAVID:** Because I'm a Hebrew. Besides, I'm practicing to be king. Look—the messenger is back. What is the news from Nabal? Let's see...Why, that vile dog! How DARE he treat me this way?

**HELPER:** Messenger, you gave the message to the DOG?

**MESSENGER:** No, vile dog is a way of saying that Nabal isn't very nice.

**HELPER:** What did he do?

**MESSENGER:** He said he wasn't going to share any food with a worthless slave who was running away from his master.

**HELPER:** What worthless slave?

**DAVID:** ME! HE WAS TALKING ABOUT ME!

**HELPER:** You seem a little tense, David. How about a nice cold drink?

**DAVID:** We don't HAVE any drink! Tell my men to gird up their swords!

**HELPER:** To do WHAT with their swords?

**DAVID:** Put them on—prepare for BATTLE!

**HELPER:** Oh.

**DAVID:** I shall not rest until every man in Nabal's household is slain!

**HELPER:** Slain?

**DAVID:** Killed.

**HELPER:** Oh. OH!

## ACT TWO

**MESSENGER:** My lord, servants approach with laden donkeys.

**HELPER:** Laid in what? (DAVID glares at him.) Never mind.

**ABIGAIL:** Please, let your maidservant speak into your ears.

**MAID:** Me? But what do I say?

**ABIGAIL:** Not you, ME. I'm humbling myself before him so he won't kill us all.

**MAID:** Oh.

**DAVID:** You may speak.

**ABIGAIL:** My lord, I am Abigail, wife of Nabal. I beg that you pay no regard to this foolish man.

**MAID:** Don't you want David to ignore Nabal?

**ABIGAIL:** That's what I just said. Now be quiet so I can finish.

**MAID:** Oh. OK.

**ABIGAIL:** Please accept my most humble apology. My husband, Nabal is a fool. Unfortunately, I did not see the young men when they came, for I would have given them the food they desired. I know you are the Lord's chosen one. Please put aside your anger and do not risk your good name by venting your anger on my husband and his household.

**HELPER:** What did she say?

**MAID:** I don't know.

**DAVID:** She's asking me not to do anything foolish, like taking revenge on her husband.

**HELPER:** Revenge is foolish?

**DAVID:** Revenge belongs only to the Lord. Abigail, I accept your gift, and I promise not to hurt anyone in your household. And I thank you for reminding me of what is good in the eyes of the Lord. Come, join us as we feast on your generosity.

**MAID:** What?

**HELPER:** We're going to kill the fatted calf.

**MAID:** What?

**HELPER:** We're going to PARTY!

**For the real deal read 2 Samuel 11—12:25**

# Gabby's Game Show

### Characters:

**JOE,** an all-around nice guy; **JENNY,** an average kid who tries hard; **RICHARD,** looks like someone you might want to avoid; **GABBY,** host of Gabby's Game Show; **GEORGE,** the Narrator of Gabby's Game Show; **DR. NATE,** an author and the guest judge on Gabby's Game Show; **AUDIENCE**

**Scene:** *The studio set of Gabby's Game Show.*

**GEORGE:** Let's all welcome Gabby Grip, the host of Gabby's Game Show, where people compete to find out whose sin is the MOST unforgivable.

**GABBY:** Thank you, George, and welcome to our audience! Today our judge will be Dr. Nate, the author of that best-selling book, "How to Tell When Someone Is Lying." It's a pleasure to have you here with us today, Dr. Nate.

**DR. NATE:** I'm sorry Gabby, but you're lying. You are NOT happy to be here today. You'd rather be home. AND you aren't happy to see me. In fact, you think I'm a pompous wind-bag.

**GABBY:** Well, that much is true. But let's meet our contestants, shall we? George, who's our first contestant?

**GEORGE:** Our first contestant is Joe Joy. A straight-*A* student at Podo Middle School, Joe spends his spare time helping out at the Elder Care Center, leads the Clean Up Our Town committee and is president of the after-school club at his church.

**GABBY:** Welcome, Joe!

**JOE:** Thanks, Gabby.

**GEORGE:** Our second contestant is Jenny Jones. Jenny is an average student at Podo Middle School who spends her spare time trying out for the track team.

**GABBY:** Welcome, Jenny! I guess you must know Joe since you're at the same school.

**JENNY:** Um, well, a little...

**DR. NATE:** I'm sorry, Jenny, but you're lying!

**GABBY:** Dr. Nate, how about we listen to their stories, and THEN you can do your judging?

**GEORGE:** And our final contestant is Richard Smudge, a straight-*D* student at Podo Middle School, who spends his spare time stealing spare change from people who walk by.

**RICHARD:** Hey, you can't prove it!

**GABBY:** Welcome to you all! Now, let's begin our contest. First, we will have the voting round where the audience decides who is most likely to have the most unforgivable sin. Next you tell your stories, and then Dr. Nate decides which sin is the most unforgivable.

**GEORGE:** Audience, based on what you know about these people, who do you vote for?

**AUDIENCE:** *(Votes.)*

**GABBY:** All right. Let's hear your story, Richard.

**RICHARD:** Okay, well, I never STOLE anything, but I saw this man drop a ten, and I wanted it for myself.

**GABBY:** That's pretty bad.

**DR. NATE:** And not quite the truth.

**GABBY:** Hmm. All right, let's hear your story, Jenny.

**JENNY:** Well, my mom asked me to clean my room, but I just yelled at her, saying it was unfair and that I hated her. Then I ran out of the house to see my friend.

**GABBY:** Being disrespectful and disobedient is pretty serious stuff.

**DR. NATE:** And not the whole truth.

**GABBY:** All right, Joe, what could you have possibly done?

**JOE:** I cheated on a test. I'd forgotten to study, and the girl next to me had all the answers, so I copied them. When the teacher asked us why our answers were exactly the same, I said I'd seen the girl looking at my paper. Of course, the teacher believed me. The girl got an *F* on her test and her parents grounded her for a month!

**GABBY:** I'm sure that isn't the truth.

**DR. NATE:** But it is!

**EVERYONE:** Gasp!

**GABBY:** Well, I guess Joe wins, then.

**DR. NATE:** Not so fast, Gabby. You said the sins had to be unforgivable.

**GABBY:** Yes...

**DR. NATE:** What Joe didn't tell you is that yesterday he went to his teacher, the girl's parents and his parents and told them all that had happened. Then he asked for God's forgiveness. So his sin was forgiven!

**GABBY:** I see. Well, then the winner is Jenny.

**DR. NATE:** Nope! Jenny didn't finish telling her story, either. After she cooled down, Jenny went back and apologized to her mom. Then she cleaned her room. She also asked God to forgive her and was forgiven.

**GABBY:** So Richard, I guess you are the winner.

**DR. NATE:** Tell them the TRUE story, Richard.

**RICHARD:** Okay, okay, I didn't keep the ten, I wanted to, but I didn't.

**GABBY:** Are you telling me we don't have a winner? We can't have a game show without a winner!

**DR. NATE:** As long as people are willing to ask God for forgiveness and change their ways, no sin is too great to be forgiven.

**GABBY:** Thank you so much for your help, Dr. Nate.

**DR. NATE:** You're lying, again, Gabby.

**GABBY:** Oh, fine! You've destroyed my show with your truth telling and I'm not glad I met you! Hmm, "Truth Telling," or "To Tell the Truth," now there's a game show idea...

**For the real story read 1 Kings 3:16-28**

# Case No. 212: To Tell the Truth

**Characters: BOB PARKER**, TV Court host, very excitable; **MS. TATE**, defendant, trying to put on a good front for the camera, but whines a lot; **MS. FORSHUN**, plaintiff, trying to put on a good front for the camera; **SOLOMON**, king and judge, wise and dignified bailiff; **OBSERVER**, Female Audience Member, very enthusiastic; **RALPH,** show director, very calm

**Props:** Characters may wish to pantomime the use of props.

**Scene:** *The set of King* SOLOMON'S *TV Court.*

**BOB:** Welcome, ladies and gentlemen. Bob Parker here. Today in King Solomon's TV Court, we will be hearing the case of Ms. Tate versus Ms. Forshun in a custody battle. But first a word from our sponsors. *(RALPH does a cut sign and takes off earphones.)*

**MS. TATE:** How long will this take? I have a...um...appointment in an hour.

**BOB:** Depends on how much evidence you have, how many witnesses—

**MS. FORSHUN:** But there aren't any witnesses.

**BOB:** What? Ralph, what happened to the witnesses?!

**RALPH:** No witnesses listed. No evidence, either.

**BOB:** NO EVIDENCE? NO WITNESSES? The king can't decide a case with no evidence and no witnesses! And what are we going to SHOW?

**RALPH:** *(Shrugs, and puts headphones back on.)* We're on in five, four...

**BOB:** Who booked this case? I'm ruined. No evidence. No wit—*(RALPH cues BOB to begin.)* Welcome back, ladies and gentlemen. Our trial is ready to begin.

**BAILIFF:** All rise for the entrance of the king! Ms. Tate and Ms. Forshun, please take the stand. Raise your right hands. Do you solemnly swear to tell the truth?

**MS. TATE and MS. FORSHUN:** I do.

**BAILIFF:** The plaintiff, Ms. Forshun, may state her case.

**MS. TATE:** Why does she get to go first? Look, I'm on a tight schedule here—

**SOLOMON:** The plaintiff ALWAYS goes first. Proceed, Ms. Forshun.

**MS. FORSHUN:** Yes, your honor, ah, well, Ms. Tate and I, we don't make much money. Have to live in a tiny apartment on Ninth Street—filthy, noisy place—

**MS. TATE:** Are you going to let her go on forever?

**SOLOMON:** Your point, Ms. Forshun?

**MS. FORSHUN:** Well, when our babies came, we couldn't afford a hospital or nurse or anything. So we just had the babies by ouselves.

**SOLOMON:** Surely a friend would have helped you!

**MS. FORSHUN:** Most people don't like to associate with us.

**SOLOMON:** I see. Go on.

**MS. FORSHUN:** Well, last night I laid down to sleep, holding my precious baby next to me, and in the morning, my baby was GONE. In its place was Ms. Tate's DEAD baby. I guess something happened during the night—maybe she rolled over on it.

**MS. TATE:** LIES! VICIOUS LIES!

**SOLOMON:** Ms. Forshun, do you have any witnesses or evidence that this baby is yours?

**MS. TATE:** No, she hasn't, your honor.

**SOLOMON:** I asked Ms. Forshun!

**MS. FORSHUN:** No, your honor, I don't.

**MS. TATE:** What did I tell you? She's lying. HER baby died, not mine. Hey, I'd never roll over and...

**SOLOMON:** *(To* MS. TATE.*)* Do YOU have any evidence or witnesses?

**MS. TATE:** Well, like she said, we live alone, and don't have much money...

**SOLOMON:** DO YOU HAVE WITNESSES?

**MS. TATE:** No. But—

**SOLOMON:** Quiet while I think this over.

**BOB:** Let's talk with someone from our studio audience. *(To* OBSERVER.*)* Your name, please?

**OBSERVER:** *(Gives name.)*

**BOB:** And what do you think of these proceedings?

**OBSERVER:** I think King Solomon is SO-O-O handsome!

**BOB:** Uh, yes. But which woman do you think is the mother of the baby?

**OBSERVER:** Who KNOWS? There's no evidence, no witnesses, and they both look like liars! Even King Solomon won't be able to figure this one out.

**BOB:** Uh-huh. Well, let's find out how our audience would decide this case. *(All audience members vote on which mother they'd give the baby to.)* Thank you, everyone.

**SOLOMON:** I have decided. Cut the baby in two and give one half to each woman.

**MS. TATE:** Seems fair. Can I go now?

**MS. FORSHUN:** NO! Don't kill the baby! Let HER have the baby! But PLEASE don't kill it!

**SOLOMON:** Give the baby to Ms. Forshun. SHE is the baby's real mother.

**BOB:** King Solomon, how were you able to make your decision?

**SOLOMON:** Only the child's real mother would be willing to give it up so that it would live.

**BOB:** And that's it for today. Next week, two brothers fight over an inheritance. See you then!

**For the real story read 1 Kings 11:1-13, 29-40**

# Not Another Statue!

**Characters: X,** palace servant; **Y,** palace servant; **NARRATOR**

**Scene:** *A palace corridor.*

**NARRATOR:** Two servants cross paths in a corridor of a palace.

**X:** He's getting married again.

**Y:** Oh no!

**X:** You know what that means.

**Y:** Yep.

**X & Y:** Another statue!

**X:** Where will we put it?

**Y:** He'll probably build another building. He's good at that, you know.

**X:** Yeah, we'll soon be known as the City of Temples.

**Y:** Well, gotta go dust the west wing. With all those statues, it may take DAYS.

**X:** See ya.

**NARRATOR:** Some time later, the servants cross paths again.

**X:** Did you hear?

**Y:** What?

**X:** He's getting married.

**Y:** Oh no, not again!

**X:** Yep, and you know what that means—

**X & Y:** Another statue!

**Y:** I sure hope this one isn't as ugly as the last one. Gives me the willies every time I have to dust it.

**X:** You think DUSTING them is bad, you should try cleaning up after the rituals. Well, gotta go, wife number 53 is celebrating some harvest ritual tonight. I hear he plans to be there.

**Y:** See ya.

**NARRATOR:** And a little later than that, the servants cross paths again.

**X:** Guess what?

**X & Y:** He's getting married again!

**Y:** I suppose that means...

**X & Y:** Another statue!

**Y:** You wouldn't think he'd put up with it. They're not part of his religion, you know.

**X:** Guess he wants to make his wives happy.

**Y:** Yeah. But it seems strange. Well, gotta go. I'm doing the east wing today, tomorrow, and probably the rest of the week.

**X:** See ya.

**NARRATOR:** And much later, the servants cross paths again.

**X:** You're not going to believe this!

**Y:** He's getting married again?

**X:** Yep.

**Y:** How does he remember all their names?

**X:** Don't know.

**Y:** I suppose she'll bring...

**X & Y:** Another statue!

**Y:** You know, I was dusting off the Torah the other day...

**X:** The what?

**Y:** The Torah—the books of Law. And I happened to read that God wants His people to worship only one God—Him.

**X:** ONE God? We sure have a lot more than that around here. Maybe it's just one god per PERSON?

**Y:** No, just one God, the God of the Torah.

**X:** But we don't even have a statue built for Him.

**Y:** The Torah says those statue gods aren't real, they're just idols.

**X:** Huh. Wonder if HE knows?

**Y:** He should—he's the wisest man around.

**X:** Then I wonder why he allows all these statues—er, idols?

**Y:** Don't know. Maybe he doesn't want to offend his wives. Maybe he's trying to impress people. Maybe he's forgotten about the God of the Torah.

**X:** Maybe he just doesn't care.

**Y:** Yeah, maybe. Well, gotta go dust the north wing this month.

**X:** See ya.

**NARRATOR:** And, quite a bit later, the servants meet again.

**X:** Guess what?

**Y:** Not another wife! Not another statue! I can't stand it! All day, cleaning statues. Statues here, statues there—

**X:** No, no, it's about the prophecy.

**Y:** What prophecy?

**X:** That his kingdom will be divided into two kingdoms.

**Y:** Why would he want to do THAT?

**X:** It's not HIS idea.

**Y:** Then whose is it?

**X:** God's. God said that because HE hadn't followed the laws of the Torah, and because HE hadn't put God first in his heart, God was going to give most of the kingdom to someone else!

**Y:** Who would have thought?

**X:** Yeah, he was such a wise man.

**Y:** To lose his kingdom and his favor with God, just because of all of those wives and...

**X & Y:** STATUES!

**For the real deal read 1 Kings 17:1-6**

# The Reliable Ad Agency

**Characters: MORT,** the editor in chief, who yells most of the time; **MERT,** an ad writer; **CURT,** another ad writer; **SQUIRT,** the ad agency gofer, who speaks softly

**Props:** Characters may wish to pantomime the use of props.

**Scene:** *The editor-in-chief's office at the Reliable Advertising Agency.*

**MORT:** *(Yelling.)* Mert! Curt! Squirt! Get in here! My in-basket's overflowing. My phone's ringing off the hook! Where IS everybody? Doesn't anyone WORK around here?

**MERT:** *(Entering.)* Calm down, Mort! Don't have a stroke! Good morning!

**CURT:** *(Entering.)* Mornin', Mort. Didja sleep well? We've got great ads!

**MORT:** Where's Squirt? Where's my coffee?

**SQUIRT:** Mornin', Mort. Glad to see you're not cranky! Here's your coffee.

**MORT:** Let's get down to business! Let me hear your ideas for the Reliable Computer ad campaign!

**CURT:** *(Reading ad.)* Has your hard drive gone soft? Has your RAM turned into jam? Has your Internet access become inaccessible? Reliable Computer has the TOTAL answer for you! The new TOTAL computer NEVER freezes, NEVER loses access and has memory increased by adding a single chip! It does everything—

**MORT:** *(Interrupting.)* Hold it. Is any of this TRUE?

**MERT:** Oh, come on, Mort! This is ADVERTISING!

**SQUIRT:** Sounds like it's a TOTAL lie!

**CURT:** Well, how about this new ad campaign for the four-wheel drive vehicle? *(Reading the ad.)* "If you want to go ANYWHERE, do ANYTHING, the NEW Crusader is for YOU! It goes through lakes. It climbs rocks. It—"

**MORT:** *(Interrupting.)* Hold it. How much of this is true?

**MERT:** Listen, Mort! We have some terrific statistics to back up our claims! This Crusader is really reliable and it can go a lot of places!

**MORT:** It climbs rocks? It SWIMS?

**MERT:** Oh, come on, Mort! This is ADVERTISING!

**SQUIRT:** Why don't you just tell people that it's a good vehicle and leave it at that?

**CURT:** Squirt, that's why you'll always be the gofer and never an ad writer! This is

ADVERTISING! We get people to want what they don't need and buy what they can't afford! It's what makes this country GREAT!

**SQUIRT:** Mert, I think we better move on to the Brite Spot Detergent account. I have an idea—

**MERT:** Oh, so now YOU'RE an ad writer? Well, don't forget how to make coffee!

**MORT:** *(Laughs.)* Let's hear it, Squirt!

**SQUIRT:** *(Pulls a paper out of his pocket and reads.)* Is your laundry looking mean? Let Brite Spot detergent make it beam! Now used by the All Star baseball team to get their uniforms sparkling clean!

**MORT:** It just doesn't grab me.

**CURT:** See, Squirt? You just don't have the knack for advertising!

**SQUIRT:** Well, at least the things I said in MY ad are TRUE! I didn't lie about the detergent. I never said it would make old clothes new or make your family love you—which was what you said in Brite Spot's LAST ad, if I remember right! You can't make such impossible claims and expect people to listen!

**MERT:** What a concept. What do you think, Mort? Doesn't it just frost you? The nerve of this guy!

**MORT:** *(Quietly.)* You know, the kid may have something. What's REALLY reliable in this world, kid? Give me something I can BELIEVE in!

*Note: 1 Kings 17:1-6 tells the story of a time Elijah relied on God.*

**For the real story read 2 Kings 5:1-16**

# In Service of the Master

**Characters: HANNAH,** teenage slave girl from Israel, serving in Naaman's house; **JUDITH,** teenage slave girl from Israel, serving in Naaman's house; **BETH,** 11-year-old slave girl from Israel, serving in Naaman's house; **SHEBA,** 11-year-old servant girl from Aram, serving in Naaman's house; **MRS. NAAMAN,** wife of Naaman—commander of the Aramean army

**Props:** Characters may wish to pantomime the use of props.

**Scene:** *The home of Naaman.* BETH *kneels near a window.*

**HANNAH:** *(Enters talking with JUDITH.)* And then the master tried a mixture of honey, herbs and mud and smeared it on himself. Yuck! *(Sees BETH.)* Beth! What are you doing?

**JUDITH:** Daydreaming again! You'd better get to work, young lady, or you're gonna catch it.

**HANNAH:** Catch what?

**JUDITH:** Trouble! She'll be in trouble. *(To BETH.)* You know how strict our mistress is!

**BETH:** I wasn't daydreaming; I was praying.

**HANNAH:** Praying?!

**JUDITH:** You'd better not let the master catch you praying! He doesn't believe in our God.

**BETH:** But aren't we supposed to obey God over anyone else?

**HANNAH:** In our own country, sure. But our master changed all that when he kidnapped us and forced us to work in this foreign country as his slaves.

**BETH:** But isn't our God everywhere?

**JUDITH:** I guess so. Look, I've got work to do! And so do you! Get busy!

**BETH:** *(Starts sweeping.)* How is our master today?

**JUDITH:** *(Annoyed.)* He has leprosy. How do you think he is?

**BETH:** Maybe we could help him.

**HANNAH:** You have a cure for leprosy?

**BETH:** No. Not me. But there is someone who could help him.

**JUDITH:** Who?

**BETH:** The prophet of God, Elisha. I've heard about all the wonderful things he's done in God's name. Perhaps if I told the master—

**HANNAH:** Hold it!

**JUDITH:** Don't even think about it!

**BETH:** But why not?

**JUDITH:** Well, we aren't allowed to talk to the master.

**HANNAH:** And if he doesn't believe in our God, he's not going to believe that a prophet of our God can help him.

**JUDITH:** (Whispers.) And if our master dies of leprosy, we could be free to return home.

**BETH:** Well, I'd like to see my mother and father again. But I'm sure God wants to help our master. It's not right for us not to tell him.

**HANNAH:** Hmph! Listen to you, wanting to help the master! You are nothing! You are a slave! And just a kid slave at that! Now, get to work and leave us alone.

**BETH:** (To herself.) I'm more than a slave. I'm a servant of God.

**SHEBA:** (Enters and whispers.) Beth! Over here!

**BETH:** Hello, Sheba. How are you today?

**SHEBA:** Why do you let those two boss you around?

**BETH:** They don't really mean any harm. Have you seen our master today?

**SHEBA:** Yes. And he's awfully upset. Here he is, one of the most admired men in our country, and he's got this horrible disease. I wish I could help him!

**BETH:** If he would go to see the prophet of God in my country, I know God would heal him.

**SHEBA:** Why would your God heal our master? We don't follow Him or obey His laws. If our master went there, your prophet would laugh at him.

**BETH:** Sheba, God loves everyone, including our master. The prophet knows that.

**SHEBA:** Yeah, right.

**MRS. N.:** (Entering.) What is going on in here? Why aren't you working?

**JUDITH:** (To BETH.) See? I told you that you'd catch it!

**HANNAH:** Catch what?

**JUDITH:** (To HANNAH.) Do you ever listen to yourself?

**MRS. N.:** Silence! Explain yourself, Beth!

**BETH:** Ma'am, I was just saying that if our master would go visit the prophet of God in our country, I know my God would cure him of his leprosy.

**MRS. N.:** (Angrily.) Are you making fun of my husband?

**BETH:** Oh no, ma'am. I wouldn't do that. I know how sad and worried you are.

**MRS. N.:** (Sighs.) I'm sorry for being angry, Beth. You're right. I'm very worried about my husband. So you really think this prophet would help?

**BETH:** Yes, ma'am.

**MRS. N.:** Well, the prophet certainly can't make things worse. (Smiles.) Thank you, Beth. I'll tell my husband right away! (Exits.)

**SHEBA:** I can't believe our mistress apologized! (BETH kneels by the window.)

**JUDITH:** I haven't seen her smile in weeks. (To BETH.) What are you doing now?

**BETH:** I'm praying for my master.

**HANNAH:** Didn't we tell you to get to work?

**JUDITH:** Leave her alone, Hannah. Who knows? Maybe praying will help.

**For the real story read 2 Kings 6:8-23**

# Two Kings and a Prophet

**Characters: AHADAD**, Aramean soldier; **BEN-HADAD**, king of Aram; **MIHADAD**, Aramean soldier; **UHADAD**, Aramean soldier

## ACT ONE

**Scene:** *The king of Aram's headquarters.*

**AHADAD:** *(Enters with* MIHADAD, UHADAD *marching behind.)* Your most honorable majesty called for us?

**BEN-HADAD:** Yes, I have a problem.

**MIHADAD:** Tell us, your problem, O wondrous king! Your problem is our problem.

**BEN-HADAD:** Exactly!

**AHADAD:** I am not familiar with Exactly. Is he a new recruit? Tell us where to find him and we will eliminate your problem!

**BEN-HADAD:** MY problem isn't Exactly. Exactly it's YOUR problem.

**MIHADAD:** We understand that. Point out this Exactly fellow, and we'll get rid of him immediately.

**BEN-HADAD:** No, no, no! Can't you see?

**AHADAD:** I have perfect vision, sir!

**BEN-HADAD:** It's not your vision I'm worried about. Now listen! There is a spy in our camp.

**MIHADAD:** We KNOW how to deal with spies! Which one is Exactly?

**BEN-HADAD:** There is NO Exactly! Now LISTEN! Someone, I don't know WHO, is telling the King of Israel our secret attack plans.

**MIHADAD:** But we're the only ones who know our secret attack plans.

**BEN-HADAD:** Precisely!

**AHADAD:** I think I've met Precisely.

**BEN-HADAD:** THERE IS NO PRECISELY! One of US is the spy!

**MIHADAD:** And you're sure it's not Exactly or Precisely?

**BEN-HADAD:** AUGH!

**UHADAD:** I think, sir, I know what's going on.

**A & M:** You?!?

**UHADAD:** Yeah, me. The king of Israel has a prophet—Elisha. This Elisha seems to always know our plans.

**AHADAD:** Aha! And he gets information from Precisely and Exactly.

**UHADAD:** No, it's said that his God tells him.

**BEN-HADAD:** God tells Elisha our battle plans?

**UHADAD:** Yes, sir!

**BEN-HADAD:** Well, what are YOU going to do about him? *(AHADAD and MIHADAD shrug their shoulders.)*

**UHADAD:** Perhaps if we take the army and sneak up on him at night, we could capture him.

**BEN-HADAD:** Excellent idea! Uhadad, I'm putting you in charge!

**A & M:** Him?

**BEN-HADAD:** Yes, him!

## ACT TWO

**Scene:** *The king of Israel's palace in Samaria.* (ELISHA *enters leading* UHADAD, AHADAD *and* MIHADAD.)

**UHADAD:** It's sure nice of you to lead us to Elisha.

**AHADAD:** Yeah, especially with this sudden blindness.

**MIHADAD:** Didn't know we'd meet such a nice stranger.

**ELISHA:** Thank you. OK, you can open your eyes now.

**A, M & U:** *(Open eyes and scream.)*

**UHADAD:** The king of Israel's palace? We're in Joram's palace?

**ELISHA:** Yup!

**MIHADAD:** Well, in case you hadn't noticed, we're Aramean soldiers. I don't think King Joram will be too happy to see us.

**JORAM:** Elisha! My buddy, my pal!

**UHADAD:** You're Elisha?

**ELISHA:** Yep!

**AHADAD:** Oh great! Wait till our king hears about this one.

**JORAM:** So did you bring them here for me to kill?

**ELISHA:** Joram! You are NOT going to kill them!

**A & M:** He's not?

**JORAM:** I'm not?

**ELISHA:** No, these men are God's prisoners.

**JORAM:** Is He going to send down fire from heaven and burn them up, like He did for Elijah?

**ELISHA:** No.

**A, M & U:** Whew!

**JORAM:** OK, so He'll send a plague that will kill them instantly?

**ELISHA:** NO!

**JORAM:** Well, what IS He going to do to them?

**ELISHA:** He wants YOU to feed them and give them water.

**JORAM:** Well, that seems like a waste, when they're going to die anyway. But if that's what God wants...

**ELISHA:** Joram, listen to me carefully. God doesn't want YOU to kill the Aramean army, and God isn't going to kill the Aramean army. God wants you to treat the Arameans with KINDNESS and send them home.

**JORAM:** Treat them with kindness and send them home? Are you sure you heard God right?

**ELISHA:** Yes, I'm sure!

**JORAM:** Well, OK. Servants, get these men some food and some fresh water. And make it snappy; they've got a long journey! (JORAM *exits.*)

**UHADAD:** Wow! What kind of a God have you got?

**ELISHA:** A very powerful God. A loving God. The ONLY God. And don't you forget it!

**A, M & U:** We won't!

**UHADAD:** *(To* AHADAD *and* MIHADAD.) But our king may not be so easy to convince. Mihadad, you tell the king.

**MIHADAD:** Not me! Have Ahadad do it.

**AHADAD:** Not me! No way!

**UHADAD:** Well, someone's got to do it!

**AHADAD:** Hey, let's get Exactly and Precisely to do it. The king doesn't seem to like them anyway.

# Dinner Fit for a King

**Characters: SERVANT,** queen Esther's servant; **ESTHER,** queen of Persia; **XERXES (ZERK-SEES),** king of Persia; **HAMAN (HAY-MAN),** King Xerxes' right-hand man

## ACT ONE

**Props:** Characters may wish to pantomime the use of props.

**Scene:** *A corridor in the Persian palace of* KING XERXES.

**SERVANT:** *(Enters carrying plates of food.)* Go here. Do that. Dust this. Bring that. That's all I hear. One big fancy dinner for the king wasn't enough for Esther. Oh no! She's got to have TWO big fancy dinners. You know, I was in the same harem* as her. If Xerxes had chosen me instead, I'd be queen! *(Exits.)*

**ESTHER:** *(Enters, checking off a list.)* Meat cooked. Table set. Fruit washed. Beautification done. Everything's GOT to be perfect!

Imagine if Mordecai (MOR-duh-KI) hadn't warned me about this disaster! I just hope and pray my plan works. Otherwise, that Haman will have all my people destroyed, including Mordecai and myself! May God be with us. *(Exits.)*

**XERXES:** *(Enters.)* I wonder what it is that Queen Esther wants. It must be something very important for her to risk her life coming to me. And now she's not only invited me to one dinner but to two. Hm...*(Exits.)*

**HAMAN:** *(Enters.)* I am the second-most important man in the kingdom. You want proof? Last night, the queen had a private banquet; today, she's having another. Do you know who was invited? The king and I. That's all. No princes, no foreign royalty. I would be the happiest man in the world were it not for that Mordecai. But I have plans to take care of him! *(Exits.)*

## ACT TWO

**Scene:** *The banquet room in* QUEEN ESTHER's *chamber.*

**XERXES:** *(Leaning back from the table.)* Queen Esther, that was a magnificent meal you prepared.

**ESTHER:** Thank you, my king.

**SERVANT:** *(To herself while clearing away dishes.)* Meal SHE prepared. I'll tell you who did all the work—ME. You know, I could have been queen.

**XERXES:** Don't you think it was a great meal, Haman?

**HAMAN:** My most mighty king, ruler of Medes and Persians, may you live forever,

---

* In Bible times, it was common for a king to have many wives. These wives lived together in a separate part of the palace, called a harem.

may I say that I am honored to even be dining with you.

**XERXES:** A simple yes will do.

**HAMAN:** Of course, my most excellent king, conqueror of the known world—

**XERXES:** Yeah, yeah, thanks, Haman.

**SERVANT:** (*To herself while continuing to clean.*) I have no idea why Esther would invite that pompous windbag, Haman, to her dinner. I wouldn't have, if I were queen, which I could have been.

**XERXES:** My beautiful queen, the dinners last night and tonight have been wonderful. But I know there's something on your mind. Whatever it is that you want, you can have it.

**SERVANT:** Anything she wants? Even, say, if she asked for half of your kingdom?

**XERXES:** Yes, you impudent servant, even if she asked for half of my kingdom.

**SERVANT:** (*To herself.*) And to think, I could have been queen.

**ESTHER:** All I ask, my gracious king, is for my life and for the lives of my people.

**XERXES:** That's it? Well, of course you can have that. Don't you already have it?

**ESTHER:** My king, a death sentence has been issued against my people.

**XERXES:** Death sentence? I don't remember issuing a death sentence against you.

**HAMAN:** (*Gets up to leave.*) Well, I'd better be going. Have to get home to the wife and kids, you know.

**XERXES:** Sit down. I may need your help and advice.

**HAMAN:** (*Sitting down.*) Of course, my king, may you live forever. (*Whispers.*) Or for no more than 30 seconds, if I'm lucky.

**ESTHER:** My king, you were tricked into issuing a death sentence.

**XERXES:** By whom?

**HAMAN:** (*Standing.*) I must really be going.

**XERXES:** Sit down! (HAMAN *sits.*)

**ESTHER:** Haman. He wanted the death of my people. All because he has a grudge against my cousin Mordecai.

**HAMAN:** Mordecai's your cousin? Oh, great!

**XERXES:** (*To* HAMAN.) Now I understand why you wanted to leave, you vile snake.

**HAMAN:** Your majesty, I can explain.

**XERXES:** Explain it to your executioner!

**HAMAN:** Executioner? Surely your majesty doesn't mean...look, it was all a mistake... (XERXES *drags* HAMAN *offstage.*)

**SERVANT:** Whoa! That was a sticky situation! I'm sure glad I'm not queen! (*Exits.*)

**ESTHER:** (*Calls offstage.*) Mordecai! Mordecai! I have great news! Our people are safe! God has helped us once again!

For the **real deal** read Psalm 23

# Camp Swampy

## Characters: DENNY; JAMIE; BUDDY

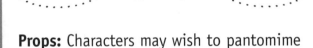

**Props:** Characters may wish to pantomime the use of props.

**Scene:** *A leaky tent in Camp Swampy.*

**DENNY:** *(Writing a letter.)* "Dear Mom and Dad...," no, "Dearest Mom...," no, "To the most wonderful fantastic parents in the world...,"

**JAMIE:** Whatcha doing?

**DENNY:** Writing a letter home. "Things are AWFUL here! Yesterday, the alligators ate one of the counselors!"

**JAMIE:** I don't remember that happening.

**DENNY:** It didn't. Let's see...aha! "The mess hall served us something green and slimy with purple spots on it. It was the only thing to eat, but I didn't eat it, and boy, am I glad. The kids who did eat it got really sick."

**JAMIE:** I don't remember any green stuff! It was pizza! And it was good!

**DENNY:** Quiet. You're distracting me! I know, "You would have been proud of the way I fought the grass fire..."

**JAMIE:** I don't remember any grass fire! Why are you writing all this stuff to your parents?

**DENNY:** Because everything here is TERRIBLE! I'm never picked first for anything. Not even kitchen duty!

**JAMIE:** You WANTED kitchen duty?!

**DENNY:** That's not the point! This place stinks! Yesterday, I got stung by a bee, and had to go to the emergency room to get a shot!

**JAMIE:** I was wondering why you missed the popcorn party.

**DENNY:** Don't rub it in. And speaking of rubbing things in, I lost that poison oak and ivy cream. I'm starting to itch!

**JAMIE:** I have it. But it sure was a lot of fun exploring off the trail.

**DENNY:** Aw, it was muddy. And today I got in trouble because I wouldn't eat that green mush they call vegetables.

**JAMIE:** Maybe you're right. Now it's raining and the tent's leaking. I think I'll write a letter home, too.

**DENNY:** Write it right, or they'll just say all this rotten stuff "builds character."

**JAMIE:** How's this: "To my fabulous parents from your miserable son!"

**DENNY:** That's pretty good. I think I'll change that on my letter.

**JAMIE:** OK. How's this? "I write from my

handmade lean-to, which I was forced to build after our entire camp was washed away in the flood."

**DENNY:** That's great stuff!

**BUDDY:** *(Enters.)* Whatcha guys doing?

**JAMIE:** Writing letters home.

**BUDDY:** Didja tell them about the great movie we saw last night? I never laughed so hard!

**DENNY:** Umm...I forgot about that.

**BUDDY:** Did you mention the play we're acting out?

**JAMIE:** Oh. Yeah! Well, I forgot about that.

**BUDDY:** Did you tell them about the TV crew coming tomorrow to film us?

**DENNY:** TV crew...? No, I don't remember mentioning that.

**BUDDY:** This camp has been so cool! I've never been to a better camp! And believe me, I've done a lot of camps! And we've learned about God, besides! What ARE you writing your parents about, anyway?

**DENNY:** Oh, just stuff.

**JAMIE:** Yeah, stuff.

**BUDDY:** Better finish those letters soon. It's almost time for the marshmallow roast! (BUDDY *exits.*)

**JAMIE:** *(Calls.)* We'll be right there.

**DENNY:** *(Looks at his letter.)* Maybe camp isn't so bad after all.

**JAMIE:** Yeah. And I just remembered, we're only going to be here one more day!

**DENNY:** Oh, no! I was having such a good time!

*Note: Psalm 23 provides encouragement in difficult situations.*

# The Trainee

**Characters: MAC,** factory supervisor; **TRAINEE,** first day on the job; **QUALITY CONTROL,** a group of people never seen, only heard over the intercom.

**Props:** Characters may wish to pantomime the use of props.

**Scene:** *The assembly room of a factory that makes something really important, but we're not sure what it is.*

**MAC:** OK, trainee, let's go over this one more time. You want to take notes?

**TRAINEE:** Oh, no, I've got a real good memory.

**MAC:** Well, OK, I guess. First you take the brown stuff and put it on the blue stuff.

**TRAINEE:** Check.

**MAC:** Then you take the red stuff and put it on the brown stuff.

**TRAINEE:** Check.

**MAC:** Then you put the yellow stuff on the orange stuff, the green stuff on the white stuff and the white stuff on the yellow stuff and the orange stuff on the red stuff. Got it?

**TRAINEE:** Check.

**MAC:** OK. Then it all goes in the box and the box is sent to Quality Control.

**TRAINEE:** Quality Control. Got it!

**MAC:** Good, now I've got another trainee to check on. I'll be back in a while. You sure you've got it?

**TRAINEE:** Oh, yes, I'm sure.

**MAC:** OK, we're counting on you. Show us what you've got! *(MAC leaves.)*

**TRAINEE:** I put the brown stuff on the blue stuff, then the yellow stuff on the orange, the, ah, white on the brown, the green on the...uh-oh, I don't remember!

**QUALITY CONTROL:** Hey, where's our next box? What's the slowdown?

**TRAINEE:** Ah, just a minute. OK, brown on blue, yellow on brown, green on white, white on yellow, but what do I do with this orange stuff?

**QUALITY CONTROL:** Do you need some help in there?

**TRAINEE:** No, no, I've got it. Brown on blue, orange on brown, yellow on orange, white on yellow, green on white. Yes, I've got it! Now I put it in the box. This is easy! Blue, brown, orange, yellow, white, green, in the box. Blue, brown, yellow, orange, green, white, in the box. Uh-oh, what's this red stuff?

**MAC:** *(Over intercom.)* Everything OK?

**TRAINEE:** Sure, sure, everything's great! No problem!

**MAC:** Well, if you have any questions, just ask.

**TRAINEE:** No, no, I'm fine.

**MAC:** Great. Over and out.

**TRAINEE:** This red stuff must be extra. Oh, well. Blue, brown, yellow, orange, green, white, in the box.

**QUALITY CONTROL:** Hey, what's going on in there?

**TRAINEE:** What do you mean?

**QUALITY CONTROL:** This stuff isn't put together right.

**TRAINEE:** It most certainly is. I'm following my instructions to the letter.

**QUALITY CONTROL:** What letter?

**TRAINEE:** It's an expression meaning I'm following the instructions EXACTLY.

**QUALITY CONTROL:** Well, you're one oar short.

**TRAINEE:** What?

**QUALITY CONTROL:** THAT'S an expression that means you don't know what you're doing! This stuff's no good. It won't work. We're going to have to send it back!

**TRAINEE:** *(To self.)* No good? But I was sure I was putting it together right. But maybe it's white, green, red, blue, brown... oh, I don't know. I wish I had written the instructions down. I'll probably be fired on my first day!

**MAC:** *(Enters.)* I understand there's a problem here.

**TRAINEE:** I didn't remember how the stuff is put together. I'm really sorry. I should have listened to you and written the directions down.

**MAC:** But when I asked you if you needed help, you said no!

**TRAINEE:** I didn't want you to think I couldn't do the job. I didn't want to look ignorant. I'm really sorry.

**MAC:** Well, there's only one thing to do.

**TRAINEE:** Yeah, I know. Go ahead and tell me. I'm fired.

**MAC:** We'll have to start over again.

**TRAINEE:** You mean with someone else.

**MAC:** No, with you.

**TRAINEE:** You mean, you'll give me a second chance?

**MAC:** Well, you seem to have learned a lot from your mistakes, and you seem ready to try to do things in a better way now. So, we'll give you a fresh start.

**TRAINEE:** What about all the stuff I messed up?

**MAC:** When you get better at this job, you'll be able to fix it in a second.

**TRAINEE:** You really think so?

**MAC:** I know so!

**TRAINEE:** Gee, thanks.

**MAC:** OK, let's take it from the beginning. The brown stuff goes on the blue stuff...

**TRAINEE:** Um, would you wait while I get a pencil and paper? I want to get it right this time!

*Note: Psalm 51:1-4, 10-12 tells us about God's promise to forgive us when we need a fresh start.*

**For the real story** read Isaiah 40:3-5, Mark 1:1-8, John 1:15-34

# A Voice Calling

**Characters: SANDY,** narrator and guide to the Sunshine Sunday School; **ISAIAH,** a prophet of God; **ANDY,** a boy who doesn't really want to be in the Christmas play; **SUSAN,** a girl who loves doing Christmas plays; **MS. GIGGLE,** the Christmas play's director, she laughs at anything; **REV. WINKLE,** a minister with too many meetings, and a watch he keeps looking at; **EZRA,** a Bible-times boy; **BETH,** a Bible-times girl; **JOHN,** John the Baptist, the "voice of one calling" predicted by Isaiah

### ACT ONE

**Scene:** *Outside the Sunshine Sunday School Hall.*

**SANDY:** Welcome! Today we are going to visit the Sunshine Sunday School as they rehearse for their Christmas play. I have with me the famous prophet, Isaiah, who will comment on what we see.

**ISAIAH:** Thank you, Sandy. Today the Sunshine Sunday School is rehearsing the "John the Baptist" portion of the play.

**SANDY:** Who exactly was John the Baptist?

**ISAIAH:** He was the voice calling out from the desert, "Prepare the way for the Lord."

**SANDY:** Could you be a little more specific?

**ISAIAH:** It's all in my book.

**SANDY:** Oh yes, your book, which I believe is part of the Bible and available at most bookstores.

**ISAIAH:** Yes.

**SANDY:** Well, let's just take a look inside the Sunshine Sunday School Hall.

### ACT TWO

**Scene:** *Modern church Sunday School room.*

**ANDY:** I don't even see how this John the Baptist fits into the Christmas story. Can't we just leave his part out?

**SUSAN:** He wouldn't be in the skit if he weren't important.

**ANDY:** Yeah, but why was he important? I mean, he's gross—living out in the desert, eating bugs and honey. How come I have to play his part?

**MS. GIGGLE:** *(Entering and giggling.)* All right everyone, we're going to take this from the top. Andy! Why aren't you in costume? *(She giggles.)*

**ANDY:** THAT CAMEL FUR ITCHES!

**SUSAN:** Camel HAIR, not fur. *(To MS. GIGGLE)* Andy doesn't want to play John the Baptist.

**MS. GIGGLE:** Why not? *(She giggles again.)*

**ANDY:** He was just some crazy guy shouting a bunch of stuff in the desert.

**REV. WINKLE:** Hm, I guess some people might have thought that, but John the Baptist had a very important job. He came to tell everyone to prepare themselves to meet the Messiah. Without John's preparation, people might not have been ready when Jesus started His teaching. Now, let's get this rehearsal moving. I've got a meeting with the Decorations Discussion Group at 10:32.

**ANDY:** It might be easier to play this part if I had some motivation.

**SANDY:** *(To audience.)* Hm, it looks like trouble brewing among the players. I wonder if Andy will do a good job as John the Baptist! Let's watch and see.

## ACT THREE

**Scene:** *Judea, right before Jesus' ministry begins.*

**EZRA:** Hurry up, Beth, it's time to go to see that man named John.

**BETH:** John? Why go hear him? Isn't he, well, a little crazy?

**EZRA:** Beth, I hear he has important news for us.

**BETH:** Hmph! YOU may have time to go running all over the countryside listening to crazy men, but I don't! I have a house to clean, bread to bake, clothes to weave...

**EZRA:** BETH, this is MUCH more important than all that.

**BETH:** Oh fine. Let's go. But I'm not staying long.

*(BETH and EZRA walk off and on stage.)*

**EZRA:** Well, here we are. Look Beth, there he is!

**JOHN:** Prepare your hearts! Repent! Wash away your old evil ways of doing things! Prepare to do good things instead! The One who comes after me is the One we have waited for!

**BETH:** What on earth is he talking about, Ezra? I told you he was crazy!

**EZRA:** The Messiah, Beth, the Messiah is coming!

**BETH:** The Messiah? He's coming? If the Messiah's coming, I've got to make new carpets, new clothes, I can't have Him seeing me like this...

**EZRA:** Snap out of it, Beth. What the Messiah wants for us to have is new attitudes.

**BETH:** Oh. How do you make those? I've never made a new attitude in my life!

**EZRA:** Then listening to John is REALLY important. *(To audience.)* Boy, Isaiah sure wasn't kidding when he said we'd need someone to help us prepare the way for the Messiah.

*Note: Combine skits from pages 77-84 for a Christmas production.*

For the **real story** read Isaiah 9:6-7; Luke 2:1-7

# Room for a Baby

**Characters: SANDY**, narrator and guide to the Sunshine Sunday School; **ISAIAH**, a prophet of God; **ANDY**, a boy who doesn't really want to be in the Christmas play; **SUSAN**, a girl who loves doing Christmas plays; **MS. GIGGLE**, the Christmas play's director, she laughs at anything; **REV. WINKLE**, a minister with too many meetings, and a watch he keeps looking at; **SARAH**, the innkeeper's wife; **JAMES**, the innkeeper

## ACT ONE

**Scene:** *Outside the Sunshine Sunday School Hall.*

**SANDY:** Welcome! We're here observing the Sunshine Sunday School rehearse their Christmas play. Isaiah, in your book you've given this Messiah a lot of names: Wonderful Counselor, Mighty God, Everlasting Father, Prince of Peace...How could one baby have so many names?

**ISAIAH:** Because He's the Son of God, no one name can fully describe Him.

**SANDY:** So, the Son of God came to earth as a baby? I'll bet nobody expected that!

**ISAIAH:** That's why I wrote "For to us a CHILD is born," to let the people know what to expect.

**SANDY:** I see. Well, let's see how the Sunshine Sunday School is doing.

## ACT TWO

**Scene:** *Modern church Sunday School room.*

**ANDY:** An innkeeper? Now I have to play an INNKEEPER? How important can an innkeeper be?

**SUSAN:** Hey, you could be playing the part of the donkey.

**ANDY:** Oh, very funny.

**MS. GIGGLE:** *(Entering and giggling.)* Alright everyone, we're going to do the scene at the inn. Andy! Why aren't you in costume?

**ANDY:** That old bathrobe smells like mothballs!

**SUSAN:** Andy doesn't want to play the innkeeper.

**REV. WINKLE:** Why not?

**ANDY:** It's such a boring part. It never has very many lines: "No room at the inn." And NO ONE likes the innkeeper.

**SUSAN:** There are no SMALL parts, only SMALL actors.

**ANDY:** Oh yeah! Beats playing the innkeeper's wife. Now THERE'S an important part!

**MS. GIGGLE:** *(Giggles.)* Children! No fighting! ESPECIALLY not at Christmas. And, who knows, Andy, your part might be better than you expect. *(Giggles.)*

**REV. WINKLE:** Places, everyone! I've got a Super Sunday Seminar at 11:02.

**SANDY:** *(To audience.)* Hm, I don't expect this part of the rehearsal to go well at all. But let's see what happens.

**ACT THREE**

**Scene:** *An inn in Bethlehem.*

**JAMES:** There's a young couple at the door looking for a room. I just can't turn them away!

**SARAH:** You don't have a choice. There's not a speck of room left...watch out! You're going to kick the Benjamins!

**JAMES:** Why are they sleeping on the kitchen floor?

**SARAH:** There's no where else to put them. Now, exactly where do you propose we put this young couple?

**JAMES:** Sarah, she's going to have a baby at any time! We've got to find some place for them. Maybe we could ask someone to leave?

**SARAH:** Not a chance. The guests have paid and I've used the money to feed them all.

**JAMES:** I'll tell them. (JAMES *sadly leaves and returns seconds later.)*

**SARAH:** What happened?

**JAMES:** I told them they could stay in the stable.

**SARAH:** The stable? The stable is no place for a baby!

**JAMES:** There wasn't anywhere else for them to go. Could we give them some food?

**SARAH:** I suppose I could find something.

**JAMES:** There's something different about them, Sarah. I've just got a strange feeling something special is happening.

**SARAH:** Tell you what I'd find special is the Messiah coming and getting rid of all these Romans and their bad ideas, like taxes and the census.

**JAMES:** Wouldn't it be something if the Messiah was being born in our stable right now?

**SARAH:** I don't know what's got into you tonight. The Messiah isn't going to be a baby born to a poor couple in a stable. He's going to be the Mighty God. It says so in Isaiah.

**JAMES:** It also says that for us a CHILD is born.

**SARAH:** But THIS child, James?

**JAMES:** I don't know, Sarah, but something special is happening.

**SARAH:** Why don't I just warm up some bread and take them some yogurt dressing for dinner. Then I can see what I can do to help the woman with her baby.

**JAMES:** Let's both go.

*Note: Combine skits from pages 77-84 for a Christmas production.*

## For the real story read Isaiah 40:9; Luke 2:8-20

# Shepherds and Angels

**Characters: SANDY,** narrator and guide to the Sunshine Sunday School; **ISAIAH,** a prophet of God; **ANDY,** a boy who doesn't really want to be in the Christmas play; **SUSAN,** a girl who loves doing Christmas plays; **MS. GIGGLE,** the Christmas play's director, she laughs at anything; **REV. WINKLE,** a minister with too many meetings, and a watch he keeps looking at; **ISAAC,** a twelve-year old Bible-times boy shepherd; **SAM,** for Samantha, a twelve-year old Bible-times girl shepherd

## ACT ONE

**Scene:** *Outside the Sunshine Sunday School Hall.*

**SANDY:** Here we are, outside the Sunshine Sunday School, waiting to report on another Christmas play rehearsal. What do you suppose we'll see today, Isaiah?

**ISAIAH:** Today we'll hear about the angels who sang the glad tidings of the Messiah's birth.

**SANDY:** I'm guessing that was a pretty spectacular simulcast across the world for all the great nations to see.

**ISAIAH:** Actually, Sandy, God sent His messengers to some EVERYDAY people—shepherds.

**SANDY:** Well, you sure can't get much more everyday than shepherds. Let's see how preparations are going in the Sunshine Sunday School.

## ACT TWO

**Scene:** *Modern church Sunday School room.*

**ANDY:** A shepherd. I'm a dumb ol' shepherd.

**SUSAN:** What did you want to be?

**ANDY:** An angel! They get all the glory.

**SUSAN:** Hmph! No one would give you glory no matter what part you played. Let's face it, you stink!!

**MS. GIGGLE:** SUSAN! I can't believe I just heard you say that!

**SUSAN:** NOW Andy doesn't want to be a shepherd. He's complained about EVERY part he's had and I'm tired of it!

**ANDY:** It wasn't my idea to be in this DUMB play!

**REV. WINKLE:** Ms. Giggle, why aren't we rehearsing? I'm a busy man, you know!

**MS. GIGGLE:** *(Starts to laugh.)* This is so absurd. I mean, this part of the play is about peace and everyone is getting angry about it. *(Laughs uncontrollably.)*

SUSAN: *(Tries to stifle a giggle.)* Well, it's not really funny. But I am sorry I got angry.

REV. WINKLE: Can we *(starts to giggle)* please get on with this rehearsal? I have a Christmas Chorale Committee meeting at *(giggles more)*, at...*(giggles harder)*, at 7:16.

ANDY: *(Laughing.)* A shepherd, I get to play a shepherd!

SANDY: *(Giggling.)* With all this bickering, things just don't seem too peaceful, do they? Let's see what happens during the rehearsal.

## ACT THREE

Scene: *Bethlehem at the time of Jesus' birth.*

ISAAC: Did you hear what I heard?

SAM: Yup. What did you hear?

ISAAC: I heard a choir of angels. Didn't you see them?

SAM: Yup. What did they say?

ISAAC: Weren't you here? They said a baby had been born.

SAM: Yup. But, what's so exciting about that? Babies are born all the time.

ISAAC: Yes, but THIS baby is going to bring us peace.

SAM: Yup. Hey, Isaac, how's a baby going to bring us peace?

ISAAC: I don't know. Maybe He'll wipe out all our enemies.

SAM: Yup. That's what He'll do, zap all our enemies. Hey, Isaac, that doesn't sound too peaceful.

ISAAC: No, it doesn't. Well, maybe He'll make sure everyone has what they need.

SAM: Yup. That's what He'll do, give us everything we need. Hey, Isaac, we already have everything we need, but we're still not too peaceful.

ISAAC: Okay, well, maybe he'll give us everything we WANT.

SAM: Yup. That's it! That's what He'll do. But, if we get what we want, won't we want more?

ISAAC: Look, Sam, I don't know what He'll do.

SAM: He must care about us a whole lot.

ISAAC: Who?

SAM: God. I mean, to send us such a special gift and all.

ISAAC: Yup, I guess you're right.

SAM: Ya know what, Isaac?

ISAAC: Yup?

SAM: Knowing God loves me that much makes me feel kinda peaceful.

ISAAC: Yup. Me too. You know what Sam?

SAM: Yup?

ISAAC: Let's go to that stable the angels told us about and see this Prince of Peace!

SAM: Yup.

*Note: Combine skits from pages 77-84 for a Christmas production.*

For the **real story** read Isaiah 35:5-6; John 10:11

# The Beginning

**Characters: SANDY,** narrator and guide to the Sunshine Sunday School; **ISAIAH,** a prophet of God; **ANDY,** a boy who doesn't really want to be in the Christmas play; **SUSAN,** a girl who loves doing Christmas plays; **MS. GIGGLE,** the Christmas play's director, she laughs at anything; **REV. WINKLE,** a minister with too many meetings, and a watch he keeps looking at; **SENIOR ANGEL,** in charge of all heavenly paperwork; **ANGEL #1, ANGEL #2, ANGEL #3, ANGEL #4**

## ACT ONE

**Scene:** *Outside the Sunshine Sunday School Hall.*

**SANDY:** Welcome! We're here at the Sunshine Sunday School where we're observing the rehearsal of a Christmas play. Isaiah, maybe you can give us more information on this Messiah everyone is talking about.

**ISAIAH:** Well, Sandy, that would take more time than we have here. I would suggest that everyone read my book. It has lots of clues about the Messiah in it.

**SANDY:** Yes. And that book can be found in the Bible, which is available in most bookstores. Let's have a peek at rehearsal preparations, shall we?

## ACT TWO

**Scene:** *Modern church Sunday School room.*

**ANDY:** Senior Angel! YES! I finally get a good part!

**SUSAN:** Congratulations! NOW, maybe we can rehearse in peace.

**ANDY:** Or, you could be the Senior Angel if you want.

**SUSAN:** Then who will you be?

**ANDY:** Whatever. The important thing is that the play goes well.

**SUSAN:** Who are you? And what have you done with Andy?

**REV. WINKLE:** Good news, everyone! I've canceled all my meetings so that we can have a party after the program! Promptly at 8:26. Or whenever!

**MS. GIGGLE:** This certainly is turning out to be a "good news" day!

## ACT THREE

**Scene:** SENIOR ANGEL'S *Office.*

**ANGEL #1:** Whew! I'm glad that's all over! All those choir rehearsals! Taking messages here, there and having to talk to wide-mouthed, open-eyed humans! Not to mention the paperwork!

**ANGEL #2:** Yeah, this birth of the King sure has been a lot of work!

**ANGEL #1:** Now the work is done!

**SENIOR ANGEL:** Have you completed all three of your forms?

**ANGEL #1:** Of course I've filled them out! See...

**ANGEL #3:** OUR work is over, but not His.

**ANGEL #2:** You mean, the King's?

**ANGEL #3:** Yes, now the King's work begins. And if you think WE had a hard time getting people's attention...

**SENIOR ANGEL:** I only see two copies of the request for a stable.

**ANGEL #1:** I'm sure there's another copy, yes, here it is!

**SENIOR ANGEL:** What did you need a stable for, anyway?

**ANGEL #2:** But the King may still need our help.

**ANGEL #3:** Yes, in fact I'm putting together a huge guardian force to watch over Him; to be there at His every command.

**SENIOR ANGEL:** You'd better have your paperwork filled out for the guardians!

**ANGEL #3:** Yes, I do. Here it is.

**SENIOR ANGEL:** Hm, this is what I like, three neat copies of the form!

**ANGEL #4:** You seem to be losing sight of the big picture.

**SENIOR ANGEL:** Not if I have three copies of the big picture!

**ANGEL #4:** Actually, I wasn't talking to you. The King has gone to LIVE among the humans.

**ANGELS #1, #2, and #3:** WHY??

**ANGEL #4:** Because He loves them!

**ANGEL #1:** Having visited those humans, I doubt they are worth it.

**ANGEL #2:** I wouldn't love them for all the wealth in heaven!

**ANGEL #3:** Hmph! I'd take a BIG army of angels and straighten them out in a hurry!

**SENIOR ANGEL:** You'd better have the paperwork for that army!

**ANGEL #4:** Well, the King thinks they are important enough to die for.

**ANGEL #1, #2, and #3:** NO!!!

**SENIOR ANGEL:** YES! And I have three copies of that order here!

*Note: Combine skits from pages 77-84 for a Christmas production.*

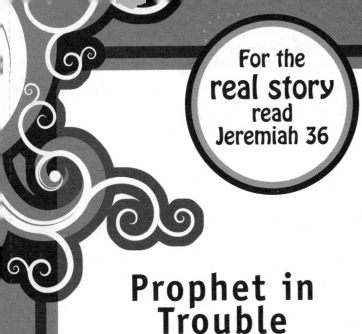

For the **real story** read Jeremiah 36

# Prophet in Trouble

**Characters: JEREMIAH,** a prophet of God; **BARUCH (BEHR-UHK),** Jeremiah's secretary; **MICHAIAH (MIH-KY-AH),** an Official in king's court; **OFFICIAL 1, 2 and 3,** Officials in king's court; **JEHOIAKIM (JEH-HOY-AH-KIHM),** King of Judah; **NARRATOR**

**Props:** Characters may pantomime props.

**Scene One:** JEREMIAH'S *house, Judah.*

**NARRATOR:** Long ago in the land of Judah, God's people were disobedient and disloyal to Him. So God gave His Prophet, Jeremiah a special assignment.

**JEREMIAH:** Baruch, my friend! God wants us to write down everything—ALL the messages He has given me.

**BARUCH:** Everything?

**JEREMIAH:** Everything. Maybe if God's people see all of His messages together, they'll finally get it.

**BARUCH:** Oh, boy...*(Opens scroll and takes out a thin stick to use as reed pen.)* Ready!

**JEREMIAH:** "My wrath will break out and burn like fire because of the evil you have done. Flee for safety without delay!" *(BARUCH pretends to write on scroll.)*

**Scene Two:** *God's Temple.*

**NARRATOR:** When the scroll was finished, Baruch took it to the Temple and read it aloud for everyone to hear.

**BARUCH:** Here are God's words for you, just as He told them to Jeremiah: "My wrath will break out and burn like fire because of the evil you have done."

**MICHAIAH:** Oh, no! This doesn't sound good!

**BARUCH:** *(Still reading.)* "Flee for safety without delay! For I am bringing disaster from the north, even terrible destruction."

**MICHAIAH:** Does it say anything about the king? Like maybe what a great king he is, and how he'll live forever?

**BARUCH:** *(Still reading.)* "He will have the burial of a donkey—dragged away and thrown outside the gates of Jerusalem."

**MICHAIAH:** That's terrible! Please tell me that's all there is!

**BARUCH:** Oh, no. There's more. Lots more!

**MICHAIAH:** I'll have to see what the king's scribe and officials have to say about this.

**Scene Three:** *Office of the King's Scribe.*

**NARRATOR:** Meanwhile, in the office of the king's scribe, many officials were gathered.

**MICHAIAH:** I have terrible news! Jeremiah's secretary, Baruch, has read God's words to us. If Jeremiah's right, we're toast!

**OFFICIAL 1:** Uh, oh. The king will be furious! But we'd better tell him ourselves before someone else does!

**OFFICIAL 2:** First let's find out exactly what Jeremiah's saying this time. The king will have our heads if we get this wrong!

**NARRATOR:** So they sent someone to find Baruch. (OFFICIAL 3 *exits, and then immediately returns with* BARUCH.)

**MICHAIAH:** Go ahead. Read it.

**BARUCH:** (*Opens scroll and reads.*) "My wrath will break out and burn like fire because of the evil you have done."

**MICHAIAH:** Read the part about the king!

**BARUCH:** (*Reading.*) "He will have the burial of a donkey—dragged away and thrown outside the gates of Jerusalem."

**OFFICIAL 2:** Oh, the king won't like that last part—not one little bit!

**OFFICIAL 3:** Baruch, you and Jeremiah have to go into hiding! Don't tell anyone where you're going! Leave the scroll with me.

**Scene Four:** *The King's Apartment.*

**NARRATOR:** Meanwhile, the king was warming himself by the fire in his apartment.

**JEHOIAKIM:** What brings you out on such a cold night?

**OFFICIAL 1:** We've come with some important news! Jeremiah—

**JEHOIAKIM:** Him again? That man's been claiming something bad will happen as long as anyone can remember!

**OFFICIAL 2:** Yes, your highness, but we really think you ought to hear this! It sure scared me when I heard it!

**JEHOIAKIM:** Alright, already! Let's hear it!

**OFFICIAL 3:** Very well, sir. (*Reading scroll.*) "My wrath will break out and burn like fire because of the evil you have done."

**JEHOIAKIM:** Burn like fire? I'll show you what will burn like fire! (*Takes out knife. Grabs scroll, cuts off a section and throws it into fire.*) Burn, baby, burn! (*Hands scroll back to* OFFICIAL 3.) Keep reading!

**OFFICIAL 1:** (*Worried.*) Are you sure that's a good idea, your highness?

**JEHOIAKIM:** READ!

**OFFICIAL 3:** (*Reading.*) "Flee for safety without delay! For I am bringing disaster from the north, even terrible destruction."

**JEHOIAKIM:** Oh, yeah? Give me that! (*Repeats pretend grabbing, tearing and burning of scroll. Pretends to hand scroll back to* OFFICIAL 3.) Read on!

**OFFICIAL 2:** (*Nervously.*) Sir, do you HAVE to burn it? Maybe we could just hide it!

**JEHOIAKIM:** Leave me alone or the scroll won't be the only thing burning! (*To* OFFICIAL 3.) What does it say about me?

**OFFICIAL 3:** (*Reading reluctantly.*) "He will have the burial of a donkey—dragged away and thrown outside the gates of Jerusalem."

**JEHOIAKIM:** The burial of a donkey? (*Grabs, cuts up and burns rest of scroll.* OFFICIALS *look horrified.*) We'll see who's going to be dragged away! Be gone, all of you! And send in my special guards! They won't sleep until Jeremiah has been captured!

**OFFICIAL 3:** Yes, sir.

**NARRATOR:** (*Steps forward.*) But the king's guards could not find Jeremiah and Baruch, because God had hidden them. But even in their hiding place, God had another assignment for them. God wanted them to rewrite the scroll Jehoiakim had burned. And just as they'd done before, Jeremiah and Baruch did exactly what God told them.

For the **real story** read Daniel 1

# Food Issues

**Characters: DANIEL,** a teenage Israelite boy who has just been taken captive by the Babylonians; **ABED-NEGO (AH-BEHD-NAY-GO),** Daniel's friend, also a teenage Israelite boy; **MESHACH (ME-SHAHK),** Daniel's friend, also a teenage Israelite boy; **SHADRACH (SHAHD-RAHK),** Daniel's friend, also a teenage Israelite boy;

**Scene:** *Royal rooms in Babylon.*

**ABEDNEGO:** *(Looking around.)* You know, this isn't half bad.

**MESHACH:** If you don't count the fact that we're PRISONERS, miles away from our homes, with some dumb new foreign names, it's great!

**SHADRACH:** Yeah, but did you expect this when they dragged us away from home?

**MESHACH:** I expected to end up dead! And that still might happen, if we're not careful.

**ABEDNEGO:** Look at all these books! This is a great library!

**MESHACH:** Too bad we don't read the language.

**SHADRACH:** They said they're going to teach us the language.

**ABEDNEGO:** Yeah. They're going to train us to be leaders!

**MESHACH:** We were leaders at home. We were the smartest kids around. Everyone said that.

**ABEDNEGO:** True. Well, we weren't smarter than Daniel.

**SHADRACH:** Where is Daniel anyway?

**ABEDNEGO:** He went to talk to that head guy—the one who gave us all those tests.

**MESHACH:** *(Alarmed.)* What?

**SHADRACH:** Daniel had better be careful. I don't think these guys are too tolerant.

**MESHACH:** Which is why Daniel is in real danger!

**ABEDNEGO:** Daniel? In danger? I doubt it. He's too smart.

**SHADRACH:** Why'd he go see the guy anyway?

**ABEDNEGO:** Something about changing the dinner menu.

**MESHACH:** That's it! We're all going to die!

**SHADRACH:** What IS your problem?

**MESHACH:** I heard one guy say the king was giving us food from his own table! He's going to be pretty angry if Daniel turns it down!

**DANIEL:** *(Entering.)* Oh, good. You're all here.

**MESHACH:** And we're happy to see you're still alive. Or is this a farewell visit?

**DANIEL:** Huh?

**SHADRACH:** Don't mind him. He's been doom and gloom ever since we left Israel.

**DANIEL:** I see. Anyway, I've discussed the food problem with the guy in charge.

**SHADRACH:** Food problem? What food problem?

**DANIEL:** Well, they were planning on serving us food from the king's table.

**MESHACH:** Told you!

**SHADRACH:** So why's that a problem?

**DANIEL:** The king dedicates his food to one of his idols.

**SHADRACH:** Food is food, isn't it?

**DANIEL:** Don't tell me you've already forgotten our laws?

**SHADRACH:** Hard to forget our laws when I still have a knot on my head from Rabbi Levi's constant rapping. "Young man, you will recite those laws until they stick in your head." (SHADRACH *knocks on MESHACH's head in demonstration.*)

**MESHACH:** Ow!

**DANIEL:** (*Knocks on SHADRACH's head.*) OK, "young man," tell us why we aren't supposed to eat meat dedicated to idols.

**SHADRACH:** (*Rubbing head.*) Because Rabbi Levi will rap on your head if you do.

**DANIEL:** (*Knocks on SHADRACH's head again.*) Wrong! Because we're not to worship or have any part in worship to any gods other than the one, true God!

**ABEDNEGO:** So what did that official guy say?

**DANIEL:** At first he said no way! The king would cut off the official's head if he let us starve. But I made a bargain with him.

**SHADRACH:** What kind of a bargain?

**DANIEL:** We eat nothing but vegetables for the next ten days. If we're still strong and healthy, he'll let us keep eating only vegetables.

**MESHACH:** Whoa! Nothing but vegetables?

**SHADRACH:** No meat?

**DANIEL:** Nope! Just vegetables! We'll show them that following God's laws is good for us! Now I'm going to go work in the gardens!

(MESHACH, SHADRACH *and* ABEDNEGO *watch as* DANIEL *exits.*)

**SHADRACH:** Eat nothing but vegetables? I think not!

**ABEDNEGO:** Daniel's right. We can't go against God's laws!

**MESHACH:** (*Sadly.*) Nothing but vegetables?

**SHADRACH:** (*Sadly.*) No meat?

**ABEDNEGO:** Oh, cheer up guys! At least we get to eat. This won't be so bad.

(ABEDNEGO, SHADRACH *and* MESHACH *stare at each other.*)

**MESHACH, SHADRACH and ABEDNEGO:** We wanna go home!

**For the real story read Daniel 3**

# Four in the Fire

**Characters: NARRATOR; KING NEBUCHADNEZZAR,** King of Babylon; **JACKAL,** King Nebuchadnezzar's faithful sidekick and astrologer; **MESHACH, SHADRACH, ABEDNEGO,** young Israelite men

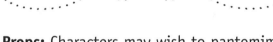

**Props:** Characters may wish to pantomime the use of props.

**Scene One**

**NARRATOR:** One day King Nebuchadnezzar came up with a plan to show everyone how wonderful he was! *(NEBUCHADNEZZAR enters.)*

**NEBUCHADNEZZAR:** *(Pacing the floor.)* Jackal!

**JACKAL:** *(Enters.)* Yes, your greatness.

**NEBUCHADNEZZAR:** I have decided to have a golden statue built. It will be taller and greater than any building in my kingdom.

**JACKAL:** *(Aside.)* A modest statue for a modest man.

**NEBUCHADNEZZAR:** What was that?

**JACKAL:** Uh...are you going to strike up the band?

**NEBUCHADNEZZAR:** Band? Yes! That's a fantastic idea! And when the band plays, everyone will bow down and worship the golden statue.

**JACKAL:** I'm sure they'll be pleased.

**NEBUCHADNEZZAR:** They'd better be! If they're not, why, I'll...have them thrown into the furnace. Now, let's go find my... uh...statue builder.

**JACKAL:** Yes, your greatness. *(NEBUCHADNEZZAR and JACKAL exit.)*

**Scene Two**

**NARRATOR:** Now, Meshach, Shadrach and Abednego were not from Nebuchadnezzar's kingdom. When they were teenagers they'd been taken from their homes in Israel and forced to come to Babylon. But because they were so smart, Nebuchadnezzar had selected them to learn how to do government work. *(MESHACH and ABEDNEGO enter.)*

**SHADRACH:** *(Enters holding a piece of paper.)* Look at this! We've been given positions as administrators!

**ABEDNEGO:** Hey, that's great! God has really been helping us!

**JACKAL:** *(Enters.)* I have a message from King Nebuchadnezzar. *(Hands the three an important-looking document, which they read together, sadly shaking their heads.)* Don't you wish it weren't so? *(They all nod.)* Well, it is. Live with it! *(Pauses.)* Or don't. (JACKAL *chuckles as he exits.)*

**SHADRACH:** There's something about that guy I don't trust.

**MESHACH:** Forget about him! We're in SERIOUS trouble! This says we have to bow down to the king's statue. Remember what we were taught in Israel about the one true God? He's commanded that we should never worship anyone or anything except Him.

**ABEDNEGO:** *(Nodding in agreement.)* We can't just turn our backs on God. *(Grabs the others' arms and starts to walk off stage.)* C'mon guys, we've got to figure out what to do! *(They all exit.)*

**Scene Three**

**NEBUCHADNEZZAR:** *(Enters followed by JACKAL.)* Isn't it a truly magnificent sight? Look at my statue! Listen! There go the trumpets, and the flutes. Look, everyone is bowing down to my statue!

**JACKAL:** Well, not everyone.

**NEBUCHADNEZZAR:** Who isn't bowing down to my statue?

**JACKAL:** Looks like Meshach, Shadrach and Abednego.

**NEBUCHADNEZZAR:** Bring them here immediately! *(JACKAL departs and then returns with the three guys.)* You have a choice. You either bow down to my statue right now, or you'll be thrown into the fiery furnace. Which will it be? *(SHADRACH, MESHACH and ABEDNEGO look at each other.)*

**NARRATOR:** What will Meshach, Shadrach and Abednego do?

**SHADRACH:** *(Turns to NEBUCHADNEZZAR.)* If we are thrown into the blazing furnace, our God is able to save us. But even if He doesn't we will NOT worship your gods. We will serve only Him! *(MESHACH and ABEDNEGO nod in agreement.)*

**NEBUCHADNEZZAR:** Very well! Throw them into the furnace! But heat it seven times hotter before you toss them in!

**JACKAL:** *(Smiles.)* Very good, your greatness. *(JACKAL hustles the three offstage.)*

**NEBUCHADNEZZAR:** *(Looking offstage.)* That's it, throw them in. Wow! That fire's hot! *(Looks puzzled.)* Jackal, what do I see? Didn't we throw three men into the furnace?

**JACKAL:** *(Enters.)* Yes, your greatness.

**NEBUCHADNEZZAR:** But I see four! *(JACKAL looks at the furnace and shrugs shoulders.)* And all of them are walking about, unharmed! How can that be? *(JACKAL shrugs shoulders again.)* You are of no use to me! Be gone!

**JACKAL:** As you wish, *(aside)* your pompousness.

**NEBUCHADNEZZAR:** Shadrach, Meshach and Abednego! Come out of the fire! Come out of the furnace! *(NEBUCHADNEZZAR brushes at their clothes and sniffs their hair.)* You aren't burned! You don't even smell singed! Praise to your God, Shadrach, Meshach and Abednego! You were willing to give up your lives rather than worship any god except your own God. You trusted in Him and He sent His angel to rescue you! I see how wrong I was! Your God is the One who is the greatest, not I!

For the **real story** read Daniel 6:1-9

# Daniel's Promotion

**Characters: SHAZZAR,** Persian satrap (SAY-trap); **SHEM,** Persian satrap; **SAM,** Persian satrap; **JOE SOLO,** Persian private investigator

**Props:** Characters may wish to pantomime the use of props.

**Scene:** *The satraps' secret headquarters in the palace of King Darius.*

**SHAZZAR:** Attention! Attention! I call the meeting of the satraps to order. (SHEM raises hand.) Yes, Shem. What is it?

**SHEM:** What is a satrap? Is that a new kind of music?

**SHAZZAR:** WE are the satraps!

**SHEM:** Oh. I thought we were governors.

**SHAZZAR:** We are! It's just that since Persia conquered Babylon, we're now called satraps.

**SHEM:** But why?

**SAM:** Can we get on with our business?

**SHAZZAR:** Excellent suggestion. First item of business—a report from the palace.

**SAM:** Plans for the hanging-garden renovations have been approved by the Babylon Beautiful Committee; now they need to pass the Disaster Safety Commission.

**SHAZZAR:** They've been working on those plans for over a year. I hope they get them approved before the gardens go completely to pot.

**SHEM:** Aren't they already in pots?

**SHAZZAR:** It's just an expression. Continue with the report.

**SAM:** Major road work is expected to begin next month.

**SHEM:** Oh, great! That'll mean more traffic jams. It's already tough to get a camel through these streets!

**SAM:** And Daniel has been appointed head administrator. He's now second-in-command to King Darius.

**SHAZZAR:** No! Not another promotion!

**SHEM:** I suppose that means he'll be checking our books for evidence of cheating, lying and stealing. It's getting so hard to cover up those activities.

**SHAZZAR:** He's not even a Persian! Or a Babylonian! How can Darius keep promoting him?

**SAM:** Like Shem said, Daniel keeps everyone under him honest—which is big trouble for us!

**SHAZZAR:** He can't be THAT good! I'm sure he pockets a little from the taxes, collects a few bribes.

**SAM:** I've hired an investigator for just that purpose—Joe Solo!

**SHAZZAR:** I've heard he's the best! If Daniel's got any dirt, Joe will find it!

**SAM:** *(Calls off stage.)* Joe! Come on in!

**JOE:** Afternoon, gentlemen.

**SAM:** So give us the report, Joe. What's Daniel been up to?

**JOE:** Sorry, gentlemen. This guy is clean— squeaky clean. He doesn't even take home quills from the office. I mean, everyone does that!

**SHAZZAR:** Are you saying Daniel is COM-PLETELY honest?

**JOE:** Absolutely!

**SAM:** Well, Daniel's getting older. Maybe his memory's slipping. Does he fall asleep on the job?

**JOE:** I had to hire two guys to help me keep up with this guy! He's on top of everything! One of his secretaries forgot to send a pay-ment to a local merchant. Daniel found the error in the middle of the night and marched right over to the merchant with it.

**SHEM:** In the middle of the night?

**JOE:** Yep! And remember that accountant Daniel caught stealing? Well, let's just say he learned his lesson.

**SHAZZAR:** Oh dear!

**JOE:** Yep! I feel sorry for you guys. You're all gonna have to clean up your act.

**SAM:** Ahem! Well, thank you for your report. *(JOE hands written report to SAM and exits.)*

**SHAZZAR:** Gentlemen, we are in serious trouble.

**SHEM:** Maybe we'd better start praying like Daniel.

**SHAZZAR:** What did you say?

**SHEM:** Maybe we'd better start praying like Daniel.

**SHAZZAR:** Of course! That's it!

**SHEM:** Well, I wasn't serious.

**SHAZZAR:** Daniel prays every day, doesn't he?

**SAM:** According to Joe's report, three times a day.

**SHAZZAR:** OK. Here's the plan. *(SHAZZAR whispers in the ears of the other satraps.)*

**SAM:** You think Darius will fall for it?

**SHAZZAR:** We'll tell Darius that it's Daniel's idea. Darius won't even think to question it!

**SHEM:** All right!

**SHAZZAR:** Sam, you write it up and we'll present it to Darius together.

**SAM:** I'll do it this afternoon!

**SHAZZAR:** Great! Now on to new business.

**SHEM:** I'd like to suggest we take up dona-tions for the widows and orphans.

**SHAZZAR and SAM:** WHAT?!?

**SHEM:** Well, we'd keep most of the money for ourselves.

**SHAZZAR:** Oh. That's better. All in favor? *(SAM and SHEM raise their hands.)*

For the **real story** read Joel

# Loads of Locusts

**Characters: OREN,** a Bible-times man; **GABE,** a Bible-times man; **EBEN,** a Bible-times man; **JED,** a Bible-times man

**Scene:** *A small town in Judah around the time of the prophet Joel.*

**OREN:** Hey, Gabe, how's it going?

**GABE:** How's it going?! How do you think it's going? My grape crop was completely wiped out by those ravenous locusts! And our vegetable garden is gone!

**OREN:** Whoa! Gabe! It was just a way to say hello. I didn't mean to upset you.

**GABE:** "How's it going?" he asks. My grain crop is completely gone! Not only will my family be without bread and my animals without food, but those priests will probably still want grain offerings. "How's it going?" Humph.

**OREN:** Gabe! Calm down!

**GABE:** Calm down?! How do I calm down? Those pesky locusts were EVERYWHERE! They were in the fields, in the house, in my bed! How can anyone be calm?

**OREN:** Look, Gabe, the locusts are gone now.

**GABE:** There's nothing left to eat! Why should they stay where there's no food?

**OREN:** Gabe, I was trying to point out that we can start replanting.

**GABE:** And what good would that do? We haven't had rain in weeks. No grapes. No grains. No vegetables. No rain. No food. And he asks, "How's it going?!"

**OREN:** I'm sorry I asked.

**EBEN:** *(Entering.)* Hey, Oren. What's Gabe so upset about?

**GABE:** What's Gabe so upset about?! I'll tell you what Gabe's so upset about. That plague of locusts—that's what Gabe's so upset about!

**EBEN:** Er, yeah, those locusts were really bad, all right.

**GABE:** Really bad?! We've got nothing to eat and he says "really bad!"

**JED:** *(Enters. To OREN.)* What's wrong with Gabe?

**OREN:** *(To JED.)* Don't ask. And don't mention locusts!

**JED:** OK. Um, have any of you heard Joel's book?

**EBEN:** Joel wrote a book? About what?

**JED:** It's a prophecy. You know, a message from God.

**GABE:** Unless it had something to do with recovering from the locusts, why waste our time?

**JED:** Gabe! A message from God is ALWAYS important! And yes, Joel's prophecy did have something to say about the locusts.

**GABE:** It did? What did it say?

**JED:** Joel's prophecy said that if we don't change our ways and repent, God's going to punish us with a plague worse than locusts.

**GABE:** There's nothing worse than locusts.

**EBEN:** Why would God want to punish us? I mean, I go to the Temple every religious holiday.

**JED:** Do you talk to God every day?

**OREN:** Talk to God?

**GABE:** He's talking about prayer. And I did a lot of praying while those locusts were here. I went up in the front of the Temple and shouted, "O God, take away these locusts!" at least twice a week. But did that make those locusts go away? No.

**JED:** Yelling at God isn't exactly praying.

**EBEN:** You know, I had just gotten a new tunic, and the priest asked us to tear our clothes to show God how upset we were over the locusts. So what I want to know is—what do I tear to show how upset I am over my ruined new tunic?

**OREN:** You think OUR rituals are bad, you should hear about the rituals my wife has to perform to her god. And, of course, I have to help her.

**JED:** You help your wife worship a false god?

**OREN:** Hey, I don't believe in it. So what's the problem?

**JED:** Whew! Joel was right!

**GABE:** Right about what?

**JED:** Well, Joel said we just go through the motions of worshiping God—that we really don't care about a relationship with Him.

**EBEN:** A relationship?

**JED:** Yeah. Sort of like we have with each other. We get together to talk, to enjoy each other's company, to learn more about each other—all that stuff.

**OREN:** God wants us to have that kind of relationship with Him?

**GABE:** I don't understand what's wrong with the old way of doing things. It was good enough for my father and my grandfather and my great-grandfather.

**JED:** But it isn't good enough for God. God's been patient with us, but no more.

**EBEN:** Great. We've blown it big time and God's going to punish us. That cheers me up.

**JED:** Hey, guys. Joel says that God really cares about us, that God will send us help and that His love will be shared by everyone. But if God's got to use punishment to get our attention, He'll do it.

**GABE:** Hm. I think I'll just pop over to Joel's for a while and see what that book of his says.

**EBEN:** Well, wait up. I'll go with you.

**OREN:** Maybe I'd better go, too. But my wife isn't going to like this.

**JED:** Maybe you should take her with you to hear Joel's book.

**For the real story read Jonah 1–4**

# Wrong-Way Jonah!

**Characters: NARRATOR; JONAH; GOD; SAILOR**

**Props:** Characters may wish to pantomime the use of props.

## ACT ONE

**NARRATOR:** A very long time ago, the wicked people in the city of Nineveh did many evil deeds that deserved God's punishment. So God decided to warn them to change their ways. In another city there lived a man named Jonah. *(JONAH enters.)* God had given Jonah the job of a prophet. This meant he was *supposed* to tell God's messages to everyone.

**GOD:** Jonah, I want you to go to Nineveh and preach to the people.

**JONAH:** Nineveh? That wicked, evil place? Why?

**GOD:** Because I want to warn them to change their evil ways.

**JONAH:** Yeah, yeah, I'm going. *(To AUDIENCE.)* But not to Nineveh! I'm going the other way, to Tarshish! Then Nineveh will be punished as they deserve!

**NARRATOR:** So Jonah hurried to the nearby port and got on a ship sailing to Tarshish. Pretty soon, the wind began to blow. Then it started to rain. The waves splashed higher and higher. And before anyone knew it, a heavy storm had hit. The sailors worked as hard as they could to save the ship. But where was Jonah during all this excitement?

**JONAH:** *(Rubbing eyes sleepily.)* Sleeping. In the bottom of the boat.

**NARRATOR:** One of the sailors ran down to the bottom of the boat and woke up Jonah.

**SAILOR:** Jonah, wake up! Wake up! If you care about your life, wake up and pray to your God that we will be saved!

**JONAH:** Huh? What?

**SAILOR:** Can't you hear the storm raging? Do you want to die? Wake up and pray to your God like the rest of us.

**JONAH:** God? Uh-oh. Look, God is angry with me for running away and disobeying Him. If you throw me overboard, you will all be saved.

**SAILOR:** Throw you overboard? What good would that do?

**NARRATOR:** Just then the storm got louder and stronger.

**JONAH:** Look, this is my fault, not yours. You shouldn't die for my mistake. Just throw me overboard. God will stop the storm if you do.

## ACT TWO

**NARRATOR:** So the sailors took Jonah up to the deck of the ship where the storm was raging, the rain was pounding, the waves were splashing, the wind was howling and the fish were gurgling in anticipation of dinner. And they threw Jonah off the ship. The sea was calm!

**JONAH:** I was sinking to the bottom of the ocean, I was drowning, choking, calling out to God...and then, I was swallowed by a great fish.

**NARRATOR:** Jonah sat in the belly of the great fish for three days. He had a lot of time to think and pray.

**JONAH:** I think it stinks.

**NARRATOR:** I meant he had time to think about what he'd done.

**JONAH:** Oh yeah, that. But if I'd gone to Nineveh, those people might have listened to God's message and changed their ways. And then God would have forgiven them. They don't deserve to be forgiven!

**NARRATOR:** Don't you have faith that God knows best?

**JONAH:** Well, I suppose.

**NARRATOR:** And you don't believe that God's love is for everyone?

**JONAH:** Maybe. Maybe not.

**NARRATOR:** So, what did you pray about?

**JONAH:** I told God that He had saved my life.

**NARRATOR:** And?

**JONAH:** (Sighs.) And, I said I'd go to Nineveh.

## ACT THREE

**NARRATOR:** The great fish spit Jonah up on a beach near Nineveh.

**JONAH:** Yuck!

**GOD:** You've got a job to do, Jonah. (JONAH nods head in disgruntled way and walks off stage.)

**NARRATOR:** Jonah walked to Nineveh. It took a while because it was 500 miles away! But he finally got there and told God's message to the Ninevites.

**JONAH:** (Offstage.) If you don't change your ways in the next 40 days, God's going to destroy you. (Comes back onstage.) I can't believe this! Those Ninevites believed God. They said they were sorry for doing evil. They actually changed their ways. And God forgave them! I'm so mad! (JONAH sits down.)

**GOD:** Jonah, why don't you want me to show my love and forgiveness to so many people?

**NARRATOR:** God wanted Jonah to learn that faith in God means not just knowing that God is real and powerful, but telling others about God's love as well.

# New Testament

**For the real story read Matthew 4:1-11**

# Whatta Bargain!

### Characters: JESUS; SATAN

**Props:** Characters may wish to pantomime the use of props.

**Scene:** JESUS *sits reading the Bible, somewhere in the desert*.

**SATAN:** *(SATAN approaches JESUS.)* Fancy meeting YOU here! Been out here in the desert for months? Well, have I got the solution for You! This state-of-the-art rock can be turned into bread. Yes, for a very small price, You can have food any time You want. Simply pick up any rock by the side of the road and...presto! Instant bread! Doesn't it look wonderful? Yummy, yummy!

**JESUS:** God says in Deuteronomy 8:3 that people don't live on bread alone, but that they need every word that comes from the mouth of God to live forever.

**SATAN:** OK, fine...Bungee-jumping leave You cold? Roller coasters lost their rush? Now

You can experience the thrill of a lifetime! It's simple! Just throw Yourself off the top of the Temple into the ravine below, and You're in for the heavenly ride of a lifetime. No need to worry. God will send His angels to catch You. He would never let YOU down! See? It says so right here in Psalms 91:11-12.

**JESUS:** It also says here in Deuteronomy 6:16 that we should not try to make God prove His love for us.

**SATAN:** OK, OK...how 'bout this: Ever dream of a nice little universe to call Your own? Complete with riches beyond compare and kingdoms of people to bow down to You? Well, I have one right here. And I have got a deal for You! It's easy! All I ask is that You bow down and worship me. Just this once! Whatta bargain! It beats having You give up Your life for these silly humans. Why go through all that pain and suffering?

**JESUS:** It says here in Deuteronomy 6:13 to worship and serve only God. Now, get lost, Satan!

For the **real story** read Matthew 4:23-25, 26:3-4; Luke 2:4-7, 52; 23:33-34; 24

# A Wonderful Life!

**Characters:** CHUCK SMILEY, Host; **JOE SCHMOE**, Contestant; **KASPAR**, King from the East; **PERRY LYZED** and **SUZI SICKLY**; **CLYDE CENTURION**; **AUDIENCE**

**Props:** Characters may wish to pantomime the use of props.

**Scene:** *Game Show set.*

**CHUCK:** Welcome to your favorite game show, "A Wonderful Life!"—where someone learns just how wonderful his life has been! I'm your host, Chuck Smiley, and our special guest today is Mr. Joe Schmoe! *(AUDIENCE cheers as JOE enters.)*

**CHUCK:** Welcome, Joe!

**JOE:** Glad to be here, Chuck.

**CHUCK:** Backstage, we have some people to remind you of your wonderful life! Let's begin with this voice from your past.

**KASPAR:** *(Offstage.)* I traveled far to see you when you were a small child. I wanted to worship the child that God sent to show love to the world.

**CHUCK:** Do you recognize that voice?

**JOE:** Well, no.

**CHUCK:** This is one of the wise kings who followed a star to find you! Come on in, Kaspar, King from the East! *(KASPAR enters. Both he and JOE look puzzled.)*

**JOE:** But I never met a king.

**CHUCK:** Sure you have. At least three of them, in Bethlehem.

**KASPAR:** Um...it was Jesus we came to see, not Joe.

**CHUCK:** Oops. Both of their names begin with a J. Uh, well, thanks for coming anyway, Kaspar. *(CHUCK quickly shoos KASPAR offstage.)*

**CHUCK:** A little mix-up in the research department. No problemo. Here are voices I know you'll remember! *(Offstage many voices say "Thank you. Thank you.")*

**CHUCK:** Quick! Who do you think they are?

**JOE:** Well, they sound really joyful. And grateful. But I can't remember doing anybody any big favors.

**CHUCK:** Come on out, Perry Lyzed and Suzi Sickly. *(PERRY and SUZI enter and wave.)*

**CHUCK:** You must want to say something to Joe. *(PERRY and SUZI look puzzled.)*

**PERRY and SUZI:** *(In unison.)* Who are you?

**JOE:** I'm Joe Schmoe.

**PERRY and SUZI:** *(In unison.)* Nice to meet you.

**CHUCK:** That's all you can say? After your miraculous healing? Come on—tell us what happened.

**PERRY:** Well, I was paralyzed; and a man came along and suddenly, I could walk.

**SUZI:** I was sick for many years, and a man reached out and healed me.

**CHUCK:** *(To PERRY and SUZI.)* And you were healed by...

**PERRY and SUZI:** *(In unison.)* Jesus.

**CHUCK:** Well, it was wonderful meeting you. *(CHUCK shoos PERRY and SUZI offstage and then mutters.)* I'll have to have a little talk with our research department. *(To JOE.)* But here's a voice I'm sure you'll know.

**CENTURION:** *(Speaks from offstage.)* Surely, this was a righteous man.

**CHUCK:** Mystery guest, come on in! *(CENTURION enters. CHUCK looks at JOE, but JOE continues to look stumped.)*

**CHUCK:** *(To CENTURION.)* Tell us who you are and what you do.

**CENTURION:** My name is Clyde Centurion. I oversee crucifixions for the Roman government.

**CHUCK:** What was your most memorable crucifixion?

**CENTURION:** There were three men being crucified. The two on the outside were criminals. But there was something different about the One in the middle.

**CHUCK:** Go on.

**CENTURION:** He had been betrayed by one of His closest friends. All of His other friends ran away. He should have been cursing everyone. They all do.

**CHUCK:** But He didn't?

**CENTURION:** No. He seemed full of peace. While He was being crucified, He said things like, "Father, forgive them, for they don't know what they're doing."

**CHUCK:** So, His father was there at the crucifixion?

**CENTURION:** No, He was talking to God when He said "Father."

**CHUCK:** But something else remarkable happened, didn't it?

**CENTURION:** It sure did. Three days after He died, He came back to life. And I learned that He suffered that death on the cross so that all people who would believe in Him could have their sins forgiven. What a kind and loving man!

**CHUCK:** *(Pointing to JOE.)* And here he is!

**CENTURION:** I don't know him. He wasn't the One who was crucified!

**CHUCK:** *(To JOE.)* You weren't crucified?

**JOE:** Nope. I never died.

**CHUCK:** Then what did you do?

**JOE:** Well, one time I saw a traffic accident and fainted.

**CHUCK:** Nothing else?

**JOE:** Nope. I'm just your average Joe. *(To CENTURION.)* Tell me about Jesus. He sounds like a great guy to know.

**CENTURION:** He is! Not only was He a man, but He was also God. It's kind of hard to describe...*(Pantomimes talking to JOE as CHUCK closes the show.)*

**CHUCK:** That's all the time we have. This is Chuck Smiley reminding you to have "A Wonderful Life!" *(To somebody offstage.)* Are we clear? Hey, can we get this Jesus to be on the show? THAT'S the kind of life we're looking for.

For the **real deal** read Matthew 5:1-3,5

# Attitude Check

**Characters: ROBBIE BARKER,** the host of "TV Star Quiz"; **JENNY,** a girl who knows EVERYTHING, or so she thinks; **ERIK,** a boy who doesn't know ANYTHING, or so he thinks; **JOE,** a boy who knows what he knows; **JAMIE,** the stage manager

## ACT ONE

**Scene:** *Backstage in the Green Room (the waiting room for actors or contestants).*

**JAMIE:** *(Enters with* JENNY, ERIK *and* JOE.*)* You're on in one minute, thirty seconds. Wait here 'til I call for you. Got it? Good. *(Exits.)*

**JOE:** Look at all these donuts! It certainly is nice of them to give us this food.

**ERIK:** We're probably not allowed to eat any.

**JENNY:** Hmph! I don't see any strawberries! I told them I wanted STRAWBERRIES! What will I eat?

**JOE:** Actually, I'm not sure we have time to eat now. Maybe after the show...

**JENNY:** That eclair looks fat and yummy! *(Takes a bite, squirting filling on her dress.)* Oh no!

**JAMIE:** *(Sticks head in door.)* All right, let's go.

**JENNY:** The show's going to have to wait. I need to change my clothes.

**JAMIE:** Can't wait—live show. You go on as is or not at all. *(JAMIE exits.)*

**JENNY:** He sure needs an attitude check. I can't go on like this!

**JOE:** Let's go, Erik. Maybe we can give Jenny enough time to clean herself up.

## ACT TWO

**Scene:** *The set of "TV Star Quiz" game show.*

**ROBBIE:** Our first contestant is Jenny. *(ERIK enters.)* You're not Jenny.

**ERIK:** I'm sorry, I'll leave.

**JOE:** *(Enters.)* I apologize for the confusion, Mr. Barker, but Jenny isn't quite ready yet. I'm Joe and this is Erik.

**ROBBIE:** Uh-huh. Well, tell us about yourself, Joe.

**JOE:** I'm a student at Easton Middle School. I like to swim, play video games and go to movies.

**ROBBIE:** Great! And how about you, Erik, what can you tell us about yourself?

**ERIK:** Nothing! I don't do anything interesting. No one would want to know about me.

**ROBBIE:** Do you go to school? Play on a sports team?

**ERIK:** Yeah, but I'm the worst kid in my class and on my team.

**ROBBIE:** Oh boy. Where is Jenny?

**JENNY:** *(Enters with a big wet spot on her dress.)* Here I am!

**ROBBIE:** Great, let's begin our game.

**JENNY:** Robbie, I think you forgot to ask me to introduce myself. I was born in upstate New York and have attended only the finest schools since birth.

**ROBBIE:** It says on my card you were born in New Jersey.

**JENNY:** Well, that's NEAR upstate New York. I've won honor student awards every year. And I'm the class president.

**ROBBIE:** It certainly sounds like you've done well. Erik, why don't you pick our first question?

**ERIK:** I don't know what to pick. I'm sure I'm not going to be able to answer any of the questions. But I guess I'll pick Star Names for 200 points.

**ROBBIE:** Here's your question: Who was the star of the "Gilligan's Island" show?

**ERIK:** (Groans.) I knew I wouldn't know the answer.

**JENNY:** I know the answer, Robbie. It was John Denver!

**ROBBIE:** I'm sorry, Jenny, that's the wrong answer.

**JENNY:** You'd better check your Hollywood Encyclopedia, Robbie. I'm SURE the answer is John Denver.

**ROBBIE:** No, it isn't. Joe, do you have an answer?

**JOE:** The answer is Bob Denver.

**ROBBIE:** That's correct.

**JENNY:** THAT'S what I was trying to say! Bob Denver. I should get the points for that question, Robbie.

**ROBBIE:** You CAN'T get the points because you DIDN'T say the RIGHT name.

**JENNY:** Well, really! I had no idea you'd be so picky.

**ROBBIE:** It's your turn to pick a question.

**JENNY:** I'll take Star Names for 500.

**ROBBIE:** Here's your question: Who was the male star of the "I Love Lucy" comedy?

**JENNY:** This question is worth 500 points? The answer is SO easy. Ricky Ricardo was.

**ROBBIE:** I'm sorry, that's incorrect.

**JENNY:** Incorrect?!? I think not! You OBVIOUSLY don't know your star facts, Robbie!

**ROBBIE:** Erik, do you know the answer?

**ERIK:** ME?!? If SHE doesn't know the answer, how am I supposed to know the answer?

**ROBBIE:** (Sighs.) JOE, do you know the answer?

**JOE:** I'm sorry, Mr. Barker, I thought it was Ricky Ricardo, too.

**ROBBIE:** Desi Arnaz was the male star of the "I Love Lucy" comedy.

**JOE:** Wow! That's interesting!

**JENNY:** It's wrong!

**ROBBIE:** I think it's time for a commercial break. JAMIE!

**JAMIE:** Trouble?

**ROBBIE:** Where'd you get these contestants? There's only one here that's any good.

**JENNY:** (To ERIK and JOE.) Sorry you have to leave, guys.

**JAMIE:** OK. Erik and Jenny, it's been nice having you, but we're going to select some other contestants from the audience. Sorry, you just didn't work out.

**JENNY:** What?!?

**ERIK:** I knew it.

*Note: Matthew 5:1-3,5 describes the reward of being a humble person*

**For the real deal read Matthew 5:38-48; Luke 6:27,35**

# Love Your Enemies?!

**Characters: ABNER,** a Bible-times boy; **DAN,** a Bible-times boy; **HANNAH,** a Bible-times girl; **MASSAH,** a Bible-times bully; **JULIUS,** a Roman soldier; **CLAUDIUS,** a sick Roman soldier

**Props:** Characters may wish to pantomime the use of props.

**Scene:** *A road near the Sea of Galilee.*

**ABNER:** Wasn't Jesus great? All those wonderful things He said...

**HANNAH:** Yes. I'M going to do ALL the good stuff He talked about!

**DAN:** It won't be easy...

**ABNER:** Of course it'll be EASY! How could loving others be hard?

**HANNAH:** Oh no! Look! It's Massah! Let's run.

**MASSAH:** Hmph, like you weaklings could outrun me!

**ABNER:** Go away and leave us alone!

**MASSAH:** *(Mockingly.)* Abner, Hannah and

Dan, were sitting one day in a pan, Said Hannah, "Hey I have a plan! I think I'll become a man!" Ha! Ha! Ha!

**HANNAH:** Oh yeah? Well, at least people LIKE me!

**ABNER:** And we don't have a dumb name like "Massah."

**DAN:** Actually, Massah, that was a pretty good rhyme.

**MASSAH:** Are you making fun of me?!?

**HANNAH:** Dan, be quiet! Don't encourage him!

**MASSAH:** Yeah, Dan, you'd better not "encourage" me!

**DAN:** But, Massah, you're good at rhymes. Why shouldn't we encourage you?

**ABNER:** Dan, what do you think you're doing?

**DAN:** Go ahead, Massah. Hit us with another rhyme.

**MASSAH:** Why should I? So you can make fun of me?

**DAN:** I don't want to make fun of you, Massah. I just think if you worked at it, you could be a really clever poet.

**MASSAH:** Really?

**DAN:** Really.

**MASSAH:** Ah...thanks,...I guess. Me, a poet? Nah. *(MASSAH exits.)*

**ABNER:** OK, explain THAT to me. Why were you nice to that bully?

**DAN:** Because...

**JULIUS:** Hey, you kids! Get over here and help me!

**ABNER:** *(Whispers.)* Oh no! A Roman soldier! I hate those Romans!

**JULIUS:** *(Louder.)* Did you kids hear me? I said get over here!

**HANNAH:** We'd better go. We could get arrested if we don't.

**JULIUS:** You're carrying water, aren't you?

**ABNER and HANNAH:** *(Hiding water skins.)* Nope, no water here.

**JULIUS:** *(To DAN.)* What about you?

**DAN:** Yes, I have water.

**JULIUS:** My friend needs some water. Give him yours.

**DAN:** *(Hands water to JULIUS.)* Here. Your friend doesn't look like he feels well.

**JULIUS:** That's no business of yours!

**DAN:** Well, I have some bread. Would he like that as well?

**ABNER and HANNAH:** DAN!

**CLAUDIUS:** Thank you. That's very kind of you.

**ABNER:** Dan, why are you being nice to those Romans?

**DAN:** Because...

**JULIUS:** Hey, you kids! Pick up my friend's backpack and carry it for him.

**ABNER:** *(To JULIUS.)* What?

**HANNAH:** Abner! The law says we HAVE to carry it a mile.

**DAN:** Here, I'll carry it!

**CLAUDIUS:** It's too heavy for one boy to carry. You'll never make it a mile.

**DAN:** Who said anything about carrying it for a mile?

**JULIUS:** You kids are all alike! You'd better pick up that pack before I...

**DAN:** No, what I meant is that my friends and I will be happy to carry it to the next town for you.

**HANNAH:** The next town?!?

**ABNER:** Dan, are you nuts? The next town is over two miles away!

**DAN:** Yeah, but that Roman soldier looks pretty sick. He needs our help.

**ABNER:** No way! I'm not helping any Roman soldier.

**DAN:** OK. You guys help me carry the pack the first mile, then I'll carry it myself the second mile.

**ABNER:** Dan, WHY are you doing this?

**DAN:** Well, it's like Jesus said—we've got to love our enemies.

**ABNER and HANNAH:** Oh.

**HANNAH:** I guess I could help you carry it to the next town, since we're going there ANYWAY.

**DAN:** Great! Thanks, Hannah. You know, if we sing some songs, it'll make the trip seem shorter...

**ABNER:** Well, wait for me. This loving your enemies stuff isn't going to be as easy as I thought!

**For the real story read Matthew 6:25-34**

# Don't Worry— Have Peace

**Characters: DAVID; MATTHIAS; THOMAS; JESUS**

**Scene:** DAVID, MATTHIAS *and* THOMAS *are walking together.*

**MATTHIAS:** Will you hurry up! We don't want to be late!

**DAVID:** Don't blame me. He's the slowpoke.

**THOMAS:** Where are we going?

**DAVID:** Matthias, you're the one in a hurry. You explain it to him.

**MATTHIAS:** *(Pulls* THOMAS *along.)* We are going to listen to Jesus, a rabbi. There's always a crowd when He speaks.

**THOMAS:** *(Stops walking.)* Why?

**DAVID:** Thomas, just hurry up. You'll see when we get there. *(To* MATTHIAS.*)* If you try to explain it, we'll be here all day.

**MATTHIAS:** You're right. If we're late, we'll never get a good seat. *(Prods* THOMAS *to get moving.)*

*(*MATTHIAS, DAVID *and* THOMAS *wind around the stage area as if hurrying to the place where* JESUS *is; then they stop.)*

**MATTHIAS:** We made it. I was afraid we'd be late.

**DAVID:** You're always worrying about something.

**THOMAS:** *(Loudly.)* So where's this rabbi?

**MATTHIAS:** *(Points offstage.)* Over there.

**DAVID:** Shhh! He's starting to talk.

**JESUS:** *(From offstage.)* Listen to what I tell you. Don't get all upset and worry about what you will eat and drink, or what you will wear.

**THOMAS:** What's happening? I can't hear from here.

**DAVID:** He's telling people not to worry about food or clothing.

**THOMAS:** Well, that's silly. You have to eat something and wear clothes.

**JESUS:** *(From offstage.)* Look at the birds of the air. They don't plant or harvest or store food away in barns, and yet your heavenly Father feeds them. Aren't you much more valuable than birds? And will worrying about everything add a single hour to someone's life? Not at all!

**THOMAS:** That's easy for Him to say. What does He know about our worries?

**DAVID:** He might know. He looks like a hard worker. He's wearing ordinary clothes. I'll bet He doesn't have a lot of money.

**JESUS:** *(From offstage.)* And why do you worry about clothes? Watch how the lilies of the field grow. They don't work or sew. Yet not even Solomon in all his splendor was dressed as richly as one of these flowers.

**THOMAS:** I'm not getting this. What's King Solomon got to do with lilies?

**MATTHIAS:** He said the flowers are dressed better than Solomon ever was.

**THOMAS:** Who IS this rabbi and how does He know so much?

**DAVID:** People say He's sent from God and that He heals the sick and makes paralyzed men walk and blind people see.

**THOMAS:** *(Loudly.)* And what's His name again?

**DAVID:** *(Exasperated.)* Jesus. Now, shhh! Just LISTEN.

**JESUS:** *(From offstage.)* If God dresses the grass of the field in such finery, even though it's here today and tomorrow is thrown into the fire, won't He clothe you?

**MATTHIAS:** *(Whispering to* THOMAS *before he can ask any more questions.)* He's saying that if God cares for the grass so much that He gives it such beautiful clothing, we should trust Him to give us what we need, also.

**DAVID:** So, we don't need to worry about what to wear.

**THOMAS:** We do when it's cold. If I had known it was going to be cold, I'd have worn a coat.

**MATTHIAS:** The weather forecast said it would be cold.

**THOMAS:** Who listens to them? They're always wrong.

**DAVID:** Really, guys. Can't you be quiet? We came all the way here to listen to Jesus, not to complain.

**JESUS:** *(From offstage.)* So don't worry saying "What shall we eat?" or "What shall we wear?" Your heavenly Father knows that you need those things. Instead, try to please God and do what is right, and all these things will be given to you. So don't worry about tomorrow. Don't live in fear, for I bring you peace.

**DAVID:** He's saying we can count on God. He cares about us and will make sure we have what we need.

**MATTHIAS:** You know, it kind of gives me a peaceful feeling to realize I don't need to worry so much.

**THOMAS:** One. Two. Three. Four—

**MATTHIAS:** What are you doing now Thomas?!

**THOMAS:** I'm counting on God. Why?

**MATTHIAS:** Oh, brother! *(Rolls eyes at* THOMAS.)

**THOMAS:** *(Wondering what he said wrong, clueless.)* What?

**DAVID:** Let's get back home and tell everybody what we've heard. I think this Jesus makes a lot of sense—unlike our friend Thomas here!

For the **real story** read Matthew 9:18-26; Mark 5:22-43; Luke 8:41-56

# Galilee TV

**Characters: CINDY-SUE SADDLESHOO,** pushy TV reporter; **JACKIE T. CARBUNKLE (JACK),** ambulance-chasing lawyer; **WITNESS 1,** woman on the street; **WITNESS 2,** man on the street

**Props:** Characters may wish to pantomime the use of props.

**Scene:** *Outside a home in Galilee. A large crowd has gathered.*

**CINDY-SUE:** *(Holding microphone, speaks to audience as if to a camera.)* I'm Cindy-Sue Saddleshoo, ace reporter for Galilee TV News. For those of you just joining us, there's a sick young girl in this house. Her father is the synagogue ruler, Jairus. He has gone to ask Jesus, the famous teacher and healer, to help her.

**JACK:** *(Pushes his way through crowd.)* Excuse me! Pardon me! Important lawyer... gotta get through!

**CINDY-SUE:** *(Pushes microphone in JACK'S face.)* Sir, wait! What's your name? Are you the sick girl's lawyer?

**JACK:** *(To audience as if to camera.)* Jackie T. Carbunkle, attorney-at-law. Hurt your back? Just call Jack!

**CINDY-SUE:** *(To JACK.)* Tell me, Mr. Carbunkle, how is your client feeling?

**JACK:** Well if you must know, she isn't my client yet! But I heard she's nearly dead, and I'm here to make sure she knows her rights! *(Sees WITNESS 1. Hands her a business card.)* Jackie T. Carbunkle, attorney-at-law. Slip 'n fall? Gimme a call!

**WITNESS 1:** Well, I'm not hurt, but I was sick for years! I went to doctor after doctor, and no one could help me.

**JACK:** *(Excited.)* Really? I can make sure you never have to worry about doctor bills again!

**WITNESS 1:** But that's the thing—I'm not sick like I used to be.

**CINDY-SUE:** *(To audience.)* You heard it here first! The sick woman is now... *(Looks at WITNESS 1.)* Sicker? *(WITNESS 1 shakes her head.)* Help me out, then! What happened?

**WITNESS 1:** Well, I heard that Jesus was in the area. And I knew that He has healed many people. I knew He could heal me, too!

**CINDY-SUE:** *(To audience.)* Aha! So this brave woman marched right up to Jesus, and He healed her!

**WITNESS 1:** Well, not exactly...Jesus was on His way here to see this young girl. There were crowds all around Him. But I thought, if I can just touch the hem of His robe, I'll be healed.

**CINDY-SUE:** *(To audience.)* Another tragic story of illness making people delusional. *(To WITNESS 1.)* So what made you think clothing can heal?

**WITNESS 1:** I didn't think His ROBE would heal me...I believed that because Jesus is so powerful, even touching His robe would save me. And I knew the crowd would never let me in if they knew I was sick. So I quietly slipped through the crowd and touched Jesus' robe.

**JACK:** *(Excited.)* So did the crowd get angry? Were you injured?

**WITNESS 1:** Not at all. Jesus stopped and asked who had touched Him. I was terrified! But I admitted I had touched His robe. Jesus was so kind and patient that He said because of my faith, I was healed!

**JACK:** *(Disappointed.)* Well, if you start to feel sick again, call me.

**WITNESS 1:** I won't! I'm all better. I'm right as rain! Healthy as a horse! My friends and family won't believe it! I'm on my way home right now to tell them all about Jesus and how He helped me. *(WITNESS 1 exits.)*

**CINDY-SUE:** *(WITNESS 2 enters as CINDY-SUE is speaking to audience.)* For those of you just joining us, on Jesus' way to heal a young girl, a sick woman sneaked through the crowd, touched Jesus' robe and was healed!

**JACK:** *(Sees WITNESS 2. Hands him a business card.)* Jackie T. Carbunkle, attorney-at-law. Is your donkey broke? I'm your bloke!

**WITNESS 2:** Actually, I don't have a donkey. I just know that when the young girl died—

**CINDY-SUE:** She's dead?! *(To audience.)* What a tragic turn of events! You heard it here first, folks. The sick girl is now dead.

**WITNESS 2:** No, no. You don't understand. She WAS dead, but she isn't anymore!

**CINDY-SUE:** *(To audience.)* You heard it here first, folks! The dead girl is now just sick!

**JACK:** Hold on! Is she sick or is she dead?

**WITNESS 2:** She was sick. Then she was dead. Now she isn't sick or dead.

**CINDY-SUE:** *(To JACK.)* How do you think this will affect your case?

**JACK:** I'm not sure. But I'll definitely look into it. *(To WITNESS 2.)* So what happened with the girl?

**WITNESS 2:** When the girl died, I went to get Jairus. I told him the girl had died. So Jairus and Jesus hurried here. But Jesus said that the girl wasn't really dead. She was only sleeping.

**CINDY-SUE:** So Jesus was confused?

**WITNESS 2:** No! He meant that He could still heal her—even from death! He went inside the house. She was lying on her bed, dead. But I hear that Jesus told her to get up, and she DID! She was completely healthy!

**CINDY-SUE:** *(To audience.)* You heard it here first, live on Galilee TV News! Jesus healed Jairus's daughter AND a sick woman, all in one day. This is Cindy-Sue Saddleshoo. Goodnight. *(Pauses for a moment, smiling widely and then exits.)*

**JACK:** *(Disappointed.)* So you mean to tell me that there are NO sick people here? *(WITNESS 2 shakes his head, no.)* And NO dead people? *(WITNESS 2 shakes his head, no.)* And nobody is even injured?

**WITNESS 2:** Well, it looks like you're not needed here.

**JACK:** *(Excited.)* That's alright. While I'm down this way, I'm going to talk to some fishermen. *(WITNESS 2 and JACK exit, as JACK continues talking.)* They want to sue the mayor because they didn't catch any fish all day! And one of them says he got seasick...

**For the real story read Matthew 12:9-14**

# The Plot

**Characters: LEADER,** Snaps fingers in rhythm with spoken lines; **CHORUS,** Snaps fingers in rhythm with spoken lines; **JOE,** Man with a crippled hand; **BART,** Joe's friend; **PHARISEE,** Religious leader

**Scene:** *A street just outside the Temple on a sunny Sabbath day. JOE sits alone. CHORUS and LEADER speak lines as they slowly walk by JOE.*

## ACT ONE

**LEADER:** There once was a man...

**CHORUS:** A man? What man?

**LEADER:** ...with a crippled hand.

**CHORUS:** Oh, the crippled man!

**LEADER:** No, the HAND is crippled, not the man!

**CHORUS:** Poor man with the crippled hand.

*(BART enters and sits next to JOE.)*

**BART:** Hey, you look blue! What's down with you?

**JOE:** Oh, nothing new.

**BART:** Is this about your hand?

**JOE:** You'd think someone would care, have some feelings for me. I can't even beg because today's the Sabbath! Another day of going hungry.

**BART:** Just between you and me, some of these rules are stupid.

**PHARISEE:** *(Sneaking up.)* Excuse me!

**BART:** Ulp! Yup, that's what he said to me, but I told him...

**PHARISEE:** I have no time for your prattle. Come with me.

**BART:** Oh, I wasn't prattling, sir. I know it's against the laws to prattle on the Sabbath!

**PHARISEE:** As far as I know prattling is not against any Sabbath law, yet. But I can see that it SHOULD be. You, Joe, come with me.

**JOE:** But, I wasn't begging—

**PHARISEE:** There's a man I want you to meet. *(Insincerely.)* He might be able to heal you.

**BART:** Heal you? Hey, that's great! *(PHARISEE drags JOE offstage. BART starts to follow but stops to listen to LEADER and CHORUS.)*

**LEADER:** You'd better beware of those Pharisees there.

**CHORUS:** Can't trust those Pharisees anywhere.

**LEADER:** They want to catch Jesus in a trap.

**CHORUS:** They want to break Jesus on a rap.

**BART:** What trap? What rap?

**LEADER:** Gonna make Him break the rules, those Sabbath rules.

**CHORUS:** Or make Him look bad, make the people mad.

**BART:** How? What can they do?

## ACT TWO

**JOE:** Look, Bart, look!

**BART:** What is it?

**JOE:** Look at my HAND! It's healed! Jesus healed my hand!

**BART:** Jesus healed you on the SABBATH?

**JOE:** Yup. Look! I can wiggle my fingers!

**BART:** Yeah, great! Um, what did the Pharisees say? I mean, about Jesus.

**JOE:** Oh, they asked Him some question about whether or not a person should heal on the Sabbath. Look! I can finally clap! *(Tries to clap hands, but misses.)*

**BART:** So all this was OK with them?

**JOE:** Who? Guess I need a little practice yet.

**BART:** WHAT ABOUT THE PHARISEES? Concentrate, will you?

**JOE:** Well, they were kind of huddled up when I left. And they did tell me to keep this quiet. Hey, look at this! *(Does motions for "Itsy Bitsy Spider" and sings.)*

**BART:** Joe, listen to me! The Pharisees were planning some kind of a TRAP for Jesus. What happened!?

**LEADER:** There once was a Man...

**CHORUS:** A man? What man?

**LEADER:** ...who healed Joe's hand.

**CHORUS:** Yeah, Jesus the Healer is our Man!

**LEADER:** Now the Pharisees—

**CHORUS:** So tough to please!

**LEADER:** —want Him to die!

**CHORUS:** Those nasty guys!

**BART and JOE:** But WHY?

**For the real story read Matthew 14:13-36; John 18:1-11; 19:17-30; 20**

# Wise Up!

### Characters:

**JOHN,** a disciple of Jesus;
**PETER,** a disciple of Jesus; **PASSERBY**

**Props:** Characters may wish to pantomime the use of props.

**JOHN:** I got some good shots this time. Look at this one. *(Tries to show photo to PETER.)*

**PETER:** This camera thing is getting out of hand, John. Most of your photos are out of focus anyway. Besides—I was there. Remember?

*(PASSERBY enters.)*

**JOHN:** I'll bet he'll want to see them. *(Grabs PASSERBY and shows photo.)* Hey! See this picture? You know who this is?

**PASSERBY:** Uh, no. *(Shakes head.)*

**JOHN:** That's Jesus—a fantastic teacher! He did miracles! He wanted people to know that God loves them.

**PETER:** *(To JOHN.)* If you're going to do it,

do it right. Show these other people that picture. *(JOHN gives photo to audience to pass around.)* We always knew Jesus was an amazing person. But, boy, we had a lot more to learn about Him! Right, John?

**JOHN:** Ri—

**PETER:** *(Interrupts.)* Show him that picture of the twelve of us disciples. *(JOHN shows PASSERBY another photo.)* See me doing my Samson imitation? Pretty funny, hey? Well, I guess you had to be there. Pass it around. *(PASSERBY gives photo to audience.)* Some people think I've done some foolish things. This one time I did something my friends thought wasn't too bright, but actually that's when I began to wise up. *(To PASSERBY.)* Sit down, it's quite a story.

*(PASSERBY sits with audience.)*

**PETER:** John, show them the picture you took with all the people. *(JOHN holds up another photo for the audience to see.)* That's Jesus, there. And that's me. And that's a little kid. And see all those people! How many were there, John?

**JOHN:** Oh, proba—

**PETER:** At least 5,000. Jesus spent hours teaching and healing. Finally we told Him, "You've got to send these people away—it's nearly dinnertime." Jesus says, "Then feed them." I say, "With what?" Then this little kids says, "I've got my lunch. I'll share." Big laugh, right, John?

**JOHN:** It did seem a little small—

**PETER:** A little small? Five loaves of bread and a couple of fish. But Jesus says a blessing, breaks it into pieces and tells us to pass it around. Everyone ate and we STILL had leftovers. I thought, *Who can make food appear like that?*

**JOHN:** Then, later He—

**PETER:** John, you're getting ahead of yourself. After we ate, Jesus says to us, "Take the boat across the lake, and I'll join you later." He wanted to be alone to pray. So we took off. At first it was calm, but boy, that Sea of Galilee sure can change in a hurry. Right, John?

**JOHN:** Ri—

**PETER:** Don't hog the picture, John. Show it to them. (JOHN *shows a different photo.*) I think that picture got taken by accident. You dropped the camera, didn't you, John?

**JOHN:** Well, actually, I—

**PETER:** We rowed and rowed for hours in that storm. Suddenly, we saw something coming toward us on the water. We were scared out of our wits! Someone screamed, "It's a ghost!"

**JOHN:** But really it was—

**PETER:** Jesus. He was walking on top of the water! He knew we were in trouble. (JOHN *passes the last photo to the audience.*) I called to Him, "If it's really You, Lord, let me come out onto the water, too." Jesus told me to come. So, I stepped out of the boat and into the water. (*To* JOHN.) Now why didn't you get a picture of that?

**JOHN:** (*Shrugs.*) My flash didn't—

**PETER:** I took a couple of steps, but then I thought, *What are you doing, Peter? You can't walk on water!* I started to sink.

**JOHN:** I got a great shot of that! (JOHN *shows a photo to the audience.*)

**PETER:** Jesus pulled me out of the water just before I went under. "Why did you doubt?" He asked. I guess He wondered why I didn't trust Him to help me. As soon as we were back in the boat, the storm stopped—just like that! You got any more pictures, John? (JOHN *shakes his head no.*) After that, we were all sure that Jesus was the Son of God and I thought, *From now on, I'll always trust Jesus.* But then Jesus was arrested and killed on a cross. I started to have my doubts again. We all couldn't understand why He had to die. Right, John?

**JOHN:** Right. But later we—

**PETER:** Saw Him alive! I was pretty ashamed for not trusting Jesus—again. Now I know that Jesus had to die so that all of us can be forgiven for the foolish choices we made. Right, John?

**JOHN:** Ri—

**PETER:** The wisest thing I did was to trust Jesus and rely on Him for help. You can do it, too. Jesus loved you, and He wants you to trust Him to help you. He died for your sins, too, not just mine. Wise up! Trust in Jesus! He'll never let you down. (PETER *and* JOHN *begin to walk away.*)

**PETER:** (*To* JOHN.) I don't know why you carry that camera around all the time, John. People aren't interested in your pictures. You should take up a different hobby. Baking—bread, donuts, cookies. People would like that.

**For the real deal** read Matthew 19:16-30; Mark 10:17-31; Luke 18:18-30

# Rich Man, Poor Man

**Characters: ABNER,** a Bible-times boy; **HANNAH,** a Bible-times girl; **DAN,** a Bible-times boy

**Scene:** *A road in Bible-times Israel, not far from where Jesus has been preaching.*

**ABNER:** Boy, am I glad I'm not rich!

**HANNAH:** Why?!?

**ABNER:** Didn't you hear Jesus? He said rich men had to walk through the eye of a needle with a camel to get into heaven. I don't even have a camel!

**HANNAH:** You would if you were rich.

**DAN:** That's NOT what Jesus said. He said it was harder for a rich man to get into heaven than for a camel to go through the eye of a needle.

**ABNER:** Yeah, well, I'm still glad I'm not rich. This way I get to go to heaven! Poor people rule! Yeah!

**HANNAH:** What about the middle class? Jesus didn't say anything about US not getting into heaven. So I'll be there too! Middle-class people rule! Yeah!

**DAN:** *(Shaking his head.)* I think you two missed the point.

**ABNER:** What point? Where?

**DAN:** Jesus' point. He didn't say that ALL rich people won't go to heaven.

**ABNER:** How many camels can YOU get through the eye of a needle? Of course He meant that NO rich people would get into heaven!

**HANNAH:** Yeah! Didn't you hear Him talking to that man? Jesus told him he had to give away ALL his money and ALL his stuff.

**ABNER:** I thought Jesus told him to follow all the commandments.

**DAN:** He did! Look, Jesus didn't tell the rich man to give away all his riches so that the man would be poor.

**HANNAH:** Here's a simple math lesson, Dan: If you give away everything you have, you'll be poor.

**ABNER:** Even I could figure THAT out!

**DAN:** If you'll let me finish. I was saying that what Jesus really wanted was for the rich man to care about other people and God MORE than he cared about his stuff and himself.

**HANNAH:** Well, if that's all Jesus wanted, why didn't the man do what Jesus asked?

**ABNER:** Yeah, and why did Jesus ask him to give away ALL his stuff? I'd let the man keep the important stuff. You know, stuff with sentimental value. And just give away the rest.

**HANNAH:** Yeah!

**DAN:** *(Shaking head.)* How can I explain this to you? Abner, what is the most important thing in the world to you—the thing you wouldn't give up for anyone or anything?

**ABNER:** I don't know. I don't have much. I have this really cool rock I found.

**DAN:** Would you keep it even if it meant someone else had to go without food?

**ABNER:** How can my rock keep someone else from having food?

**DAN:** Just answer the question, Abner.

**ABNER:** Well, I guess not. But I'll tell you something I wouldn't do. I would never do anything against the law to get food!

**DAN:** See, that's what Jesus was talking about. Obeying God's laws is more important to you than even your own comfort. But that rich man loved his own stuff so much, he couldn't bear to give any of it away, even to please God!

**HANNAH:** Are you saying even a nice middle-class person like me might not get into heaven?

**DAN:** If they don't make loving and obeying God their first priority, yes.

**ABNER:** What was it Jesus said we should do?

**HANNAH:** Well, we aren't supposed to commit murder.

**ABNER:** I can do that! Oops! I guess I mean I'd NEVER do that.

**HANNAH:** We aren't supposed to steal.

**ABNER:** I can "NOT" do that.

**HANNAH:** We're supposed to honor our parents.

**ABNER:** I can usually do that.

**HANNAH:** And then we aren't supposed to give false testimony...

**ABNER:** What's "false test and money"? Is that bribing someone else to take your test at school?

**HANNAH:** "Testimony," not "test and money!" It means not to lie.

**ABNER:** Oh. Not lie? Ever? Uh-oh, I'm not sure I can do that. Maybe I better start practicing with that camel.

**DAN:** *(Groans.)*

**For the real story read Matthew 21:1-11**

# A Funny Thing Happened...

**Characters: EZRA,** a Bible-times boy on his way to see Jesus; **BETH,** a Bible-times girl; **JESSE,** a Bible-times boy; **SARAH,** a Bible-times girl; **JAMES,** a Bible-times boy

**Props:** Characters may wish to pantomime the use of props.

**Scene:** *Just outside the walls of Jerusalem.*

**EZRA:** *(Enters carrying a large palm branch and bumps into* BETH.)

**BETH:** Ow! Watch what you're doing with that thing!

**EZRA:** Sorry!

**BETH:** Why are you carrying that huge branch around anyway?

**EZRA:** I'm going to see Jesus!

**BETH:** With that? What have you got against Jesus?

**EZRA:** What? Ah...nothing...I mean...it isn't like that. You see, Jesus is coming on a donkey.

**BETH:** Big deal! Lots of people ride donkeys! *(JESSE enters.)*

**EZRA:** It IS a big deal! *(EZRA swings around and hits* JESSE *with the branch.)*

**JESSE:** Ow! Watch where you're going with that "big deal"!

**EZRA:** Oh, sorry, Jesse. But this isn't the "big deal." I was telling Beth—*(EZRA points to* BETH, *dropping the branch on both* JESSE *and* BETH.)

**BETH and JESSE:** Watch out!

**EZRA:** Sorry! *(Picks up palm branch.)*

**SARAH:** *(Enters.)* Ezra, what are you doing with that big branch?

**EZRA:** *(Swings around to see* SARAH *and hits her in the process.)*

**SARAH:** Ow!

**EZRA:** Sorry! I'm taking the branch to see Jesus—

**SARAH:** Why does the branch need to see Jesus?

**JAMES:** *(Enters.)* Hi, everybody! Where are you going with that big branch?

**EZRA:** *(Swings around to see* JAMES.)

**BETH, JESSE and SARAH:** WATCH OUT! *(JAMES ducks in time, but* EZRA *hits* BETH, JESSE *and* SARAH.)

**BETH, JESSE and SARAH:** OW!

**EZRA:** Sorry!

**BETH:** Ezra, why are you taking that branch to see Jesus?

**EZRA:** Jesus is coming! He's entering the gates of the city riding a donkey! Do you know what that means?

**SARAH:** No, what?

**JAMES:** Oh! Oh! I know this! I know this! I just learned this at school.

**SARAH:** So tell us, oh learned one.

**JAMES:** When a king's coming to a city in peace, he rides on a donkey.

**JESSE:** Yeah, well, I've heard that when an important visitor or king comes to a city, the people greet him by putting branches and coats on the ground for his donkey to walk on.

**EZRA:** There! See—THAT'S what I'm doing with the palm branch!

**JESSE:** So, Jesus is a king?

**SARAH:** Of course He is, silly! He's the One that is going to save us all.

**JESSE:** Save us all from what?

**JAMES:** From the Romans. That's what my dad says. He says the Messiah's going to take over Jerusalem and wipe out all the Romans. Then we'll be in charge again.

**SARAH:** Don't be silly. The King is going to make sure we're always healthy and have enough to eat. I mean, Jesus has been doing that already.

**EZRA:** Well, I don't know... *(EZRA drops branch and it hits BETH, SARAH, JESSE and JAMES on their feet.)*

**BETH:** Ow! EZRA! Will you PLEASE watch what you're doing with that thing? What I'd like the King to do is to make sure I never feel pain again!

**JESSE:** Hey, I'd like the King to give me all the money in the world.

**SARAH:** Oh sure—the King's going to give you all the money and keep nothing for Himself? Right!

**EZRA:** *(Picks up branch from ground, bumping into each of the other characters.)*

**BETH, JESSE, SARAH and JAMES:** EZRA!

**JESSE:** Let's get out of here before he REALLY hurts us with that thing. *(All exit except EZRA.)*

**EZRA:** I sure hope Jesus is more forgiving than my friends.

For the **real story** read Matthew 21:12-16

# What's Wrong with That?

**Characters: ANNAS** (AH-nahs), the chief Pharisee; **ALEXANDER,** a Pharisee; **MATTHIAS** (math-EYE-us), a Pharisee; **SIMON,** a Pharisee who's wiser than he appears

**Scene:** *The Court of Gentiles in the Temple in Jerusalem.*

**ANNAS:** He must be stopped!

**ALEXANDER:** I agree!

**SIMON:** Who must be stopped?

**ANNAS, ALEXANDER and MATTHIAS:** That man, Jesus!

**SIMON:** Why? What has He done?

**MATTHIAS:** Don't tell me you didn't see Him?

**SIMON:** I can see Him right now. See, He's over there.

**ANNAS:** Don't point!

**SIMON:** What's wrong with...

**ALEXANDER:** He'll know we're talking about Him! Of course, He always seems to know when we're talking about Him, anyway...

**ANNAS:** That's not the point!

**SIMON:** I guess it ISN'T polite to point.

**MATTHIAS:** Simon! The point is we don't want the people in the Temple to know we're talking about Him.

**SIMON:** Oh, why not?

**ALEXANDER:** They might mistake our discussion for approval of what He's done.

**SIMON:** And what was it He did?

**MATTHIAS:** He chased out the money changers!

**ALEXANDER:** AND the sellers!

**ANNAS:** And called them THIEVES!

**SIMON:** What's wrong with that? I've been telling you for months we should get rid of those people. It makes it difficult to pray with all that shouting going on.

**MATTHIAS:** Shouting?

**SIMON:** Yes, you know, when people argue over the prices. And Jesus is right about them being thieves! They've been overcharging people for years.

**ANNAS:** Fool!

**SIMON:** Well, now, I don't think they're fools...

**ALEXANDER:** He meant YOU are a fool.

**MATTHIAS:** Where do you suppose all that extra money goes?

**SIMON:** Well, now, I'm just guessing here, but I'd say it goes to the money changers and the sellers.

**ALEXANDER:** Yes, but WE get to tax the money changers and sellers and take some of the money for ourselves, and for the repair of the Temple.

**SIMON:** Repairing the Temple? Isn't that what the Temple tax is for?

**MATTHIAS:** Yes, but we've found the Temple tax just isn't enough to support a lifestyle that is...um...appropriate for our positions.

**SIMON:** But the money changers and the sellers are taking the money from people who can't really afford to spend it...

**ALEXANDER:** Exactly HOW did YOU get to be a Pharisee?

**SIMON:** Well, I...

**ANNAS:** Enough! We have bigger problems on our hands. Listen!

**SIMON:** All I hear is a group of children singing.

**ALEXANDER:** Yes, but they're singing to that Jesus.

**SIMON:** What's wrong with that? He cleared God's Temple of the noisy money changers and sellers who were taking advantage of the people, AND He healed the sick, lame and blind that were here. That's pretty impressive!

**MATTHIAS:** They think He's the Son of God.

**ALEXANDER:** How could Jesus be the Son of God? He doesn't follow OUR rules!

**SIMON:** What's wrong with that? He seems to be following God's rules. I mean, He talks about loving others and loving God. Isn't that what God wants us to do?

**MATTHIAS:** You just don't understand ANY-THING, do you?

**ALEXANDER:** We have RULES for how people are supposed to do EVERYTHING!

**MATTHIAS:** Including loving others. And that sort of thing must be carefully regulated, or it could get out of hand.

**SIMON:** What's wrong with loving others?

**ANNAS:** Imbecile!

**ALEXANDER:** Listen, Simon, we can't have people loving EVERYONE—how would we make a profit?

**MATTHIAS:** Or stay in power?

**ANNAS:** Or keep ourselves separate from other undesirable people like the Samaritans and the Romans?

**SIMON:** I'm not sure that's what God wants.

**ANNAS, ALEXANDER and MATTHIAS:** How DID you get to be a Pharisee?

**SIMON:** *(To himself.)* I was wondering the same about you!

For the **real story** read Matthew 25:14-30; Luke 19:12-27

# Classy Talents

**Characters: NARRATOR; MRS. SNODGRASS; PRUDENCE PERFECT; RICHIE RIGHTEOUS; WENDY WHINER; CLASS**

**Props:** Characters may wish to pantomime the use of props.

**Scene:** *A fifth-grade classroom in Wise Acres School.*

**NARRATOR:** Once upon a time there was a teacher named Mrs. Snodgrass. One day Mrs. Snodgrass had important news for her class.

**MRS. SNODGRASS:** Class! I must leave and attend an important meeting in the principal's office. Prudence Perfect, while I'm gone, you will be in charge of the class for thirty minutes.

**PRUDENCE:** What an honor! Thank you, Mrs. Snodgrass!

**MRS. SNODGRASS:** You're welcome. Richie Righteous, I want you to be in charge of the class for the next twenty minutes.

**RICHIE:** Really? Me? This is great! Thanks, Mrs. Snodgrass!

**MRS. SNODGRASS:** You are welcome. And Wendy Whiner, you will be in charge of the class for the last ten minutes.

**WENDY:** Me? Why did she pick me?

**NARRATOR:** And with that, Mrs. Snodgrass left the classroom. Prudence Perfect was very talented in the art of origami so she gave the class a paper project.

**PRUDENCE:** OK. Since it's spring, I think it would be a great idea to decorate this room with origami flowers and birds. Michael and Lisa, you pass out the paper. Then everybody watch what I do.

**NARRATOR:** Soon the class had made enough flowers and birds to decorate ALL the walls in the room.

**PRUDENCE:** Now I think it would be nice if we wrote some poems about spring to go with the flowers. I'll be happy to help anyone who needs it.

**NARRATOR:** Before the class knew it, Prudence Perfect's thirty minutes were up, and it was Richie Righteous's turn. Richie Righteous was very good at singing and music. So he stepped up to the piano.

**RICHIE:** All right. Let's write a special song to go with some of our poems. First, we'll each read our poems and then pick one to set to music. If we have time, we'll set everyone's poem to music.

**NARRATOR:** Well, in twenty minutes, the class was only able to get five poems set to music, but everyone agreed it was a good effort. Now it was Wendy Whiner's turn.

**WENDY:** OK. Nobody move! If you do, I'm writing your name on the board! Then you'll be in BIG trouble! And remember, talking is moving your lips!

**NARRATOR:** That was the longest ten minutes that class had ever had to sit through. The class was sure glad to see Mrs. Snodgrass when she finally returned.

**CLASS:** Yeah! It's Mrs. Snodgrass!

**MRS. SNODGRASS:** What's been going on here?

**NARRATOR:** Prudence Perfect came up to Mrs. Snodgrass.

**PRUDENCE:** While you were gone, we made flowers and birds to decorate the room and wrote poems about spring.

**NARRATOR:** Mrs. Snodgrass looked around the room and read a few of the poems and was very impressed.

**MRS. SNODGRASS:** Prudence Perfect, you have done an excellent job of leading our class. I'm going to let you be in charge of the class for an hour every day!

**NARRATOR:** Then Richie Righteous played the songs the class had written on the piano.

**MRS. SNODGRASS:** Richie Righteous! What an excellent job! I'm going to let you be in charge of the class for forty minutes every day!

**NARRATOR:** Next, Mrs. Snodgrass wanted to know what the class had done while Wendy Whiner was in charge.

**WENDY:** Well, Mrs. Snodgrass, I knew you were a real strict teacher and you wouldn't want anyone misbehaving, so I made everyone sit real, real still, so they couldn't get into trouble.

**MRS. SNODGRASS:** You mean everyone just SAT there?

**WENDY:** Yeah. Well, Susan Smart almost got up to sharpen her pencil, but I wrote her name on the board. See?

**MRS. SNODGRASS:** Wendy Whiner, I am very disappointed in you. If you know I am such a strict teacher, you should also know that I don't want my students wasting time! At least you could have had the students read a book while they were sitting. I was hoping you'd teach the class how to make those cute cartoon figures you draw on all your papers.

**WENDY:** You were?

**MRS. SNODGRASS:** Yes, I was. Now the rest of us are going to enjoy singing the songs Richie Righteous helped write. But YOU, Wendy Whiner, are going to write me a five-hundred-word essay on putting your talents to good use!

**For the real deal read Matthew 28:16-20**

# Keeping Up the Paperwork

**Characters: SUPERVISOR;
PETER,** disciple of Jesus;
**CLERK; JOHN,** disciple of Jesus;
**PAUL,** disciple of Jesus

**Props:** Characters may wish to pantomime the use of props.

**Scene:** *A heavenly office.*

**SUPERVISOR:** State your name and occupation, please.

**PETER:** Peter, Simon Peter. Fisherman.

**SUPERVISOR:** Fisherman? My book says you were some kind of preacher. There must be an error here. CLERK!

**CLERK:** Yes, sir?

**SUPERVISOR:** There's an error in these books. It says here he's some kind of preacher and now he's telling me he's a fisherman. How could such an error occur?!

**CLERK:** I don't know, sir. I'm sorry, sir. I'll fix it at once!

**PETER:** But wait!

**SUPERVISOR:** What is it?

**PETER:** I did more than catch fish. I also caught men for Jesus, just as He asked me to.

**SUPERVISOR:** Jesus wanted you to TRAP men?

**PETER:** No, no! My job was to help people get to know about Jesus, just as He asked us to do before He returned to heaven.

**SUPERVISOR:** So where have you been spreading this message?

**PETER:** In Jerusalem, and I did go see a man in Caesarea *(ses-uh-REE-uh).*

**SUPERVISOR:** You went all the way to Caesarea for one man?

**PETER:** And his family and servants. That one man became a great servant of Jesus. Because of him, other people heard about Jesus.

**SUPERVISOR:** I see. Anything else?

**PETER:** I wrote a couple of letters.

**SUPERVISOR:** You WROTE? CLERK!

**CLERK:** Yes, sir?

**SUPERVISOR:** It says nothing here about this man being a writer, yet he just told me he wrote two letters.

**CLERK:** Lots of people write letters, sir.

**SUPERVISOR:** Were those letters important?

**PETER:** Well, they're in the Bible...

**SUPERVISOR:** BOOKS in the Bible?

**PETER:** Yes.

**CLERK:** I'll add that note into his record right away.

**SUPERVISOR:** Good! Mr. Peter, I guess we're

finished with you. You may go now. (PETER *walks offstage.*) NEXT! (JOHN *walks up.*) What's your name and occupation?

**JOHN:** John, and I'm a messenger.

**SUPERVISOR:** No, no, no! This is all wrong! CLERK!

**JOHN:** I assure you I am a messenger.

**CLERK:** Yes, sir?

**SUPERVISOR:** This paperwork is all wrong! Look here: It says he's a writer, and now he's saying that he's a messenger.

**CLERK:** But he wrote several books in the Bible, sir.

**SUPERVISOR:** Did you write some books?

**JOHN:** Well, yes, they told people about Jesus.

**SUPERVISOR:** This job would sure be a lot easier if you people actually knew what you were doing!

**JOHN:** But I do know what I was doing. I was telling everyone about Jesus, just as He asked us to do the day He returned to heaven.

**SUPERVISOR:** So you spread the word by writing books?

**JOHN:** I wanted to make sure everyone would know the true story about Jesus.

**SUPERVISOR:** Very well. So you were a messenger because you told the message about Jesus, is that your point?

**JOHN:** Yes, sir.

**SUPERVISOR:** CLERK!

**CLERK:** Right here, sir. I'll add that to his records right away!

**SUPERVISOR:** Next person, please. State your name and occupation.

**PAUL:** Paul, servant of God and tentmaker.

**SUPERVISOR:** Are you sure you're one of the disciples of Jesus?

**PAUL:** Yes, sir.

**SUPERVISOR:** We don't seem to have you listed. CLERK! I need a file for this man.

**CLERK:** Yes, sir. Right away, sir.

**SUPERVISOR:** All right, Paul, I guess you heard Jesus' message to His disciples just before He returned to heaven—

**PAUL:** Sadly, sir, I did not.

**SUPERVISOR:** But our records show all of the disciples were there. CLERK!

**CLERK:** I found his file, sir.

**PAUL:** I was not one of the ORIGINAL disciples. I became a disciple much later.

**SUPERVISOR:** But it says here that you were a great leader in the church. How could you become a great leader? How could you tell the message of Jesus if you weren't there when He gave His Great Commission?

**PAUL:** I was fortunate enough to see Jesus personally. But many of Jesus' followers have spread the message about Him even though they'd never seen Jesus.

**SUPERVISOR and CLERK:** Really?

**PAUL:** Yes, in fact, most people witness about Jesus just in the things they do and say. They aren't preachers or writers or even leaders.

**SUPERVISOR:** CLERK!

**CLERK:** Yes, sir. I'll fix the records, sir.

For the **real story** read Mark 1:35-37

# Where'd He Go?

**Characters: JAMES,** a disciple of Jesus; **SIMON,** a disciple of Jesus; **ANDREW,** Simon's brother; **JOHN,** James's brother; **BETH,** Simon's wife; **SERVANT,** definitely not a "morning person"

**Scene:** *Early one morning at the home of* SIMON *and* ANDREW.

**JAMES:** Simon! Andrew! Wake up! He's gone!

**SIMON:** Who's gone?

**JAMES:** Jesus!

**ANDREW:** Oh great. Well, I guess it's back to grimy fishing.

**SIMON:** Have you looked in the town square? Maybe He went back to heal some more people.

**JOHN:** *(Enters, breathless.)* I checked...the center...of town....He's...not there!

**ANDREW:** Great. It's back to stinky fishing for me.

**SIMON:** Did you check the well? Maybe He went to get some water.

**BETH:** *(Enters, sleepily.)* What's all this racket? How do you expect my mother to sleep?

**SIMON:** Jesus is gone!

**BETH:** Oh no! I hope it wasn't something you said.

**SIMON:** I don't think it was something anyone SAID. Have you sent our servant down to the well to get the water yet?

**BETH:** Of course. She should be back by now.

**SERVANT:** *(Enters.)* Here's some water. Boy, is it early!

**SIMON:** Did you see Jesus at the well?

**SERVANT:** Nope.

**BETH:** There! You see! He isn't at the well.

**SERVANT:** Haven't been to the well. This is yesterday's water. *(Yawns.)*

**SIMON:** Well, then, go! And come back immediately if you see Jesus!

**SERVANT:** Jesus?

**BETH:** Our guest.

**JOHN:** I'll go! *(JOHN exits.)*

**ANDREW:** Jesus is gone and I'm back to being a smelly fisherman.

**BETH:** That's not such a bad way to earn a living. I mean, how much are you going to make being a disciple?

**SIMON:** Beth, it isn't about earning money—it's about following a teacher that will make a HUGE difference in our lives.

**JAMES:** We can't FOLLOW Him if we don't know where He is.

**JOHN:** *(Enters, breathless.)* He isn't... at...the well.

**JAMES:** You don't suppose someone kidnapped Him, do you?

**SIMON:** Why would anyone want to kidnap Jesus? He must be around here somewhere.

**SERVANT:** *(Yawns.)* Awfully early to be up and out.

**BETH:** *(To SERVANT.)* Not for you! I thought you were going to the well. *(To SIMON.)* Have you checked the roof of the house?

**SIMON:** Now what would He be doing on the roof?

**JOHN:** I'll go! *(JOHN exits.)*

**BETH:** I don't know what He'd be doing on the roof! Maybe He likes sunrises. It's just a place to look.

**ANDREW:** Better get moving if we're going to catch those stupid fish.

**SIMON:** Andrew, we are NOT going back to fishing! We are going to find Jesus!

**JOHN:** *(Enters, very breathless.)* He's... not...up...there.

**JAMES:** We haven't looked down by the lake. Maybe Jesus likes to go fishing in the morning!

**JOHN:** I'll...*(Gasps.)*...go. *(JOHN exits.)*

**SERVANT:** Are you looking for that man who was here for dinner yesterday?

**BETH, SIMON, and JAMES:** YES!

**SERVANT:** Well, He went out real early this morning.

**SIMON:** Where did He go?

**SERVANT:** Over to the hill behind the stable.

**JAMES:** Why would He go there?

**JOHN:** *(Enters, extremely breathless.)* He's...*(Gasps.)*...not...*(Gasps.)*...at... *(Gasps.)*...the...*(GASP.)*...lake. *(JOHN collapses on the ground.)*

**SERVANT:** No, He's not. He went toward the hill behind the stable.

**JOHN:** *(Struggles to get up on his feet.)* I'll...go-o-o. *(JOHN collapses again.)*

**SIMON:** No, no. We'll go. I wonder what He's doing on the hill?

**ANDREW:** Whatever it is, I'm sure it beats fishing.

For the **real story** read Mark 2:1-12

# Coming Through!

**Characters: SHEM,** a friend of Levi; **JOE,** a friend of Levi; **SAM,** a friend of Levi; **RUEBEN,** a friend of Levi; **RUFUS; BETH; BEN and NAOMI; NATHAN**

**Scene:** *Outside a house in Capernaum where Jesus is teaching.*

**SHEM:** OK! OK! Everyone out of the way! Sick person coming through! Excuse me!

**RUFUS:** What do you think you're doing?

**SHEM:** We're taking our sick friend, Levi, to see Jesus!

**RUFUS:** Good luck! There's at least a hundred people crowded outside the doorway, and who knows how many are packed inside.

**SHEM:** Well, we'll just have push our way through!

**RUFUS:** Not through me! I was here first!

**SHEM:** Hmph! Well, maybe we can get through around the side of the house.

**JOE:** I wonder if we could...

**SHEM:** Not right now, Joe. Excuse me! Coming through!

**BETH:** Watch what you're doing!

**SHEM:** Sorry, m'am, just trying to get our sick friend to Jesus.

**BETH:** You, me and everyone else in this town, and the next three towns, I think!

**SHEM:** Well, if you could just let us through...

**BETH:** You may not have noticed, but my Aunt Edith here has an infected, sore toe.

**SHEM:** But at least she can walk. My friend, Levi, can't even sit up! Surely, if you'll just let us through, Jesus will heal our friend.

**BETH:** My name isn't Shirley, and even if I DID let you through, you wouldn't get very far. There must be two hundred people here. And who knows how many are packed inside?

**SHEM:** OK, guys, let's try around the other side of the house.

**JOE:** Shem, maybe if we...

**SHEM:** Not right now, Joe. Excuse me! Coming through!

**BEN and NAOMI:** What do you think you're doing?

**SHEM:** We're taking our friend to see Jesus! He's paralyzed! He can't walk, or sit up or do anything.

**BEN and NAOMI:** Well, that's too bad. But he'll never get to see Jesus. There must be at least three hundred people here. And who knows how many are packed inside?

**SHEM:** Right. OK, guys, let's see if there's a window open. Maybe we can get him in through the window!

**JOE:** Shem, maybe we could...

**SHEM:** Not now, Joe! Excuse me! Coming through!

**NATHAN:** And where do you think you're going?

**SHEM:** Sick friend! Needs to see Jesus! Please let us through!

**NATHAN:** To where?

**SHEM:** We're trying to get him to the window.

**NATHAN:** Ha! There must be at least four hundred people outside the house, looking in through the doorways AND the windows! And who knows how many...

**SHEM:** ...are packed inside. Yeah, so we've heard.

**NATHAN:** There's no way inside! Forget it!

**RUEBEN:** Shem, maybe we should hear Joe's plan.

**SHEM:** Joe has a plan?

**JOE:** I was just thinking maybe we could take the stairs up to the roof, cut a hole in the roof, and then let Levi down on his stretcher with these ropes.

**RUEBEN:** Of course, on the other hand, maybe listening to Joe's plan ISN'T such a great idea.

**SAM:** It might work! Look, the stairway is on the side where there are very few people. With all these people here, Jesus will be

teaching for quite a while. We'd have plenty of time.

**RUEBEN:** Yeah, but we might make Him mad if we drop stuff from the roof on Him.

**JOE:** We'll be careful!

**RUEBEN:** And someone's likely to come out and stop us. I mean, they're going to NOTICE.

**SAM:** If WE can't get IN, how are THEY going to get OUT?

**RUEBEN:** It'll be a lot of work, and we'd have to repair the roof afterwards...

**SAM:** More work than carrying Levi here, there and everywhere?

**RUEBEN:** And what if Jesus gets mad at us for going ahead of everyone else?

**JOE:** Rueben, we've just gotta get Levi to Jesus. I KNOW He'll help!

**SHEM:** Hm, through the roof. It might just work. OK, guys, here we go. Excuse me! Coming through!

For the **real deal** read Mark 4:1-20

# Out of Focus*

**Characters: JACK,** teacher; **SUE,** a fifth grader who knows what she's thinking and always says it; **JASON,** a fifth-grade boy who's more interested in eating than in talking; **MARY,** a shy fifth grader who always speaks in a soft voice; **JIM,** a sixth-grade boy who never says much; **LIZ,** a sixth grader who's at the top of her class; **MATT,** a sixth grader who's very sure of himself, even if he doesn't know what he's talking about

**JACK:** Okay, now you all understand what we're going to do. I will read a story, and then we will focus on it and discuss what it means.

**SUE:** Gotcha!

**JASON:** No problem.

**MARY:** OK.

**JIM:** What?

**LIZ:** Just listen.

**MATT:** Yeah.

**JIM:** Whatever.

**JACK:** All right, let's begin. There was a farmer who went out and scattered his seed. Some fell on the path where the birds came and ate it, some fell on the rocky places where there wasn't much soil...

**SUE:** This guy doesn't sound like much of a farmer.

**JASON:** Yeah, why is he just throwing this seed everywhere?

**JACK:** I'm not finished with the story. Let's keep our focus here...

**MATT:** What the farmer needs to do is to purchase a seeding machine.

**JIM:** What?

**LIZ:** I don't think "seeding machine" is its technical name.

**MARY:** What does a "seeding machine" do?

**JACK:** I think you're missing the point. Now, let's try to focus on...

**MATT:** It pokes holes in the ground for the seed to go in.

**SUE:** Then what happens?

**MATT:** All the farmer has to do is drop the seed in and cover the hole with his foot.

**MARY:** I don't think that's quite right...

**LIZ:** Where did you get this information?

**SUE:** He probably just made it up.

*focus: the point of a discussion or activity

**JACK:** Um, group, can we focus and get back to the story?

**MATT:** I didn't make it up, I read it in a magazine somewhere.

**JIM:** What?

**LIZ:** If you paid attention, you'd KNOW what was going on.

**JASON:** What magazine did you read it in?

**MATT:** It was one of those magazines that goes with a TV show. My mom bought it for me.

**MARY:** Oh, I love those magazines!

**JACK:** Can we get back to the focus, here? What about the story?

**JASON:** My mom got me a great magazine with lots of stories. She ordered it from the back of a cereal box.

**MARY:** Which cereal?

**JASON:** I don't know. It was one of those cereals that kids are SUPPOSED to like and are really healthy. Yuck!

**SUE:** My mother ALWAYS makes oatmeal. Every day, more oatmeal.

**JIM:** What?

**LIZ:** You really don't have a clue, do you Jim?

**JACK:** Now, let's focus on this farmer and his seed...

**SUE:** My mother says farmers eat oatmeal to keep them strong.

**LIZ:** You're kidding!

**JASON:** That's probably why that farmer was throwing his seed all around. He was angry about having to eat oatmeal.

**JACK:** Finally we're back to the story! Now, stick with me, kids...

**MARY:** Actually, I kind of like oatmeal.

**SUE:** Every day??

**MARY:** Well, maybe not every day.

**MATT:** You know what I could eat every day? Pizza!

**JASON:** Mmm, yeah. Have you tried that new pizza restaurant?

**LIZ:** What's its name?

**JASON:** I can't remember, but it has REALLY GOOD pizza!

**MARY:** There's a pizza place next door.

**JASON:** Well, its pizza isn't as good, but at least we know where it is. Let's go!

*(Everyone exits except* JIM *and* JACK.*)*

**JIM:** What did the story mean when it talked about the seed being on the path and the birds eating it?

**JACK:** I think it meant that the seeds didn't wait around for the rest of the story.

For the
**real story**
read Mark
10:13-16

# Honest to Pete

**Characters: PETER,** a disciple of Jesus; **JUDAS,** a disciple of Jesus; **THOMAS,** a disciple of Jesus; **JESUS; MARAH,** a Judean lady, mother of Joash; **ELI,** a Judean man, father of Sarah; **Nonspeaking parts: JOASH, SARAH**

**Props:** Characters may wish to pantomime the use of props.

**Scene:** *Inside a house in Judea.*

**PETER:** *(Plopping onto a stool.)* What a day! I'm worn out! Dealing with those crowds makes me CRANKY!

**JUDAS:** Yeah, we've done enough! Pass the bread.

**THOMAS:** *(Munching.)* Uh-huh. I'm sure Jesus feels that way, too. After all, I didn't even have LUNCH! We deserve a break! Here, have some grapes.

**PETER:** And we'll never become more spiritu-al unless we spend quality time with Jesus! Is there any more sauce?

**JUDAS:** After all, we ARE the disciples—it's our JOB to spend time with Jesus. Where is He, anyway? *(A knock at the door is heard as JESUS enters the room.)*

**JESUS:** I see you were all really hungry.

**THOMAS:** Oh. We were just...snacking. Please join us.

**PETER:** *(To THOMAS.)* Get the door, Thomas. On second thought, DON'T get the door.

**JUDAS:** *(Wiping his mouth.)* I vote we DON'T get the door. We're eating. Have some bread, Jesus? I'm sure You're hungry. I was!

**THOMAS:** I'll get the door. *(Opens door a crack.)* Yes? What do you want?

**MARAH:** Is Jesus here? I'd like Him to bless my little boy, Joash.

**ELI:** And my little Sarah! There are several others here besides. I'm sure Jesus won't mind. *(To SARAH.)* Here, honey, let's wipe your nose.

**THOMAS:** Look. We're busy. We're discussing important business. The Master can't be interrupted. Maybe tomorrow. *(Shuts the door.)*

**JUDAS:** Good work, Thomas. I bet every one of those little kids has a runny nose! YECH!

**JESUS:** *(Stands up.)* I can't believe what you just did! Do you have any idea who those people ARE?

**PETER:** They're JUST little kids!

**JESUS:** Exactly!

**JUDAS:** Now, Jesus, calm down. We deserve—

**JESUS:** You deserve what?

**THOMAS:** I don't get it, Jesus. They're nobody important.

**JESUS:** Thomas! Peter! Judas! WHEN will you learn what is important? NEVER keep little children from coming to ME—the kingdom of heaven belongs to those who are like them!

**JUDAS:** What? A runny nose is the require-ment for HEAVEN? I REALLY don't get it!

**JESUS:** NO, Judas. *(Sighs.)* Listen to me, all of you. Unless you receive the kingdom of God like a little child, you will never enter it!

**PETER:** Oh, uh...like...I'm sorry. Better open the door!

**THOMAS:** Hey! All of you! Come back. Jesus will see you now! Come on in!

**JUDAS:** Wipe your noses first!

For the **real deal** read Mark 12:41-44; Luke 21:1-4

# The Committee

**Characters: PIOUS,** a translator; **BASIL,** a writer; **LEO,** a researcher; **BROTHER BOB,** a scribe

**Scene:** *A committee meeting to vote on nominations to a list of Christian heroes.*

**PIOUS:** As you know, our task is to make a list of those persons whose actions of faith in God and love warrant them special recognition. Your nominations?

**BASIL:** I nominate Paul. Certainly he showed great faith in his preaching and his life. And he was an important man in the Early Church!

**LEO:** Yes. And his letters are included in the Bible! Only a man who really knows about Christian love could have written like that.

**PIOUS:** All right. We have a motion for Paul to be included. All those in favor say "Aye."

**ALL:** Aye!

**PIOUS:** Motion carries. Paul will be included on our list of Christian heroes.

**BOB:** You forgot to ask if anyone was against the nomination.

**PIOUS:** That would be silly! Who could be against Paul?

**LEO:** Still, he's right. Rules of order MUST be followed.

**PIOUS:** Very well. All those against Paul being included on our list of Christian heroes say "Nay." *(Silence.)* NOW the motion carries. Any other nominations?

**LEO:** We can't forget Barnabas. He gave that large amount of money to the Early Church, you know. And then he went on to accompany Paul on his journeys.

**BASIL:** Hm. I'm not sure he's in the same league as Paul. After all, they had such a big argument, they split up!

**PIOUS:** It was a brief disagreement. And Paul spoke highly of Barnabas and his faith. All those for Barnabas?

**ALL:** Aye!

**PIOUS:** Motion carries.

**BASIL:** *(Clears throat loudly.)*

**PIOUS:** Look, I don't see why I need to ask if anyone's AGAINST him when I can tell that everyone voted FOR him!

**BASIL:** Rules are rules.

**PIOUS:** *(Sighs.)* Fine. All those against? *(Silence.)* Motion carries. Other nominations?

**BOB:** How about the widow?

**BASIL:** Which widow? There have been many widows—including the mother of our Lord Jesus.

**PIOUS:** Of course! Mary! Now there's a person who had a lot of faith. Imagine being asked to care for God's own Son!

**BASIL:** And then to stand by and watch His crucifixion!

**PIOUS:** A woman of great faith! All those in favor of adding Mary, the mother of our Lord Jesus to the list?

**PIOUS, LEO and BASIL:** Aye!

**PIOUS:** *(Eyeing* BOB *suspiciously.)* Against?

**BOB:** I'm not against Mary being added to our list. It's just that she wasn't the widow I was talking about.

**PIOUS:** Motion carries. Now, Brother Bob, whom ARE you nominating?

**BOB:** The widow that gave the two copper coins.

**LEO:** That's all she did? Gave two copper coins? Why, these other people dedicated their entire LIVES to serving God! And they were important people in the Early Church!

**BOB:** But our Lord Jesus thought she was important. He said that her gift was greater than all other gifts that had been given because she gave EVERYTHING she had.

**BASIL:** Everything? Who would take care of her then?

**BOB:** She believed God would take care of her. And that takes a lot of faith!

**PIOUS:** But what about love? Did she show love?

**BOB:** She obviously loved God very much if she was willing to give Him everything she had.

**PIOUS:** Well, she seems a highly unusual candidate to me. But I suppose we can vote.

**BOB:** Look. Each of you is an important man. I am only a scribe. Yet no matter who we are or what we do, God asks all of us to love Him and serve Him to the best of our ability. That's what makes a Christian hero. And that's what this woman did.

**PIOUS:** Hm. You may be right. All those in favor of including this woman on our list?

**ALL:** Aye!

**PIOUS:** Against? *(Silence.)* Motion carries. The widow is added to the list. Other nominations?

For the **real story** read Luke 7:1-10

# Hut! Hut! Hut!

**Characters: SIMON,** a merchant from Jerusalem; **JETHRO,** a Jewish elder in the city of Capernaum; **ROMAN SOLDIERS; ETHAN,** a Jewish elder in the city of Capernaum; **SETH,** Jethro's servant; **CLAUDIUS,** a Roman centurion (a man in charge of 100 soldiers)

**Scene:** *A street in Bible-times Capernaum.*

**SIMON:** *(Entering with* JETHRO *and* ETHAN.*)* Thank you for your hospitality. You certainly have a beautiful new synagogue! But I must be getting back to Jerusalem.

**JETHRO:** Please come and visit us again, Simon.

**SOLDIERS:** Hut! Hut! Hut! Hut! All 'round Palestine we strut!

**SIMON:** I see your town is infested with Roman rats, too!

**JETHRO:** *(Embarrassed.)* Well, um, yes.

**ETHAN:** Although some Romans are better than others.

**SIMON:** Hah! They're monsters, every one of them!

**JETHRO:** There might be one or two that aren't so bad.

**SIMON:** Nonsense. Those soldiers are proud of the suffering they bring to our villages.

**SOLDIERS:** Stamp! Stamp! Stamp! Stamp! In the people's homes we camp!

**SETH:** *(Entering. To* JETHRO.*)* Master, Centurion Claudius is looking for you. He said it was urgent!

**JETHRO:** Tell Centurion Claudius that I will be with him shortly. *(SETH exits.)*

**SIMON:** Urgent! Hah! There is no Roman business that's really important!

**ETHAN:** Well, Simon, Centurion Claudius is different from most Romans.

**SOLDIERS:** Crunch! Crunch! Crunch! Crunch! All your best food we will munch!

**SIMON:** Those are his soldiers, aren't they?

**ETHAN:** Yes. But I'm sure if you met Centurion Claudius, you'd feel differently.

**SIMON:** I make it a policy never to speak to a Roman unless my life depends on it.

**CLAUDIUS:** *(Entering.)* Jethro! Ethan! I'm so glad I found you!

**SOLDIERS:** Stomp! Stomp! Stomp! Stomp! Through their fields of grain we tromp!

**CLAUDIUS:** *(To* SOLDIERS.*)* What is this nonsense?

**SOLDIERS:** Uh-oh!

**CLAUDIUS:** I have told you before that you will speak only respectfully about these people. Do you understand?

**SOLDIERS:** Yes, sir! Sorry, sir!

**CLAUDIUS:** You can spend the rest of your sorry day marching double-time to Jericho and back!

**SOLDIERS:** Yes, sir! Here we go! On our way to Jericho! (SOLDIERS exit.)

**JETHRO:** That's a rather harsh punishment, Claudius.

**CLAUDIUS:** Perhaps. But they must know I mean business! Listen, I need your help.

**SIMON:** You? Need the help of Jews? Hah!

**ETHAN:** Simon, I've been trying to tell you—Claudius is our friend. That synagogue you thought was so beautiful? Claudius paid for it to be built.

**SIMON:** Hah! I can't believe you're a friend of a Roman!

**JETHRO:** (Ignoring SIMON.) How can we help you, Claudius?

**CLAUDIUS:** My slave Lucas is desperately ill! I'm afraid he will die!

**SIMON:** This is new—a Roman worried about his slave.

**ETHAN:** (To CLAUDIUS.) But we're not doctors. What can we do?

**CLAUDIUS:** There is someone I have heard of. His name is Jesus. He is a Jew like you. They say He can heal the sick.

**JETHRO:** Yes, I've heard of Him.

**CLAUDIUS:** I don't dare approach such a holy man. Would you carry my request to Him?

**SIMON:** Jesus! He's not too popular with some of the Jewish religious rulers, you know.

**CLAUDIUS:** Then perhaps the religious rulers do not know Him very well.

**ETHAN:** (To SIMON.) Just like you don't know ALL Romans very well. (To CLAUDIUS.) Of course we will help you, Claudius.

**CLAUDIUS:** Tell Him He need not come to my house; I understand. I am a Gentile. But if He will just give the command, I know my slave will be made well.

**SIMON:** Amazing faith for a Roman! Too bad it's misplaced.

**JETHRO:** Claudius, I have a favor to ask of you.

**CLAUDIUS:** Anything.

**JETHRO:** Those soldiers who are marching double-time to Jericho, could they take our "friend" Simon with them? He's in a hurry to get back to Jerusalem.

**CLAUDIUS:** Certainly. Now, please hurry to Jesus.

**ETHAN:** Of course. (ETHAN and JETHRO exit.)

**SIMON:** (To CLAUDIUS.) Your soldiers needn't bother. I'm not in that much of a hurry.

**CLAUDIUS:** Oh no! For my friends this favor is no trouble at all. Soldiers!

**SOLDIERS:** (Enter, running.) Yes, sir!

**CLAUDIUS:** This gentleman needs an escort home to Jerusalem.

**SOLDIERS:** Yes, sir! (Taking SIMON by the arms.) Run! Run! Run! Run! We'll drop him off in Jerusalem!

For the **real story** read Luke 7:11-17

# What Happened?

**Characters: NARRATOR; ABNER,** a pallbearer (someone who carries the coffin in a funeral procession); **TOBIAS,** a pallbearer; **DARA,** a professional mourner (someone hired to cry at a funeral); **GABE,** a friend of Josh's family

**Scene:** *Outside the Bible-times city of Nain.*

**NARRATOR:** Jesus has just interrupted a funeral procession and raised the dead man back to life. The man, Josh, and his mother, Josephine, have returned to the city along with most of the others. The only people left are two of the pallbearers and a professional mourner.

**ABNER:** What just happened here?

**TOBIAS:** I have no idea.

**DARA:** That man, Jesus, brought your friend Josh back to life.

**ABNER:** But that's not possible. What REALLY happened here?

**TOBIAS:** I don't know. Maybe Josh wasn't really dead after all.

**DARA:** His body was cold. He was dead. Take it from me. I'm a professional. I know.

**ABNER:** Listen. A dead man cannot sit up. He cannot talk. So what happened here?

**TOBIAS:** I'm clueless. Maybe that Jesus is a magician. Maybe He just made it look like Josh was alive. He could have tied invisible ropes on him or something.

**DARA:** Have you ever heard of invisible ropes? And getting him to sit up might not be so difficult. But talking and walking? I don't think so!

**ABNER:** OK. So Josh was dead. Now he's alive. And it was not a trick. But that's not possible! So, what happened here?

**TOBIAS:** I know. The dead guy wasn't Josh. It was someone else. And then this Jesus person had Josh switch places with the dead guy.

**DARA:** Josh's mother seemed to think it was Josh, and she prepared the body for burial.

**GABE:** *(Enters, running.)* Whoa! Sorry I'm late! I overslept, then I couldn't find my sackcloth, and then I couldn't get my donkey going, so I had to run all the way. *(Looks around.)* Where is everybody?

**ABNER:** Gone.

**GABE:** Gone? But I'm not THAT late! You should still be on the way to the graveyard.

**DARA:** They went home. Josh isn't dead.

**GABE:** That's ridiculous! I was there when he died. What really happened?

**ABNER:** That's what I've been trying to figure out.

**TOBIAS:** We've so far determined Josh was really dead and it wasn't a trick.

**GABE:** Huh?

**DARA:** Let me explain. A man by the name of Jesus came by with a group of His followers. When He saw Josephine, Josh's mom, He told her not to cry.

**ABNER:** (Interrupting.) Yeah. Which I thought was really weird. People are supposed to cry during funeral processions. That's why Josephine hired Dara here.

**GABE:** What has this got to do with what happened?

**DARA:** As I was saying, Jesus told Josephine not to cry. Then He turned to Josh and touched the coffin.

**GABE:** He touched the coffin of a dead man? Doesn't He know people aren't supposed to do that? Didn't He know that would make Him unclean?

**DARA:** Do you want me to tell you what happened or not?

**GABE:** Sorry. It's just that I don't understand why anyone would go through all those cleansing rituals for someone they didn't know.

**DARA:** As I was saying, Jesus touched Josh's coffin and then told Josh to sit up.

**GABE:** He spoke to a dead man? That's just silly.

**TOBIAS:** That's what I thought!

**DARA:** As I was saying, Jesus told Josh to sit up and Josh did.

**GABE:** I don't think I heard you correctly. Josh sat up?

**DARA:** Yes. And he walked and talked. Then Jesus took Josh by the hand and took him over to his mother.

**ABNER:** Yeah. Then there was a lot of hugging and kissing and praising God.

**GABE:** This man, Jesus, brought Josh back to life?

**TOBIAS:** We haven't been able to come up with any other explanation.

**GABE:** Jesus must be a great prophet indeed!

**DARA:** He could even be the Messiah.

**GABE:** Praise God! And Josephine won't have to worry about where her next meal will come from. This is wonderful news!

**DARA:** Yeah, I guess so. But if this Jesus keeps running around raising people from the dead, I'm going to be out of a job. (GABE and DARA exit.)

**ABNER:** (To TOBIAS.) OK. So what just happened here?

For the **real story** read Luke 10:25-37

# GSN* Newscast

**Characters: MAN,** traveler who has been severely beaten; **RAYMOND,** TV reporter who is outraged by a high crime rate; **PRIEST; LEVITE; SAMARITAN**

**Props:** Characters may wish to pantomime the use of props.

**Scene:** *A road, somewhere between Jericho and Jerusalem. A wounded man crawls to* RAYMOND *and pulls on his leg, but RAYMOND is so involved in his newscast, he doesn't notice the man or the action of the* SAMARITAN.

**MAN:** Help me! Please, someone help me!

**RAYMOND:** Here we have yet another victim of crime on the streets. Notice the bruised head and shoulders, indicating the possible use of a club in the crime. Clothes are torn and shredded. Obviously this man struggled for his very LIFE with his attackers.

**MAN:** Help.

**RAYMOND:** Many have warned that there is no security on these roads. Thieves and robbers do what they want!

**MAN:** Um, help?

**RAYMOND:** And who will help this poor unfortunate victim? It will be two thousand years before cellular phones will be invented. He may die by the side of the road if no one helps him.

**MAN:** Water? *(PRIEST enters, and walks past* RAYMOND *and the* MAN.*)*

**RAYMOND:** Excuse me. I couldn't help but notice that you walked right by this person needing help.

**PRIEST:** He might be dead! If I touched him, I would be unclean. I couldn't perform my duties as a priest. I have a duty to my congregation, you know. *(MAN faints on floor.* PRIEST *and* RAYMOND *walk away from* MAN.*)*

**RAYMOND:** Yes, of course. And what is your opinion of the state of roads in this area?

*(LEVITE enters, walks all the way around* MAN *and joins* PRIEST *and* RAYMOND.*)*

**PRIEST:** Why, it's deplorable! Look at this man. Probably has a wife and children, and he may die here by the side of the road.

**LEVITE:** Yes, disgusting, isn't it?

*(SAMARITAN enters, sees MAN and walks over to him.)*

**PRIEST:** I blame the government.

---

*Good Samaritan News

**RAYMOND:** And you, sir, why wouldn't YOU help the man?

**LEVITE:** I'm a Levite. We care for the Temple. Helping people isn't in our contract. Temple work only, that's me!

*(SAMARITAN enters and gives MAN a drink of water, then helps him up and offstage.)*

**RAYMOND:** So you feel there should be a special group of people to help others.

**LEVITE:** Absolutely!

**PRIEST:** Excellent idea!

**RAYMOND:** But what about the command to love your neighbor?

**LEVITE:** Well, THAT man isn't my neighbor. I've never seen him before in my life.

**PRIEST:** I don't recall seeing him before, either... He seems to be gone.

**LEVITE:** I guess he wasn't as bad off as we thought.

**RAYMOND:** Well, I guess that wraps it up here. Thank you, gentlemen, for your input.

**PRIEST & LEVITE:** Only too glad to help!

**For the real deal read Luke 12:13-21**

# Jordi's Stash

**Characters: NICKI PEREZ,** 10-year-old, a new girl at Anna's school; **ANNA JEFFERSON,** 11-year-old, twin sister of Jordi; **DYLAN DAGMAR,** 11-year-old, Jordi's classmate; **JORDI JEFFERSON,** 11-year-old, twin brother of Anna

**Props:** Characters may pantomime props.

**Scene:** *The playroom in the Jeffersons' large house.*

**NICKI:** *(Entering with* ANNA.) I've never SEEN a house this big!

**ANNA:** *(Laughs and opens a game cupboard.)* We can play one of these games if you want.

**NICKI:** What's in that big box over there?

**ANNA:** Hmph! That's Jordi's stash.

**NICKI:** *(Looks in box.)* Wow! My little brother would sure like to have a ball like that.

**ANNA:** Really? Well, here, I have one just like it. Take this ball.

**NICKI:** But that's the only ball you've got!

**ANNA:** Do I look like I don't have enough toys? *(NICKI shakes her head.)* Take it to him. I hardly ever play with it anyway.

**NICKI:** Thanks!

*(JORDI enters carrying wood. DYLAN follows carrying tools and nails.)*

**DYLAN:** Hey, Jordi, this stuff is heavy! Where can I dump it?

**JORDI:** Wait! I've got to plan the perfect spot!

**ANNA:** The perfect spot for what?

**JORDI:** I'm building a new toy box. A bigger and better toy box.

**DYLAN:** Hey! I thought we were going to build a doghouse for my dog.

**JORDI:** *(Dramatically pointing to the toy box.)* As you can see, I have a desperate need for a new toy box! There isn't any room in this toy box for anything more.

**ANNA:** You could try getting rid of a few of your toys. After all, we ARE a little old for most of these toys.

**JORDI:** Well, I have to plan ahead, you know. Dad always sends me a LOT of toys for Christmas!

**DYLAN:** But you SAID we were going to build a DOGHOUSE.

**JORDI:** You really have a one-track mind, don't you, Dylan? I'm looking into the future. I'm building in preparation for something bigger than dogs.

**ANNA:** And what would that be?

JORDI: The super-duper remote control aircraft carrier with planes that actually take off and land.

NICKI: Wow! Cool!

ANNA: For about 30 minutes. Then it will join all the other super-duper toys in Jordi's stash. (ANNA *goes over to* JORDI*'s toy box and begins to pull toys out.*)

JORDI: Hey! What are you doing?

ANNA: *(Holding up a toy.)* You see this super-duper toy? It lights up and flies around the room. Jordi played with it for five minutes before putting it in his stash.

JORDI: *(Grabbing toy.)* So what?

ANNA: *(Holding up several more toys.)* He spent 45 minutes talking Mom into this toy which he played with for only three minutes. He wrote Grandma FOUR letters to get this toy and after an hour he said it was boring.

JORDI: *(Grabbing toys and stuffing them back in the box.)* Leave my toys alone!

ANNA: Ha! *(She walks over to* NICKI *and they sit down together.)*

NICKI: He's sure got a lot of toys! He'd probably never even notice if one was missing.

ANNA: Don't bet on it. He spends hours just counting them. I'll show you. *(Calls to* JORDI.) Hey, Jordi, how many toys do you have now?

JORDI: 321.

DYLAN: You have 321 toys?!? Look, I've only got one dog. Can't we build a doghouse for him?

JORDI: My point exactly! You've ONLY got one dog. Why waste this stuff on him?

DYLAN: Because I bought it! Look, if we're not going to build a doghouse, I'm going home. *(DYLAN stomps off.)*

ANNA: *(Looks up at computer screen.)* Hey, Jordi, there's an e-mail for us. It's from Dad.

JORDI: He's probably out shopping for my aircraft carrier right now!

ANNA: *(Giggles.)* Oh, he's shopping for your Christmas present, all right. In fact, he's already bought it.

JORDI: Really?!?

ANNA: Yep! It says: "Dear Jordi and Anna. This year I've decided to give you a trip to visit me in the Bahamas for Christmas. And you can each bring a friend."

JORDI: WHAT?!?

ANNA: Nicki, want to go to the Bahamas with me?

NICKI: Wow! Let me call my mom!

JORDI: *(Looking at screen.)* Dylan was really mad at me. I wonder who I'll take?

ANNA: Why don't you take some of your stash?

For the **real deal** read Luke 13:10-17

# The Way It Was!

**Characters: STARSHINE BURNS,** 21st-century reporter who has traveled back in time; **SID,** Starshine's cameraman; **MAN 1,** Bible-times man; **MAN 2,** Bible-times man; **MAN 3,** Bible-times man; **MAN 4,** Bible-times man; **JUDITH,** Bible-times woman recently healed by Jesus

**Scene:** *Outside the synagogue in a Bible-times city.*

**STARSHINE:** *(Nervously.)* How do I look, Sid? This video's got to be perfect or my show will be canceled. And this is live. No second chances!

**SID:** Relax. You look fine. And you're on in 3, 2, 1. *(SID points to STARSHINE.)*

**STARSHINE:** Welcome, fans! This is Starshine Burns with "The Way It Was!"

**SID:** The show that takes you to the past and shows the way it was.

**STARSHINE:** Today we're hoping to get people's impressions of Jesus. *(MAN 1 walks out of synagogue.)* And here comes a gentleman

now. Excuse me, sir. Can I have a moment of your time? *(MAN 1 looks at STARSHINE in horror and hurries off.)* Well, Sid, he was in a big hurry. Must be hiding something.

**SID:** Sure seemed like it. *(MAN 2 exits synagogue.)*

**STARSHINE:** *(To MAN 2.)* Sir, would you take a moment to speak to our audience?

**MAN 2:** First, women in the synagogue! Then, healing on the Sabbath! And now THIS! What's this world coming to? *(Hurries away.)*

**STARSHINE:** From what this man has told us, there's been a disturbance in the synagogue. *(MAN 3 exits synagogue.)* Hello, sir. People in the 21st century would like to know what happened here today.

**MAN 3:** The 21st century? Is that a Roman army post? Why do those Romans always stick their noses in where they're not wanted? *(MAN 3 hurries off.)*

**STARSHINE:** Why are all these people so secretive? What has happened? Stay with us to find out. We'll be right back after this commercial. *(MAN 4 exits synagogue and stops to stare at SID.)*

**SID:** And we're off.

**MAN 4:** *(To SID.)* What is this strange box that protrudes from your eye?

**SID:** I'm from the 21st century, bud. This is a camera.

**STARSHINE:** Sid, roll! *(To MAN 4.)* Sir, tell us what's been happening in the synagogue.

**MAN 4:** *(To SID.)* And what manner of dress is this?

**STARSHINE:** Look, I do the interviewing around here—not my cameraman. *(JUDITH *exits synagogue and observes* SID *and* STARSHINE. MAN 4 *hurries off.*)

**STARSHINE:** I blew it. I can't face being unemployed, AGAIN!

**SID:** Doesn't look good. And we're on again in 3, 2, 1. *(Points to STARSHINE.)*

**STARSHINE:** Welcome back. We're still seeking answers here.

**JUDITH:** Is there a way I can help you, dear?

**STARSHINE:** Yes! Thank you. No one seems to want to talk about what's happened here today.

**JUDITH:** In our country, men and women don't usually speak to each other in public—especially with foreign women!

**STARSHINE:** So tell us about the excitement in the synagogue.

**JUDITH:** Well, I used to walk around like this. *(JUDITH bends over and starts to walk.)*

**STARSHINE:** That looks uncomfortable. Why'd you want to walk like that?

**JUDITH:** Oh, my dear, I didn't want to. The disease in my spine forced me to walk that way!

**STARSHINE:** But you are standing straight now. Be honest. This was just a phony insurance claim, wasn't it?

**SID:** Good joke, Starshine, since we're in the first century—long before insurance companies. Ha! Ha!

**STARSHINE:** Oh, yes! So what happened in the synagogue?

**JUDITH:** Our synagogue had a very special visitor today.

**STARSHINE:** Aha! A famous star.

**JUDITH:** A star? I don't know what you

mean. No, this was the Son of the living God—Jesus.

**STARSHINE:** Jesus! This is great! That's why we're here. So what was your impression of Jesus?

**JUDITH:** Don't you want me to tell you what happened?

**STARSHINE:** Sure. But could you toss in a few words about your impression of Jesus?

**JUDITH:** Certainly. As I was saying, I was sitting in my corner listening to Jesus speak—He says such wonderful things, you know—when suddenly He called ME forward. Then He put His hands on me. And I was healed!

**STARSHINE:** That's it?

**JUDITH:** What do you mean "That's it?!" You have no idea how much I've suffered! Just this morning I wept because I was alive to suffer through another day. But Jesus changed all that!

**STARSHINE:** So by curing your disease, Jesus made your life worth living.

**JUDITH:** No, no. Even more important, by showing how much He loved me, Jesus took my despair and turned it into hope!

**SID:** That's about all the time we have, Starshine.

**STARSHINE:** Well, fans, there you have it— a miracle by Jesus. And you saw it here on "The Way It Was!" Next week join me for the crisis in Masada...I hope.

**SID:** And we're off!

**STARSHINE:** Thanks for helping me out! Oh no! I forgot to say your name! I'm hopeless!

**JUDITH:** My name is Judith. And, my dear, you're not hopeless. Jesus loves you, too. *(STARSHINE stops, looks puzzled and then smiles.)*

For the
**real story**
read Luke
**15:11-24**

# The Prodigal Case

**Characters: NEWTON,** a private investigator; **YOUNGER SON; OLDER SON; FATHER; Nonspeaking parts: FRIEND 1, FRIEND 2**

**Props:** Characters may pantomime props.

**NEWTON:** *(To audience.)* The name's Newton —Frank Ivan George Newton, Private Investigator. The sign outside my office says "F.I.G. Newton, P.I." But everyone calls me "Fig" Newton. Let me tell you about my latest missing person case.

*(Enter FATHER, OLDER SON and YOUNGER SON.)*

**NEWTON:** *(Indicates FATHER.)* This old guy has two sons. The older son works hard on the farm. *(OLDER SON pantomimes hoeing the field.)* But the kid brother's a bad seed. One day the kid says to the old man,

**YOUNGER SON:** Look, Pops! Sooner or later you're going to kick the bucket. I don't want to wait for my inheritance. Give me my share of the money now, while I'm young and can enjoy it!

**NEWTON:** So Pops gives the kid some money and the kid takes off. *(FATHER pantomimes giving YOUNGER SON money and waves sadly as YOUNGER SON walks to the other side of stage.)* I figure eventually the old man's gonna want to find the missing kid and will probably pay BIG bucks to find him. So I go to the rich farmer's house.

**NEWTON:** *(NEWTON walks over to OLDER SON, who appears to be working in the fields.)* I'm lookin' for the rich guy that lives here.

**OLDER SON:** I'm his son. Can I help you?

**NEWTON:** *(To audience.)* I figure I'm too late. The kid's already come back. *(To OLDER SON.)* I heard you were missin'.

**OLDER SON:** Oh. You mean my kid brother. He's still gone. Good Riddance!

**NEWTON:** So, I'm not too late. Maybe you can take me to see the old man.

**OLDER SON:** Sure. *(NEWTON and OLDER SON walk over to FATHER.)*

**NEWTON:** *(To audience.)* So I talk with the old man. *(FATHER is intently looking far off.)* He's been waiting for his son to come back. I figure he must be some kind of nut case. Who'd wait around for some kid who split? So I talk to the brother instead. *(To OLDER SON.)* So what's the story?

**OLDER SON:** That kid brother of mine is rotten to the core. But he's the apple of my father's eye. I can't believe my dad's still hoping my brother will come back home, after the way my brother's treated him. I wouldn't be surprised if he's gotten into trouble already.

**NEWTON:** *(To audience, as he walks slowly to side of stage where YOUNGER SON is standing.)* Well, the old man wants his son back, and I want a cash reward for finding him, so I go looking for the boy. His trail's easy to follow.

(YOUNGER SON *and* FRIENDS 1 *and* 2 *pantomime spending money, eating and drinking.*) He's spending money right and left. Parties every night with his so-called friends. The grape soda was flowing like...well, grape soda. Peanut butter, banana and strawberry jam sandwiches. Chocolate cream pie. I figure the money won't last long. Then the kid's all mine—and so's the reward money!

**YOUNGER SON:** Another round of banana splits for me and my friends! (*Searches pockets for money.*) I must have more money somewhere. (*To* FRIENDS.) Hey, do you guys have any cash? (FRIENDS *shake their heads and leave.* YOUNGER SON *dejectedly walks to another part of the stage. He pretends to feed pigs.*)

**NEWTON:** (*To audience.*) I lost track of the kid for a while. Because all his friends deserted him, he wasn't easy to spot. Then I get a tip that leads me to this pig farm. (*Walks up to* YOUNGER SON.) I see this filthy guy feeding the pigs and ask, "You seen a rich kid around here?"

**YOUNGER SON:** Nope. No rich guys around here! Just me and these pigs. Got anything to eat? I'm starving!

**NEWTON:** (*To audience.*) This is where the trail went cold. The rich man's son just disappeared off the face of the earth. I tossed the stinky kid a stick of gum and headed back to the rich guy's farm. (*Pantomimes tossing stick of gum and walks over to* FATHER *and* OLDER SON.)

**YOUNGER SON:** (*Sarcastically.*) Wow! Thanks! A stick of gum! (*Sighs to himself.*) I've really messed up, big time! Here I am starving and even the men who work for my dad have more to eat than I have. I wonder if Dad would hire me to work for him. It would be better than feeding these pigs! I'm going home!

**NEWTON:** (*To audience.*) Back at the farm I try to get some sort of lead from the old man. But he's not paying attention to me. The poor guy's still just lookin' down the road, expecting that good-for-nothing son to return. Suddenly, he starts running down the road, and I figure he's lost his marbles. Then I see him hugging that stinky kid from the pig farm.

**FATHER:** (*Hugs* YOUNGER SON.) My son! My son! I knew you would return.

**YOUNGER SON:** Dad, I don't deserve to be called your son. But if you'd let me be one of your hired hands, I'd be grateful. I'll work really hard. I promise!

**FATHER:** Nonsense! Servants, draw a bath! Bring clothes. Prepare a feast! My son has come home! (FATHER *and* YOUNGER SON *walk by* NEWTON *and exit.*)

**NEWTON:** (*Waves hand in front of nose.*) Whew! A bath would do him good! (*To audience.*) Well, that's the story. The father's patience pays off. He waits for his kid to come home, and eventually, the boy does. But not everybody's happy.

**OLDER SON:** (*Calls after* FATHER, *annoyed.*) Hey! What about ME? I stayed here like a good son! You've never thrown a party for ME!

**NEWTON:** (*To audience.*) It's nothing but sour grapes with the older kid. But the father explains everything to him.

**FATHER:** (*Returns.*) Son, you know that everything I have is yours. But your brother, who was gone, is now back home! Come! Celebrate with us! (*They both exit.*)

**NEWTON:** (*To audience.*) So all's well that ends well. The father waited patiently; the son came home; the father welcomed him and forgave him. I didn't get paid, but oh, well. There's always another case.

For the **real story** read Luke 18:9-14

# Outstanding Sam

**Characters:** SAMANTHA; RACHEL; SARAH; JASON; DEVIN

## ACT ONE

**Scene:** *Outside a church early Sunday morning.*

**SAMANTHA:** Good morning, fellow churchgoer!

**RACHEL:** Hi, Sam. You're here early as usual.

**SAMANTHA:** Of course! I've got to get in my hour of prayer before church starts!

**RACHEL:** I wish I could be as good as you, Sam.

**SAMANTHA:** Yes, it's hard work, but I'm so good at it. Do you know last week I heard Pastor Snickey miss a word when he was quoting the Bible? Well, I of course set him straight!

**RACHEL:** Pastor Snickey? Really? Wow, I wish I could be as smart as you, Sam.

**SAMANTHA:** Yes, isn't it wonderful that I can be as fabulous as I am.

**SARAH:** *(Sadly.)* Morning, guys.

**RACHEL:** Sarah, you look awful! Are you okay?

**SARAH:** Things are a little tough for me right now.

**SAMANTHA:** Things aren't tough for me! Look at how much I'm giving for the offering. You know, I must have given more than any other kid in our class.

**RACHEL:** I wish I could be as generous as you, Sam.

**SAMANTHA:** And what do you think of my new outfit? Isn't it wonderful?

**RACHEL:** It certainly is beautiful, Sam.

**SAMANTHA:** Yes, I know. I dress this way on purpose, so when people go by the prayer chapel, they'll be inspired by such a beautiful person praying!

**RACHEL:** Always thinking of others, isn't she, Sarah? I wish I could be more like you, Sam.

**SARAH:** Yes, Samantha certainly seems to try hard.

**SAMANTHA:** Look, Sarah, your bad attitude is getting me down. What's the matter with you?

**SARAH:** I made a pretty big mistake yesterday.

**RACHEL:** What did you do?

**SARAH:** I was watering the backyard when Mom said we were going to the beach. I was so excited, I forgot about the water. When we got home, there was water everywhere. It was a horrible mess!

**SAMANTHA:** That's really irresponsible! Well, I'd love to stay and chat, but I've got some serious praying to do. *(Exits.)*

**SARAH:** Yeah, me too. I need to talk with God before I can concentrate on the rest of the day.

**RACHEL:** You're going in there with Samantha?

**SARAH:** Sure. Why not?

**RACHEL:** Well, God's gonna be pretty busy listening to Samantha's prayer. I mean, she's so good—we don't really compare.

**SARAH:** Rachel, God listens to everyone. *(Exits.)*

**RACHEL:** Well, I don't think I'm good enough for Him to listen to me. Maybe I'll just go listen to Samantha pray. *(Exits.)*

## ACT TWO

**Scene:** *Inside the church.* JASON *and* DEVIN *are praying.* SAMANTHA *enters.*

**SAMANTHA:** *(Loudly.)* Good morning, everyone! It's a great day and I'm here to celebrate!

**JASON:** *(Quietly.)* Shhh!

**SAMANTHA:** *(Goes up to the front of the church and proceeds to pray loudly.)* Oh, God, I am SO happy you have made me the wonderful person that I am!

**DEVIN:** *(Quietly.)* Shhh!

**SAMANTHA:** You made me smart and talented and generous and cheerful and responsible. I'm so glad I'm not like that Sarah who is ALWAYS forgetting things. I mean, she doesn't even wear cool clothes.

**JASON:** *(In a loud whisper.)* Could you be a little quieter? We're trying to pray.

**SAMANTHA:** *(To JASON.)* And what do you think I'M doing? *(To God.)* God, thank You for making me SO nice that I don't get angry at the RUDE behavior of other people!

**JASON and DEVIN:** *(Loudly.)* SHHH!

**SARAH:** *(Enters and sits in back. Quietly.)* Dear God, I made a BIG mistake yesterday. Please forgive me.

**RACHEL:** *(Sits beside SARAH. Whispers.)* Sarah, that was a nice prayer. Um, do you think God would listen to me, too? I mean, I'm a nobody.

**SARAH:** No person is a nobody to God, Rachel. Of course God will listen to you.

**RACHEL:** Like He listens to Samantha?

**SAMANTHA:** *(Loudly.)* And God, I'm so grateful you have made me such a good example for others!

**DEVIN:** To be honest, Rachel, I think He might prefer hearing from you.

For the **real story** read Luke 18:35-43

# A Minor Disturbance

**Characters: ZEKE,** a Bible-times man who is a friend of Barney; **BARNEY,** a Bible-times man who works nights as a shepherd; **BART,** a blind Bible-times man who is a friend of Barney and Zeke; **HULDA,** a Bible-times woman who is a merchant's wife; **JAEL,** a Bible-times woman who is a friend of Hulda

**Props:** Characters may wish to pantomime the use of props.

**Scene:** *Under a shady tree along a roadside.* BARNEY *enters and lies down to take a nap.* ZEKE *follows* BARNEY *onstage.*

**ZEKE:** So, what we gonna do today, Barney?

**BARNEY:** I don't know about you, Zeke, but I'm gonna take a nap. I'm bushed!

**ZEKE:** OK. Sure, Barney. You won't hear another peep outta me. We gonna go down to the lake today, Barney?

**BARNEY:** I'm sleeping! Quiet!

**ZEKE:** Oh, sure, sure, Barney. I'll be quiet as a mouse. *(BART enters.)* Oh, look, there's

Bart! Heh, heh. Tripping over the rocks as usual.

**BARNEY:** He can't see, and I can't sleep!

**ZEKE:** You know what I wonder, Barney? Why does he leave the house if he's blind? I'd stay where no one could see me. Hey! Bart! Over here!

**BARNEY:** Zeke, go GET him! And let me sleep!

**ZEKE:** *(Ignoring BARNEY.)* Hey! Bart! A little more to your left. Watch out for that... *(BART bumps into a rock.)* rock! You OK, Bart?

**BART:** A little bruised, but I'll be all right.

**ZEKE:** Well, just don't disturb Barney. He's trying to take a nap. Isn't that right, Barney?

**BARNEY:** I beg of you, Bart, make Zeke be quiet!

**BART:** Sorry. Got no time for that. Got to get set up. A guy's gotta make a living, you know. And I've heard a whole crowd of people are coming.

**ZEKE:** Where, Bart? Where? I don't see anybody! Do you see anybody, Barney?

**BARNEY:** My eyes are closed. I'm sleeping!

**ZEKE:** But Bart can tell. He can tell for miles if someone's coming.

**HULDA:** *(Enters with JAEL.)* I think we'll be able to see from here.

**JAEL:** This is so exciting!

**BART:** *(To HULDA and JAEL.)* Alms! Alms! Alms for the blind!

**HULDA:** *(Groans.)* Bart! What do you think you're doing? Go away! You shouldn't be here!

**ZEKE:** Hey! The guy's gotta make a living!

**JAEL:** Here. I think I have a couple of coins. *(Drops coins into BART's cup. Then turns to ZEKE.)* Now, will you take him away?

**ZEKE:** Why should he go away? He has as much right to be here as you do. *(Shakes BARNEY's shoulder.)* Isn't that right, Barney?

**BARNEY:** Leave me ALONE! I'm asleep!

**HULDA:** An important visitor is coming to our town. We don't want any riffraff spoiling the view!

**JAEL:** We can stand in front of Bart, so He won't notice.

**ZEKE:** Bart can't see if you stand in front of him. That's not right! *(Shakes BARNEY.)* Is it, Barney?

**BARNEY:** He can't see, I can't sleep, and they don't care!

**HULDA:** *(To BARNEY.)* You're going to have to move, too. We can't have any lazy people lying around when He comes to town.

**BART:** Who you expecting? Caesar?

**JAEL:** Hmph! This person is much more important!

**BART:** Better not let Caesar hear you say that. So, who IS coming?

**HULDA:** For your information, Jesus is coming to town.

**BART:** Jesus! I'd really like to see Him!

**ZEKE:** Who's Jesus?

**BART:** Haven't you heard? He can heal people! He could help me see!

**HULDA:** Don't you go bothering somebody so important as Jesus with your little problems!

**ZEKE:** *(Shakes BARNEY's shoulder.)* Wow! Did you hear, Barney? Jesus is coming here! Isn't that great, Barney? Huh? Barney?

**BARNEY:** I'm asleep. *(Sits up.)* No, I'm awake! And I'm MOVING! It's far too crowded here. *(BARNEY moves around to other side of tree.)*

**ZEKE:** Wait, Barney! Here He comes!

**BART:** JESUS, SON OF DAVID, HAVE MERCY ON ME!

**HULDA:** What are you doing, shouting like that?

**JAEL:** Cut that out! No riffraff!

**ZEKE:** Whoa! Bart! Don't make such a nuisance of yourself! You can't run around annoying others! *(Goes around tree and shakes BARNEY.)* Isn't that right, Barney?

**BART:** SON OF DAVID, HAVE MERCY ON ME!

**BARNEY:** *(Sits up and listens, and then speaks to BART.)* I think He's calling you, Bart.

**BART:** *(Reaches out hand.)* You're right! He is! Help me over there!

**BARNEY:** Help him over there, Zeke. *(ZEKE helps BART offstage.)* Good for Bart.

**HULDA:** Well, I never! Riffraff getting HIS attention. Hmph!

**JAEL:** But, look, Hulda. Jesus is...Wow! Look! Bart can see! He's looking around. And he's walking without stumbling! Praise God!

**BARNEY:** Really? Wow! Maybe I'm not so sleepy after all. I think I'll follow Jesus to find out more about Him!

For the **real story** read Luke 19:1-10

# What's Going On?

**Characters: ZACK,** a really short guy who is a tax collector; **JAKE,** a really tall guy who is also a tax collector; **BETH,** Bible-times woman; **LEAH,** Bible-times woman

**Scene:** *Street in the Bible-times city of Jericho.*

**ZACK:** Hey, Jake, what's all that commotion in the street?

**JAKE:** Zack, notice that I am sitting. To find out what's happening, I would have to get up and climb that tree in order to see ANYTHING.

**ZACK:** Aw, Jake! You're so tall you could probably see if you just stood UP.

**JAKE:** That would require me to move from my comfortable seat.

**ZACK:** Oh, yeah. Bad idea. But aren't you the LEAST bit curious?

**JAKE:** Nope. Not a bit. But whatever it is, it's NOISY! I'll never get an afternoon nap this way!

**ZACK:** I'll go see if someone else knows what's going on. (*Approaches* BETH, SETH *and* LEAH.) Shalom, good people. What's happening down the street?

**BETH:** Well, if we're GOOD people, what does that make YOU, tax collector?! Nothing's going on that would gain you more money, so go home!

**LEAH:** Besides, you've already got our last coin. You can't collect any more taxes from us!

**SETH:** Ladies! Shh! Don't make him mad!

**LEAH:** What difference does it make? We've got nothing left but the clothes on our backs!

**BETH:** Next thing, he'll be wanting those, too!

**ZACK:** I don't want your clothes, I just want...

**LEAH:** What? Our clothes aren't GOOD enough for you? You sneaking Roman thief!

**SETH:** Let's go, ladies! Excuse us, Zack, but we're on our way to the bank for a loan. (BETH, SETH, *and* LEAH *exit.*)

**ZACK:** Still awake, Jake? Boy, those three are cranky! Just because I took their goats and oxen.... Look, I left them their donkey!

**JAKE:** Yep. They just need to be more positive. Takes a bit of doing to adjust after taxes.

**ZACK:** Who do they think they ARE? Roman law says we must take what we NEED to support ourselves. Do they want me to break the LAW?!

**JAKE:** Guess that fancy new house you built kind of rubs them the wrong way. They're just jealous. *(AMOS enters.)*

**ZACK:** Hey, Amos, what's happening up the street?

**AMOS:** It'll COST you. Silver—right here in this hand, first!

**ZACK:** Just to find out what's going on?

**AMOS:** Hey, SOMEBODY took my entire savings in taxes when I bought a few goats!

**ZACK:** It's not MY idea to charge everyone taxes. It's the LAW.

**AMOS:** Yeah, but it's ROMAN law. And it was YOUR idea to overcharge me! *(AMOS exits.)*

**ZACK:** Another cranky citizen of the Empire. Maybe I should take up farming.

**JAKE:** HA! That's a good one! Then I'd get to tax YOU! I'd LOVE to have your new house!

**ZACK:** Very funny, Cutthroat Jake. SOMEONE'S gotta tell me what's going on. *(MATT enters.)* Hey, Matt, what's going on?

**MATT:** Not much. The wife's finally well. Kids need new sandals. Gotta go! Bye!

**ZACK:** No, no. What's going on up the STREET?

**MATT:** Gabe's got shoes on sale. Beth's selling yesterday's bread cheap. Gotta go!

**ZACK:** THAT'S not what all the excitement is about. TALK to me, Matt! We were BEST friends when we were young!

**MATT:** Yeah. We WERE. Past tense. Look, the commotion is about Jesus, the preacher. But I've really gotta go! Mind letting go of my robe?

**ZACK:** Jesus! I've heard of Him. He's supposed to be a fantastic speaker.

**MATT:** He is. He talks about God and forgiveness and stuff. Listen, with your reputation, I'd rather not be seen talking to you. I've gotta go.

**ZACK:** Er, right.... Well, thanks for telling me what's going on, old friend.

**JAKE:** So...your old friend, Matt, doesn't want to be seen talking to a tax collector, eh?

**ZACK:** That really hurts. We were so close! He even let me have his butterfly collection.

**JAKE:** Well, I'm your only friend now...me and the other tax collectors. Listen, after I get some sleep, we'll go take some widow's house as payment for taxes. That'll cheer you up.

**ZACK:** It just doesn't hold the same excitement it used to. But I'd sure like to see that Jesus. I just can't see past all these people!

**JAKE:** Zacchaeus, get outta here. Go climb a tree and let me sleep!

**ZACK:** Climb a tree! What a great idea!

**JAKE:** Yeah, right...*(snores)*

**NARRATOR:** Sometime later...

**ZACK:** Jake! Jake! You'll never believe what happened! JESUS is coming to MY house for dinner! Can you believe it? Jesus is coming to see ME! A tax collector!

**JAKE:** Good! Now it'll quiet down and I can get some sleep!

**For the real story read John 3:1-21**

# Nick at Night

**Characters: ANNAS,** the chief Pharisee; **ALEXANDER,** a rather elderly Pharisee (also known as Al); **MATTHIAS,** a rather ruthless Pharisee; **NICODEMUS,** a curious Pharisee (also known as Nick)

**Scene:** *A nighttime meeting of the Pharisees.*

**ANNAS:** Then it's agreed. Our official position is AGAINST this Jesus.

**AL:** Right! Against Jesus! Uh, why are we against Him?

**MATTHIAS:** We are against Him because He doesn't agree with us. He is taking away our power. He refuses to obey us!

**ANNAS:** And He claims to teach the people the way God wants them to live.

**AL:** Am I missing something? What's wrong with that?

**MATTHIAS:** Who knows what God wants for the people better than WE do?

**AL:** Jesus?

**MATTHIAS:** Augh! I give up!

**ANNAS:** No one knows better than WE do, Al. Isn't that right, Nick?

**NICK:** Huh? Sorry, I was getting my cloak.

**ANNAS:** But we're not through! We're discussing important business.

**NICK:** You certainly are. And I can see that you have the situation well under control!

**AL:** So what do YOU think of this Jesus?

**NICK:** Well, no one could do such miracles unless God was with Him.

**ANNAS:** The very IDEA! So what if He's healed people! It doesn't MEAN anything. We can always say the sick ones were faking illness, right?

**AL:** Right! After all, the common people know nothing. Right?

**MATTHIAS:** With an attitude like yours, Nick, you may find yourself in serious trouble.

**AL:** Say, did you see the old crippled lady Jesus healed yesterday? You know, the one who used to beg right outside this door?

**NICK:** I did.

**ANNAS:** Not ANOTHER one! Can't these people understand that we're doing the very best we can for them? WE are their leaders, not Jesus. They should be grateful to us and IGNORE Him. So He heals. So what?

**NICK:** Do you know anyone else who is healing the sick? Anyone who teaches with such authority?

**MATTHIAS:** Nick, you're beginning to sound like one of the common people. Remember your place. Do you really want to be put out of the Temple? Removed from the Sanhedrin*? This is dangerous talk!

**NICK:** Look, it's time for me to go.

**AL:** Oh—bedtime? Good. I'm ready! *(Yawns.)*

**MATTHIAS:** Wake up, Al! *(To himself.)* It would take a miracle to keep YOUR attention!

**AL:** You have my attention. And what about miracles? What about that old lady? Healing the blind and lame IS pretty impressive!

**MATTHIAS:** Al, if Jesus were truly sent by God, He'd be one of US. A Pharisee, a scribe, a priest. He would not be some rabble-rousing rabbi!

**NICK:** Because you think He's a nobody, He can't be the Messiah?

**ANNAS:** Oh, don't tell us you think He's the MESSIAH! This is too MUCH!

**NICK:** What proof do you have that He isn't?

**ANNAS:** He's from GALILEE. He never went to school anywhere WE would recognize. He's, He's—just a bum! A bum with a rabble of followers!

**NICK:** I'm sure that's what you'll tell the Sanhedrin.

**ANNAS:** You BET I will! Nobody's taking MY Sanhedrin seat! And you'd better watch what you say, Nick, or you'll lose yours!

**NICK:** I remember that in our youth, we eagerly awaited the Messiah—before we had power and positions to lose.

**ANNAS:** *(Growls.)* That was then, this is NOW. Jesus has to be stopped before people start believing Him!

**NICK:** Annas, if we miss the Messiah, what difference will our power and dignity make? I'm leaving. I'm going to find out more about this Jesus. *(NICK exits.)*

**MATTHIAS:** Gentlemen, a storm is brewing.

**AL:** But the sky's clear!

**MATTHIAS:** Not a RAINSTORM, you sleepy simpleton. A POLITICAL storm.

**AL:** You think Nick will really go to see Jesus?

**MATTHIAS:** If he does, the Sanhedrin may have to investigate. We may even have to put him out of the Temple! We'll teach HIM to listen to the common people!

**AL:** That's right. The common people know nothing. But tell me again—why are we against this Jesus?

---

*Sanhedrin: The "supreme court" of the Jews.

**For the real story read John 4:4-26**

# Celebrity Island

**Characters: SHELBY SEABYRD,** a reality TV show host; **CARMEN STARLETTE,** a celebrity judge; **MAX SHUTTERBUG,** a contestant; **SADIE SAPPHIRA,** a contestant

**Scene:** *An island in the Mediterranean Sea. The set of a reality TV show.*

**SHELBY:** Welcome back to *Celebrity Island*, the show where ordinary people become famous just because they've met celebrities! I'm your host, Shelby Seabyrd. With me is our celebrity judge, Carmen Starlette. Carmen has been on every single reality show from *Samaritan Star* to *Shipwreck Survivor*. She starred in 27 movies before going to jail for breaking a fan's camera.

**CARMEN:** That was all a misunderstanding. He didn't UNDERSTAND that I don't like to be photographed before noon!

**SHELBY:** Let's meet our contestants, shall we? Contestants, please introduce yourselves and tell us what famous person you met.

**SADIE:** My name is Sadie Sapphira. I met Jesus when I went to a well to get water.

**MAX:** Hi! I'm Max Shutterbug. I met Carmen Starlette one day when I took her picture and she broke my camera!

**SHELBY:** Sadie, tell us your story. Why did you go to the well to meet Jesus?

**SADIE:** I didn't know He was there! I carried my water dipper to the well around noon—

**CARMEN:** Noon? Wasn't it hot? I don't go anywhere that time of day. Wouldn't want my fans to see me all shiny and wilted!

**SADIE:** It WAS hot...but also less crowded.

**MAX:** So you were avoiding people? I don't blame you. People can be so rude! Did I tell you that a lady smashed my camera, just because I wanted her picture?

**SADIE:** It's just that...well, I've done some wrong things in my life. Things I'm not proud of. I wasn't sure the women who use that well would want to see me.

**CARMEN:** I'd like to say that I understand. But I don't! Everyone wants to see me!

**SHELBY:** So what happened when you got to the well?

**SADIE:** Jesus was just sitting there, all by Himself. He looked tired, like He'd been walking a long way.

**CARMEN:** So did you speak to Him? Do you think He would star in my next movie?

**SADIE:** I didn't say anything, at first. I was a little surprised to see a Jewish man sitting by a well in Samaria.

**MAX:** No kidding! Jewish people and Samaritans have been enemies for centuries! They worship God in the Temple; we worship on a mountain. They read the old Scriptures; we—

**CARMEN:** *(Yawns.)* Fascinating. Really. But let's get back to the part where she met Jesus.

**SADIE:** I was walking up to the well, when suddenly He looked right at me and said—

**MAX:** He SPOKE to you? Most men I know NEVER speak to women they don't know.

**SHELBY:** So tell us, Sadie. What did Jesus say to you?

**SADIE:** He said, "Will you give Me a drink?"

**MAX:** That's it? Did He yell at you and tell you to leave Him alone? Did He complain that His fans never give Him a moment's peace?

**SADIE:** No. He just asked me for water. He was very polite.

**CARMEN:** *(Scowling at MAX.)* Sadie, what did you say to Jesus?

**SADIE:** I said I was surprised someone like Him would ask for water from someone like me! But He said that if I knew who He was, I'd ask HIM for water.

**MAX:** Well if He had a water dipper, what was He doing sitting around waiting for you to get His water?

**SADIE:** That's the thing—He didn't have a dipper! But He said He could give me LIVING water, and I'd never be thirsty again!

**SHELBY:** Imagine all the time you'd save! No more trips to the well. No more standing around, drinking water...

**SADIE:** Well that's what I thought! But Jesus wasn't talking about regular water. He meant that He could give me eternal life as part of God's family. And then He did something really surprising.

**MAX:** Did He scream, "Who cares about your broken camera! I'm famous! They'll never send ME to jail!"

**CARMEN:** I SAID that was a misunderstanding!

**SHELBY:** What did Jesus do?

**SADIE:** He told me He knew about the wrong things I'd done. Even though we had just met, He knew all about me! But He still wanted to talk to me! He even told me He was the Savior we've all been waiting for!

**CARMEN:** Yeah, right. Imagine YOU meeting the Savior! I'm pretty sure if the Savior came to Samaria, He'd want to talk to someone more famous. Like, I don't know...ME, maybe?

**SADIE:** Well, I was so excited, I ran straight into town and told EVERYONE about Him! Pretty soon, everybody wanted to meet Him! Jesus stayed in town for two whole days!

**SHELBY:** Well, that's a pretty good story. But let's hear from Max.

**MAX:** Like I said, I saw Carmen Starlette and took her picture. She got really angry and broke my camera.

**CARMEN:** *(Angry.)* That...was...a... MISUNDERSTANDING!

**SHELBY:** Now it's time for the audience to vote. Who had the better celebrity sighting? Who deserves to be the Ultimate Celebrity? Who will be voted off the island? Three... two...one...Time's up. According to our InstaNet results, the next person to be voted off *Celebrity Island* will be...Carmen Starlette!

**CARMEN:** No! That can't be right! I'm not even a contestant. I'm a STAR! You can't vote me off the island!

**SHELBY:** Well that's all the time we have for today's episode of *Celebrity Island*—

**CARMEN:** No! It's not over! Recount! RECOUNT!

**SHELBY:** Tune in next week to find out who our next judge will be, and who will be... the Ultimate Celebrity!

**SADIE:** *(To MAX.)* And, Max, the best thing of all was that meeting Jesus was so much better than any reality TV show.

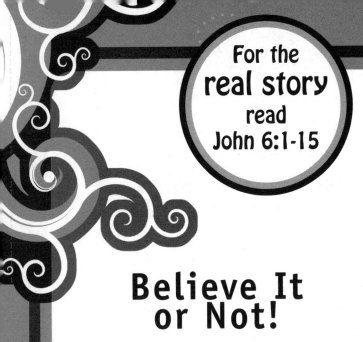

## For the real story read John 6:1-15

# Believe It or Not!

### Characters: BETH; JACOB

**Props:** Characters may wish to pantomime the use of props.

**BETH:** Jacob! Where ya been?

**JACOB:** You won't believe what happened!

**BETH:** What?

**JACOB:** Well, I've had these nasty-looking warts on my hands for months now and everyone makes fun of them. So I prayed and prayed and prayed.

**BETH:** What did you pray for, Jacob?

**JACOB:** For God to remove these warts from my hands, of course. You won't believe what happened!

**BETH:** What?

**JACOB:** Well, that same day I heard people talking about Jesus, you know, that man from Nazareth. They said He could cure anything. And you won't believe what happened!

**BETH:** What?

**JACOB:** I'm wrapping up the two fish and five loaves of bread my Mom gave me for lunch and I see a crowd of people going past.

**BETH:** Yeah?

**JACOB:** So, I followed them out of town to see what was going on, and someone said they were going to see Jesus. And this enormous crowd kept getting bigger and bigger. Must have been at least 5,000 people there. And suddenly, I saw Him. It was Jesus! So I prayed and prayed and prayed.

**BETH:** What did you pray for, Jacob?

**JACOB:** I prayed I could get close enough for Jesus to heal my dumb warts. Well, Jesus started teaching and healing people and I just kept creeping closer and closer until, well, I was so close, I could see Jesus was talking to Poor Ol' Joe. You know, the one that's never been able to walk. Poor Ol' Joe's always been very nice to me, so I prayed and prayed and prayed.

**BETH:** What did you pray for, Jacob?

**JACOB:** I prayed that Jesus would heal Poor Ol' Joe, of course. Well, you won't believe what happened!

**BETH:** What?

**JACOB:** Ol' Joe just got up and walked around. He just kept saying, "Thank You, Lord, thank You!" It was awesome!

**BETH:** I'll bet.

**JACOB:** But that wasn't even the most incredible thing that happened. I don't remember how long we'd been sitting there, listening to Jesus, when I started to get real hungry. And I was sure everybody else was hungry, too, especially when people started staring at my lunch packet. So I prayed and prayed and prayed.

**BETH:** What did you pray for, Jacob?

**JACOB:** I prayed that Jesus would notice how hungry I was and would stop for a lunch break. And you won't believe what happened!

**BETH:** What?

**JACOB:** Well, Jesus must have noticed we were hungry, because He asked His disciples, "Where shall we buy bread to feed all these people?" One of His disciples answered, "WE don't have enough money to feed all of these people. It would take eight months' wages to do that!" Well, I prayed and prayed and prayed.

**BETH:** What did you pray for, Jacob?

**JACOB:** That Jesus would find a way to feed all those people. You won't believe what happened!

**BETH:** What?

**JACOB:** A disciple told Jesus about my five loaves of bread and two fish. Then Jesus asked me if I would share my bread and fish with all those people.

**BETH:** Did you tell Him you would if He healed your warts?

**JACOB:** Of course not! That wouldn't have been right. Besides, I'd forgotten about those old warts after all the things Jesus had said. Well, you won't believe what happened!

**BETH:** What?

**JACOB:** Jesus broke the bread into parts and as He did it, there was more and more bread. Then He gave the pieces to His disciples, then the disciples gave them to groups of people, then the people gave them to each other. Then Jesus did the same thing with the fish.  And, YOU WON'T BELIEVE WHAT HAPPENED!

**BETH:** WHAT?

**JACOB:** Everyone had so much to eat that there was 12 baskets of food left over!

**BETH:** Let me get this straight. You had five loaves of bread and two fish? *(Pulls out calculator.)*

**JACOB:** Right!

**BETH:** And there were 5,000 people? *(Punches numbers on calculator.)*

**JACOB:** Right!

**BETH:** And Jesus divided YOUR little lunch among 5,000 people and there were 12 baskets of food left over? *(Punches numbers on calculator.)*

**JACOB:** Right! *(Opens can of sardines.)*

**BETH:** *(Looks at calculator.)* I don't believe it! *(Scratches head and suddenly sniffs the air.)* Eew! What's that smell?

**JACOB:** It's some of the leftover fish. Want some? I'm too full.

**BETH:** Don't mind if I do. *(Takes a bite of sardine.)* Not bad. Where'd you REALLY get it?

**JACOB:** Just like I said. It's left over from my lunch.

**BETH:** But you only had two small fish! There's more than that here!

**JACOB:** Exactly. Here, have a piece of bread. It's really good, too.

**For the real deal read John 8:1-11**

# Simon's Sandwich

**Characters: SMILEY; SID; SANDI; SIMON; JESSE**

**Scene:** *Student Court at Mid Middlevale Middle School.*

**SMILEY:** Heh, heh. I think we've finally got a case that'll fix that goody-goody.

**SID:** What goody-goody?

**SMILEY:** Jesse!

**SID:** Oh yeah, him. Why are we fixing him?

**SMILEY:** Because he's always talking about loving everyone. Well, I've found someone even HE couldn't love!

**SID:** Who?

**SMILEY:** Shabby Sandi!

**SID:** Oh yeah, Shabby Sandi. What did she do?

**SMILEY:** She stole Simon's salami sandwich! And we caught her in the act!

**SID:** You saw her steal the sandwich?

**SMILEY:** Of course! She took it off his desk.

**SID:** Why was Simon's sandwich on his desk?

**SMILEY:** Because he knew Sandi was starving!

**SID:** But why...?

**SMILEY:** So we could trap Jesse! Simon stuck his sandwich out so Sandi would see it. So when she stole it, we could accuse her in student court. And Jesse's presiding, see?

**SID:** But how does that trap Jesse?

**SMILEY:** Jesse's always saying, "Hate the sin, but love the sinner." Well, when we accuse Sandi, he'll be forced to sentence Sandi, or else say stealing's OK.

**SID:** I don't get it.

**SMILEY:** You will. Here comes Simon with Sandi the accused. And here comes Jesse.

**JESSE:** I call the Student Court to order.

**SMILEY:** Your Honor...

**JESSE:** Smiley, you don't have to call me "Your Honor."

**SMILEY:** I'm only trying to be respectful.

**JESSE:** Very well, what is your case?

**SIMON:** We caught Sandi stealing my salami sandwich! She swiped it right off my desk during social studies. According to school rules, Sandi should be suspended!

**JESSE:** *(Looks down at some papers on the desk.)*

**SMILEY:** You won't find any solutions there! Stealing is stealing!

**SIMON:** Yes, sir. And it was a super salami sandwich, too!

**SID:** He doesn't seem to be paying attention.

**SMILEY:** Say, Jesse, are you listening?

**SIMON:** Yeah, what's the sentence for Sandi?

**JESSE:** Simon, why was your sandwich on your desk during social studies? School rules say that sandwiches stay in your backpack until lunch.

**SIMON:** Well, I...um...say! Let's stick to Sandi, who stole my sandwich.

**JESSE:** So you say you broke a rule but Sandy is the sinner?

**SIMON:** I guess I wasn't that hungry, anyway. I'll be going now.

**JESSE:** And Smiley, what were you doing spying on Sandi? Weren't you supposed to be doing the homework you forgot?

**SMILEY:** Well, I...um...guess I'll be going now.

**JESSE:** And Sid...

**SID:** Hey, I wasn't even there!

**JESSE:** Then why are you pretending to be one of the witnesses?

**SID:** Well, I...um...guess I'll be going now.

**JESSE:** So, Sandi, I guess it's just you and me.

**SANDI:** Yes. I'm really sorry. I know I shouldn't have stolen that sandwich.

**JESSE:** Well, since there's no one left to

accuse you, I'm not going to accuse you either. But Sandi...

**SANDI:** Yes?

**JESSE:** Don't let it happen again. If you're that hungry, let me know. I'd be happy to share my lunch with you.

**SANDI:** Thanks, Jesse. And I promise, it WON'T happen again!

**For the real deal read John 10:1-30**

# Job Interview

**Characters: REUBEN,** applicant for the job of shepherd; **JUDE,** owner of sheep, interviewing for a new shepherd

**Scene:** JUDE's *office.*

**REUBEN:** *(Enters and shakes* JUDE's *hand vigorously.)* Hello, there. My name's Reuben. Now, some people think I'm named after the original Reuben, the one the tribe's named after. But I ain't. I'm named after my Uncle Reue. He was always wandering around the countryside an' people was always saying, "I wonder where Reue's been." Get it? Reue's been. Pretty good, huh?

**JUDE:** Ah yes, Mr. Reuben. Please have a seat.

**REUBEN:** *(Sitting down.)* I always like to start off a job interview with a joke. Helps get everyone relaxed, ya know. You wouldn't believe some of the stuffy people I've interviewed with. Say, what's your name?

**JUDE:** Jude.

**REUBEN:** Jude? Is that short for Judy? Heh, heh. Just kidding. More of that humor, ya know. It's relaxing.

**JUDE:** Yes. Now, Mr. Reuben, you're applying for the job of shepherd?

**REUBEN:** Sure am! An' I told all those other fellas to go home, 'cause I said, "I'm just what that guy's looking for! No need for you to stay." Heh, heh. Just kidding. More humor.

**JUDE:** Yes, it's relaxing. Tell me about your experience in herding sheep.

**REUBEN:** Well, none. But, hey, how much do you need to know? I mean, you just stand around and watch sheep all day. Hey, I can do that! I like to stand around all day at the well. Catch the view! If you know what I mean.

**JUDE:** No. I don't.

**REUBEN:** Well, I just stand there watching the people pass by. Some of those people are pretty funny looking! But that don't pay much. Which is why I'm looking for a job. Heh, heh. More humor there.

**JUDE:** Yes, well, shepherding is more than just watching sheep. You would be completely responsible for taking the sheep to water and food.

**REUBEN:** How far away is that?

**JUDE:** That all depends on how far away you find pure water and good grass.

**REUBEN:** You mean I gotta go looking for the stuff?

**JUDE:** Yes. And you'd need to make sure NOT to lose any sheep or lambs on the way.

**REUBEN:** How do I do that?

**JUDE:** Generally, a shepherd keeps a count of how many sheep he has. And he knows his sheep. Knows their habits. And he also keeps a watchful eye.

**REUBEN:** How many sheep are there going to be? I can't count higher than 20!

**JUDE:** There will be at least 100 sheep.

**REUBEN:** Whew! That's a lot! I'd better grow some more fingers and toes. Heh, heh. More humor.

**JUDE:** Yes. Do you consider yourself a strong person?

**REUBEN:** Sure. I can beat any one of my nine brothers in a wrestling match. Hey, if you like, I could go get one an' show you!

**JUDE:** That won't be necessary.

**REUBEN:** Say, why do I need to be strong? I'm just gonna be walking 'n watching.

**JUDE:** You will need to carry injured lambs or sheep on your shoulders.

**REUBEN:** Why?

**JUDE:** How else would they get around, Mr. Reuben?

**REUBEN:** Can't they carry each other?

**JUDE:** No, Mr. Reuben. Now, how are your fighting skills?

**REUBEN:** Fighting? I ain't applying for no fighting job. I'm looking for something peaceful!

**JUDE:** Occasionally, a shepherd must fight off a wild beast to protect the sheep.

**REUBEN:** What for? I say if the beast wants it, the beast can have it!

**JUDE:** The point is not to lose ANY sheep. Don't you have any fighting skills? You may also need to fend off thieves and robbers.

**REUBEN:** Fight off thieves and robbers? Hold it. How much does this job pay?

**JUDE:** The standard wage.

**REUBEN:** Heh, heh. That's a joke, right?

**JUDE:** No. Mr. Reuben, do you like sheep?

**REUBEN:** Sheep are sheep. They're a bunch of animals. What's to like?

**JUDE:** Mr. Reuben, you may be required to risk or even give up your life for the sake of the sheep. Are you prepared to do that?

**REUBEN:** Give up my life? For SHEEP? Are you nuts?

**JUDE:** Mr. Reuben, I'm sorry, but I don't think shepherding is the job for you.

**REUBEN:** You got that right!

**JUDE:** Send in the next person, please.

**REUBEN:** *(Stands up.)* All right. But I don't think you're gonna find anyone who'll take this job! *(Calls out the door.)* Next! But I warn you, it won't be easy to get a job with this guy! *(Turns to JUDE.)* Heh, heh. A little more humor, to help you relax for the next guy. *(Exits.)*

**JUDE:** *(Groans.)*

**For the real story read John 17—20**

# In the News...

**Characters: PAT,** a news reporter; **BARBARA,** a news reporter; **JACK,** a news reporter; **CAIAPHAS,** a high priest; **PONTIUS PILATE,** the Roman governor of Judea; **JOHN,** a disciple of Jesus

**Props:** Characters may wish to pantomime the use of props.

**PAT:** *(Sits at desk with headphones on. Looks sadly at audience.)* Who would have believed the events of these past few days? All of Jerusalem is in shock. It began Thursday night. Jesus and His disciples had just celebrated the Passover when, suddenly, the city's religious leaders had Him arrested. *(Turns toward BARBARA.)* Let's turn to Barbara for her interview with Caiaphas, the head of the religious leaders.

**BARBARA:** Thank you, Pat. Caiaphas, why did you have Jesus arrested?

**CAIAPHAS:** He was a dangerous Man!

**BARBARA:** But He preached about loving each other and loving God. What was dangerous about that?

**CAIAPHAS:** He said HE was the SON of God,

the KING of the Jews. We can't have people running around saying things like that. Suppose people believed Him? They might not listen to us anymore. We're the ones who know what God wants people to believe.

**BARBARA:** I see. What did you do after you had Jesus arrested?

**CAIAPHAS:** We conducted His trial, of course.

**BARBARA:** How could you give Him a fair trial when You were His accusers?

**CAIAPHAS:** I don't understand your question.

**BARBARA:** Never mind. What happened at the trial?

**CAIAPHAS:** We found Him guilty so we sent Him to the Roman governor to be executed.

**BARBARA:** And that's the story here. Back to you, Pat.

**PAT:** Thank you, Barbara. I've just received word that we've been able to get an exclusive interview with Pontius Pilate, the Roman governor of Judea. With Pilate is another of our hardworking reporters. Go ahead, Jack.

**JACK:** Right, Pat. Pontius Pilate has graciously agreed to answer a few questions. Can you tell us, sir, what happened when the religious leaders sent Jesus to you?

**PILATE:** The religious leaders, as you may know, have always been a problem for me. Always threatening to tell Rome this or tell Rome that...

**JACK:** Yes, about the trial...

**PILATE:** Ah, yes. Well, I examined this Jesus. He didn't seem like much of a threat to me. I tried to talk Caiaphas and his supporters out of executing Him. But, would they listen to me? Noooo, they had to have Him executed. I hoped things would settle down after that.

**JACK:** Thank you, Sir. Pat, back to you.

**PAT:** And so this Man, Jesus, who taught people to love God and help each other, was taken and crucified on a cross with common criminals. Quite strangely, there was only one disciple and a few women with Jesus at His death. It is rumored that the rest of the disciples are currently in hiding. Our reporter, Barbara, was able to interview only one disciple right after Jesus' death, just outside the city.

**BARBARA:** Your name?

**JOHN:** J-J-John.

**BARBARA:** Where is everyone else?

**JOHN:** I don't know.

**BARBARA:** What is your opinion of what happened here?

**JOHN:** What?

**BARBARA:** How do you feel about all this?

**JOHN:** Confused! I've never felt so sad in all my life.

**BARBARA:** What are your plans?

**JOHN:** I don't know.

**BARBARA:** *(To camera.)* That's the condition of Jesus' closest followers right after their leader was killed.

**PAT:** *(To audience.)* Jesus was put in a tomb and the soldiers sealed the entrance with a heavy stone. Two days have passed since then, days filled with sadness, darkness, earthquakes...EARTHQUAKES! Hang on folks, we just felt a good-sized jolt. Whoa, that was a big one. Things seem to have settled down now. It's a good thing the sun is coming up. We'll be able to check for any damage. *(Cups hand on earphones.)* We're receiving a report right now. What? *(Keeps hand over earphones.)* Ladies and gentlemen, I've just been given an update. It seems our crew talked with one of those women, Mary Magdalene, and she's reported seeing Jesus ALIVE! It seems Jesus gave her a message to tell the disciples He had risen from death! We go now to a live interview that Jack arranged with one of the disciples.

**JACK:** What is your name?

**JOHN:** He is risen!

**JACK:** Who is risen?

**JOHN:** Jesus! He is risen from the dead!

**JACK:** You mean He's alive?

**JOHN:** *(Excitedly.)* Yes! First the angel told the women, and then the women told us, and Peter and I ran to see for ourselves, and Mary talked with Him. I've got to go now. A group of us are meeting to talk about all that has happened.

**JACK:** Where is this meeting?

**JOHN:** I'd rather not say. The religious leaders, y'know. But I can tell you that Jesus is risen! Just as He said He would!

**JACK:** *(Perplexed.)* Are you saying this is all part of His plan?

**JOHN:** Yes! We didn't understand it at the time. We hadn't really paid attention to God's promises to send His Son to die for our sins! When Jesus died on the cross three days ago, we thought it was all over. But even death has no power over Him! He is risen! This proves that Jesus IS God's Son. Jesus' death paid the price for our sins!

**JACK:** Well, folks! You heard it firsthand. Now back to you, Pat.

**PAT:** Thank you, Jack. Ladies and gentlemen, this is truly the most incredible and important story I have ever had the privilege of sharing with you. After being killed three days ago, Jesus Christ is alive!

**For the real story read John 18:15—20:20**

# One Dark Sunday Morning

**Characters: JAMES; ANDREW; THADDAEUS; THOMAS; PHILIP; JOHN; PETER; MARY**

**Scene:** *Several of Jesus' disciples are gathered in the room of a home in Jerusalem the Sunday after Jesus died on the cross.*

**JAMES:** Well, I say we get together some of the other supporters and form an army! We'll show those Romans!

**ANDREW:** And exactly what would we show them? Jesus is gone! He's the One that was important! Without Him, we're nothing!

**THADDAEUS:** Well, maybe we could teach what He taught.

**THOMAS:** Our best plan of action is to hide! Don't you think they'll be coming for us, too?

**PHILIP:** Who?

**THOMAS:** (*Angrily.*) The Romans! The Pharisees! And everyone else who plotted against Jesus. Haven't you been paying attention?

**JOHN:** Haven't we learned anything over the past three years? What was it Jesus talked about most? LOVE! And here we are fighting among ourselves!

**PETER:** Don't be so hard on them, John. Fear and grief can cause the worst to come out in people.

**JOHN:** (*Quietly to* PETER.) Peter, you know Jesus would understand what you did.

**PETER:** (*Sadly.*) Jesus even warned me it would happen. When He needed me most, I denied even knowing Him. I just took care of myself. Some friend I was!

**THADDAEUS:** (*To* JOHN *and* PETER.) What are you two talking about?

**JOHN:** Just some things that Jesus said.

**PHILIP:** I'm afraid I didn't always understand everything Jesus said.

**JOHN:** Well, I know He asked us to show our love for Him by obeying His commands. That includes loving and forgiving each other.

**THADDAEUS:** I don't understand why He died. I mean, if He was the Messiah, wouldn't He have the power to stop them?

**ANDREW:** (*Glumly.*) I thought so.

**JOHN:** "Greater love has no one than this, that he lay down his life for his friends."

**JAMES:** What?

**JOHN:** It was something Jesus said. I think He was telling us why He was willing to die.

**MARY:** *(Enters, breathless.)* Peter! John! Come quick! He's gone! We don't know where He is!

**PETER:** Who? Who is gone, Mary?

**MARY:** *(Sobbing.)* Jesus! We went to the tomb and His body was gone! Oh, please come!

**JOHN:** Of course! *(PETER and JOHN exit with MARY.)*

**JAMES:** Some more Roman nastiness, I suppose.

**ANDREW:** Now why would the Romans move His body? They posted a guard there to make sure no one disturbed His grave.

**JAMES:** Apparently the guard didn't do a very good job!

**THADDAEUS:** You don't suppose, well, you know…Jesus talked about coming back. Maybe He's alive again.

**THOMAS:** Oh, be sensible! It's impossible for someone to be alive again after being dead.

**PHILIP:** Well, now, Jesus did bring several people back to life.

**THOMAS:** *(Snaps.)* Yes, but Jesus was alive to do it! *(Sighs.)* Look, I need some fresh air. I'm going for a walk. (THOMAS *exits.*)

**THADDAEUS:** Wait! Thomas! Come back!

**ANDREW:** Leave him alone, Thad. Everybody needs to grieve in their own way. Some want to be with others; others want to be alone.

**THADDAEUS:** Jesus promised we would never be alone.

**PHILIP:** Maybe Jesus didn't know this was coming.

**JAMES:** Jesus knew about everything. Maybe John was right. Maybe we should try to think about what He said. Maybe then we could make sense of all this.

**PHILIP:** I don't know. Nothing makes sense anymore!

**MARY:** *(Enters, breathless.)* I saw Him! He's ALIVE!

**JAMES:** Calm down, Mary! Who did you see?

**MARY:** Jesus! I saw JESUS!

**ANDREW:** *(Gently.)* Mary, Jesus is gone. I know it's hard to accept, but—

**MARY:** I SAW Him. I TALKED to Him. He TALKED to me. Just now. He's ALIVE, I tell you!

**JAMES:** But that can't be possible.

**THADDAEUS:** Why not? It should be possible for God's Son!

**PETER:** *(Enters with JOHN.)* I have news!

**JAMES:** Peter, Mary says Jesus is alive.

**PETER:** Mary is right. He IS alive!

**JOHN:** Think about what Jesus said! He said He'd never leave us. Believe! Jesus is alive!

**THADDAEUS:** See, I was right!

**ANDREW:** But where is Jesus?

**MARY:** He said to tell you He'd be here with you soon.

**JAMES:** *(Sits down.)* Wow! Jesus—alive! What'll the Romans think of this?

For the **real story** read Acts 1:4-5; 2

# One Family

**Characters: STARSHINE,** news reporter; **SID,** cameraman; **CYRUS,** man from Persia; **BARBARA,** woman from Greece; **AMBER,** woman from Arabia; **ISIS,** woman from Egypt; **MICHAEL,** man from Samaria; **REUBEN,** man living in Jerusalem; **Nonspeaking parts: PERSIAN MAN, GREEK WOMAN, ARABIAN WOMAN, EGYPTIAN WOMAN**

**Scene:** STARSHINE *and* SID *are interviewing people on a Jerusalem street on the day of Pentecost. The year is approximately A.D. 33.*

**STARSHINE:** *(Facing camera.)* There seems to be a great deal of excitement here today!

**SID:** Right you are, Starshine. It's the day of Pentecost, and people from all over the world have gathered here to celebrate!

**STARSHINE:** Yes, it may be difficult to find someone who can speak a language our viewers can understand! *(CYRUS and PERSIAN MAN walk by. STARSHINE speaks to PERSIAN MAN.)* Excuse me, sir. But can you tell me what all the excitement is about?

**CYRUS:** My friend only speaks Persian, but I can translate for you. *(CYRUS and PERSIAN MAN whisper to each other.)* My friend says he has heard a most incredible speaker in town today. This man has told him that knowing Jesus will change his whole life! My friend is on his way to be baptized right now. *(CYRUS and PERSIAN MAN exit.)*

**STARSHINE:** To be baptized? But why? Who was this speaker? *(BARBARA and GREEK WOMAN walk by. STARSHINE speaks to GREEK WOMAN.)* Excuse me, but can you tell me where you are going and why?

**BARBARA:** My friend only speaks Greek, but I can translate for you. *(BARBARA whispers with GREEK WOMAN.)* My friend says she just heard a remarkable speaker. She is going to be baptized! *(BARBARA and GREEK WOMAN exit.)*

**STARSHINE:** But what did this speaker say? *(AMBER and ARABIAN WOMAN walk by.)* Excuse me, ladies. Did you hear a speaker today?

**AMBER:** My friend only speaks Arabic, but I can tell you that she did hear a fabulous speaker today! In fact, now her life is changed, and mine, too. We're on our way to be baptized right now. *(AMBER and ARABIAN WOMAN exit.)*

**STARSHINE:** *(To camera.)* There certainly have been a lot of speakers here today! It seems there was a Greek, a Persian and an Arab—and ALL of them urged people to be baptized. *(ISIS and EGYPTIAN WOMAN walk by.)* Excuse me, ladies, but would you take some time to answer a few questions?

**ISIS:** My friend speaks only Egyptian, but I can translate for you.

**STARSHINE:** Well, thank you. Tell me, did you hear any speeches today?

**ISIS:** Oh yes! A wonderful man spoke!

**STARSHINE:** So you heard speeches, too?

**ISIS:** I only heard the end of the speech, but my friend told me what happened first. At first all these people were speaking in many different languages, even though they'd never spoken in them before. Then this one man, Peter, got up and told us about Jesus, the Messiah!

**AMBER:** *(Entering.)* Are you talking about Peter?

**ISIS:** Yes!

**BARBARA:** *(Entering.)* Wasn't his speech wonderful? Such great news!

**CYRUS:** *(Entering.)* What a speaker! My life has changed!

**STARSHINE:** Wait a minute! Are you telling me you all heard the same speaker? How is that possible? You don't speak the same languages!

**MICHAEL:** *(Enters with REUBEN.)* So this Jesus was the Messiah our ancestors talked about? What great news!

**REUBEN:** Yes, and now we have become members of the same family.

**STARSHINE:** You're members of the same family? But Jews and Samaritans hate each other!

**BARBARA:** *(To REUBEN.)* Yes, we've all become members of the same family!

**STARSHINE:** I'm so confused! How can people from different countries be members of the same family? How can people who speak different languages all understand the same speaker? It doesn't make any sense.

**CYRUS:** It's a miracle!

**AMBER:** Just like God's love is a miracle! But come and listen to Peter. He'll explain it much better. *(All exit except STARSHINE and SID.)*

**STARSHINE:** What do you make of all this, Sid?

**SID:** I don't know, Starshine, but it has something to do with people being adopted, I think.

For the **real story** read Acts 3

# Heard the News?

**Characters: RACHEL; MIRIAM; REBECCA; STEPHEN; MICHAEL; ISAAC; LEVI; PHILIP; NICOLAS**

**Scene:** *The Court of the Gentiles in the Temple of Jerusalem.*

**RACHEL:** *(To* REBECCA *and* MIRIAM.*)* Have you heard the news?

**REBECCA and MIRIAM:** What news?

**RACHEL:** The crippled man was healed!

**REBECCA and MIRIAM:** How?

**RACHEL:** Some guys named Peter and John just said, "In the name of Jesus, get up and walk."

**MIRIAM:** Who's Jesus?

**REBECCA:** He's that criminal the Romans crucified a few months ago.

**MIRIAM:** Um, excuse me, but how could a dead person heal someone?

**RACHEL:** He isn't DEAD. God raised Him from the dead. He's ALIVE!

**REBECCA:** Why would God raise a criminal from the dead?

**RACHEL:** But He WASN'T a criminal. He was the Son of God!

**MIRIAM:** Why would the Romans crucify the Son of God?

**RACHEL:** Because they didn't KNOW He was the Son of God.

**REBECCA:** How do you know that He WAS?

**RACHEL:** Peter and John explained it all. Jesus was the Messiah the prophets had talked about, and He died to take the punishment for our sins, and Jesus' rising from the dead PROVES He's the Son of God.

**MIRIAM:** And you believed all this?

**RACHEL:** Yes. Just look at the crippled man now! See how he's LEAPING in the air! If Jesus was just a crazy guy or a criminal, how could that happen?

**REBECCA and MIRIAM:** Wow! You're right! But what do we do now? Won't God be angry because of what was done to Jesus?

**RACHEL:** No, it was all part of His plan. Peter and John said that we should repent.

**MIRIAM:** Re-who?

**RACHEL:** Repent! Give up our old ways, and live the way Jesus wants us to. I'm going to tell ALL my friends!

*(RACHEL faces away from audience. MIRIAM turns to STEPHEN, and REBECCA turns to MICHAEL.)*

**REBECCA and MIRIAM:** Have you heard the news about the crippled man?

**STEPHEN and MICHAEL:** What news?

**REBECCA and MIRIAM:** He was healed by the power of Jesus!

**STEPHEN and MICHAEL:** Jesus? The criminal?

**REBECCA and MIRIAM:** No, Jesus was God's Son. Peter and John said that Jesus was the One the prophets told us about. They said that Jesus came back to life! And look, the crippled man is walking!

**STEPHEN and MICHAEL:** Wow! Jesus really MUST be the Son of God to do all that!

**REBECCA and MIRIAM:** I'm going to go listen to Peter and John to see if I can learn more!

*(REBECCA and MIRIAM face away from audience. STEPHEN turns to ISAAC and LEVI, and MICHAEL turns to PHILIP and NICOLAS.)*

**STEPHEN and MICHAEL:** Have you heard the news?

**ISAAC, LEVI, PHILIP and NICOLAS:** What news?

**STEPHEN and MICHAEL:** The news about how the crippled man was healed by the power of Jesus!

**ISAAC and PHILIP:** Wasn't Jesus a criminal?

**PHILIP and NICOLAS:** That's what I heard.

**STEPHEN and MICHAEL:** No, Jesus is the Son of God.

**ISAAC and PHILIP:** How do you know?

**STEPHEN and MICHAEL:** Peter and John, the men preaching over there, said that Jesus rose from the dead! And now, by His power, the crippled man is walking!

**ISAAC, LEVI, PHILIP and NICOLAS:** Wow!

*(RACHEL, REBECCA and MIRIAM face audience.)*

**ALL:** *(To audience.)* Have you heard the news?

## Most Generous

**For the real story read Acts 4:36—5:11**

**Characters: MIRIAM,** member of the early Christian church who owns only two shawls*; **SAPPHIRA,** member of the early Christian church who likes people to notice her; **ANANIAS,** Sapphira's husband and a guy who likes to be in charge; **PHOEBE,** (FEE-bee) wealthy neighbor of Ananias and Sapphira; **REUBEN,** (ROO-ben) Phoebe's wealthy husband who buys all the latest inventions; **SIMON,** somewhat dishonest neighbor who borrows things from Ananias and Sapphira

**Scene:** *In front of* SAPPHIRA'S *and* ANANIAS'S *house.*

**MIRIAM:** Sapphira, have you heard? Barnabas sold his field and gave ALL the money to the disciples for the poor. He's the MOST generous man!

**SAPPHIRA:** MOST generous...oh, yes.

**MIRIAM:** He's totally inspired me to share! I'm taking my extra shawl to the widow Anna.

**SAPPHIRA:** Yes, MOST inspiring. *(MIRIAM exits.)* Ananias! Ananias! Come quick!

**ANANIAS:** *(Enters.)* Yes, yes, what is it? Is something wrong?

**SAPPHIRA:** Not exactly wrong...just GENEROUS. Barnabas sold his field and gave ALL the money to the disciples for the poor.

**ANANIAS:** ALL the money? That IS most generous!

**SAPPHIRA:** Yes. Now everyone thinks HE'S the MOST generous person around.

**ANANIAS:** Oh dear. I was so hoping to be chosen as an elder. But if Barnabas is the MOST generous...he's sure to be chosen instead.

**SAPPHIRA:** It's just like him. MOST generous! I can't stand HIM being the MOST generous!

**ANANIAS:** I know what—we'll be even MORE generous! Let's sell some of OUR property!

**SAPPHIRA:** Wonderful idea! We can sell some of our beach-front property for far more than that field of Barnabas's! Then WE'LL be...the MOST generous people in the congregation! Everyone's sure to be impressed.

**ANANIAS:** No sooner said than done. I'm on my way, MOST generous wife!

**SAPPHIRA:** Get the highest price you can, MOST generous husband! *(ANANIAS exits, PHOEBE enters.)* Hello, Phoebe. What a lovely shawl! Where did you get it?

**PHOEBE:** Down at the marketplace. It's expensive, but worth every shekel, don't you think? You really should get one for yourself. But hurry—there are only a FEW as nice as this. Well, I must get home and make sure my servants are keeping busy. There's just no end to my work. *(PHOEBE exits, ANANIAS enters.)*

**SAPPHIRA:** Ah, MOST generous husband and future elder of the congregation! How much, eh, profit did we make?

**ANANIAS:** We made a BUNDLE! Ha! We made SO much, we could give HALF of it and STILL beat Barnabas's gift!

**SAPPHIRA:** Beat Barnabas...look like the MOST generous couple around...and still have money left for that lovely designer shawl! Hm...I like the sound of that!

**REUBEN:** *(entering)* Hey Ananias, what's the word?

**ANANIAS:** The word, my man, is generous—MOST generous!

**REUBEN:** Generous, huh? Did I hear you made a killing on that beach-front property?

**ANANIAS:** News travels fast in this little city! Yes, indeed. We made a killing!

**REUBEN:** Good for you! Well, if you look MOST generous to the disciples, maybe you'll win that elder's seat! But hey! I came to show you my new sandals! Expensive, but guaranteed to last 500 miles or three years, whichever comes first. They're great! You oughta get yourself some. And now you can AFFORD them! Well, gotta walk! *(Exits.)*

**SAPPHIRA:** Oh, Ananias! I was thinking...

**ANANIAS:** ...about the money? We made so MUCH. Do we have to give it ALL to the disciples? If we just give part of it, we'll still be MORE generous than Barnabas!

**SIMON:** *(Offstage)* Hello, hello, hello! Anyone home?

**ANANIAS:** Oh no, it's that Simon! He probably wants to borrow something he won't return.

**SIMON:** Hi, guys! I heard you just unloaded some property. Made a killing, hey? How much?

**ANANIAS:** Well, um...it was a fair price. Did you want to borrow something, Simon?

**SIMON:** *(Sees money.)* Wow! That's a pretty BIG fair price! What are you going to buy?

**SAPPHIRA:** Um...nothing. We'll give it to the disciples for the poor.

**SIMON:** Give ALL that money to the POOR? Not keeping any of it? *(Pauses.)* Oh, I see. I heard about Barnabas. Brought every shekel from that land sale to the disciples! Just gave it all up. Amazing.

**ANANIAS:** Well, we intend to give even MORE than he did, Simon.

**SIMON:** *(Stares at money.)* That should be easy! In fact, you could keep some and still give more than Barnabas did. After all, it's not HOW you give but how MUCH you give that makes an impression—right?! It's the GIFT, not the thought, that counts!

**ANANIAS:** I don't know, Simon...er, look, you DID want to borrow something, didn't you?

**SIMON:** Oh, yeah! Almost forgot! That plow of yours isn't around anywhere, is it?

**ANANIAS:** It's...uh, in the repair shop, Simon.

**SIMON:** Repair shop, huh? Too bad. Guess I'll just have to wait. See ya! *(Exits.)*

**SAPPHIRA:** *(Looks at money.)* We'll look MOST generous if we give even HALF...

**ANANIAS:** We'll say we are giving the whole price. We're still MOST generous.

**SAPPHIRA:** Then I can buy that new shawl...you can get some new sandals... and you'll be an elder and we'll sit up front where everyone can see us.

**ANANIAS:** *(Smiles and looks at money again.)* MOST generous! A killing, indeed!

**For the real story read Acts 6:1-7**

# If It Happened Today

**Characters: BART,** short for Bartholomew, one of the twelve apostles; **TOM,** short for Thomas, also one of the apostles; **JIM,** short for James, he's one of the apostles, too; **THAD,** short for Thaddaeus, another of the apostles; **MRS. LEE,** Bartholomew's secretary; **NARRATOR**

**Props:** Characters may wish to pantomime the use of props.

**Scene:** BART, TOM, JIM *and* THAD *are sitting around a table in Bart's office.*

**NARRATOR:** What if the apostles were modern businessmen? Our scene opens at a meeting of the twelve apostles' Committee for Handling Difficulties.

**BART:** So where is everybody?

**TOM:** Pete's speaking at some club today, and Andy had some business to take care of.

**THAD:** Big Jim and John are involved in that citywide prayer meeting. And I think I heard Matt say something about working on his book.

**JIM:** Phil's out of town.

**BART:** What about Matthias and Simon?

**TOM:** Don't know.

**JIM:** Haven't heard from them.

**BART:** Perhaps they called in. *(Into intercom.)* Mrs. Lee?

**MRS. LEE:** *(Pokes head in door.)* Yes, Mr. Bartholomew?

**BART:** *(Into intercom.)* Mrs. Lee, have we received any messages from Matthias or Simon?

**MRS. LEE:** I'll go check. *(Exits.)*

**BART:** *(Into intercom.)* Thank you, Mrs. Lee. *(To others.)* Well, we might as well get started. What's our first item of business?

**TOM:** I have a letter here from the Hellenists.* *(Reading from letter.)* "To the apostles, those especially chosen by our Lord to establish His church here on Earth, those who spread the news about our Lord throughout the region."

**THAD:** Whew! They must really want something! They're really buttering us up.

**BART:** Or reminding us of our responsibilities.

**TOM:** *(Continues reading.)* "We wish to make you aware of a serious problem. One that has left us feeling unfairly treated."

**THAD:** They sound upset. I wonder what they want.

**BART:** Perhaps if we allow Tom to finish reading the letter, we'll find out.

---

*Hellenists: Jewish people who spoke Greek and followed Greek customs.

**TOM:** (Reading.) "As has always been the custom, donations are collected at the markets every Friday morning to give to the poor and the widows."

**MRS. LEE:** (Entering.) Mr. Bartholomew, I called Mr. Simon's secretary and she said he was out with the sick today, so she didn't expect him to be here for the meeting.

**THAD:** Simon's sick? What's the matter with him?

**JIM:** One of us really should stop by and make sure he's all right. But I've got another meeting right after this one.

**BART:** My schedule's full, too. How about you, Thad?

**THAD:** No can do. I'm scheduled to speak at the marketplace. Tom?

**TOM:** Well, I'm busy, but I guess I could make time. There's just so much important work to do.

**MRS. LEE:** Excuse me, sirs, but Simon's VISITING the sick. He's not sick himself! (Exits.)

**BART:** Oh. I see. Um, where were we?

**TOM:** (Reading from letter.) "This is done because they have no other way to get food."

**JIM:** What's done?

**BART:** I think they're referring to the food collection.

**TOM:** (Reading.) "However, many of the Hellenistic widows are NOT receiving enough food. Please take care of this problem as soon as possible!"

**BART:** Not getting food—why that's awful! Who's in charge of food distribution?

**JIM, TOM and THAD:** Not me!

**JIM:** We're all too busy with teaching, preaching and praying to even get to a meeting.

**THAD:** But we've got to do something. How can we encourage other people to join us if we aren't even helping the members of our church?

**BART:** Thad's right. We've got to do something. But what?

**TOM:** What if we selected some special people to make sure the food's given out fairly? And to take care of the people's physical needs? That will leave us free to worry about their spiritual needs.

**JIM:** That's an excellent idea, Tom!

**BART:** I agree. Now we'll need someone to write a letter telling the Hellenists of our plan. Can you handle that, Thad?

**THAD:** I've got no time this week. How about next week?

**JIM:** I might be able to squeeze it in on Friday, but it would be better if someone else could do it.

**TOM:** Don't look at me! I've got a month of back-to-back speaking engagements.

**BART:** Hm. (Into intercom.) Mrs. Lee, will you come in here a minute? We need you to write a letter.

**NARRATOR:** Now a question for our audience: How would you describe the attitude of these businessmen? Read Acts 6:1-7 to find out about the real apostles.

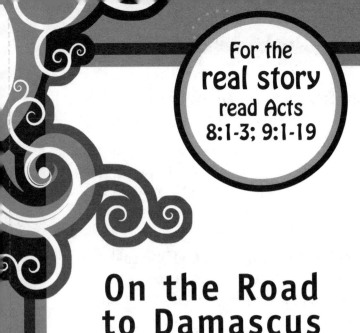

**For the real story read Acts 8:1-3; 9:1-19**

# On the Road to Damascus

**Characters: NABAL; SAUL; ANANIAS; WIFE; VOICE (Voice of Jesus)**

**Props:** Characters may wish to pantomime the use of props.

**Scene One:** SAUL *and* NABAL *enter, walking slowly on the road to Damascus.*

**NABAL:** *(Excitedly.)* So tell me. Where are we going?

**SAUL:** *(Exasperated.)* I've already told you. We're going to Damascus.

**NABAL:** Why? What're we going to do there?

**SAUL:** The same thing we do everyday. Try to stop these people who follow The Way from destroying the one true religion.

**NABAL:** Oh, I know them! They sell that stuff called Zap It! It makes grape stains disappear!

**SAUL:** That's not The Way, Nabal. I'm talking about the followers of that blasphemer, Jesus.

**NABAL:** They're blasphemers? Oooh, that sounds bad! What's a blasphemer?

**SAUL:** A blasphemer is someone who says things about God that are lies and disrespectful.

**NABAL:** Well, then, it's a good thing I didn't buy anything. Or sign up.

**SAUL:** *(Shaking his head in exasperation.)* It's like talking to a wall.

*(Flashlight shines at* SAUL *and* NABAL. *They shield their eyes.* VOICE *begins to speak to them from offstage.)*

**VOICE:** Saul, Saul, why do you persecute Me?

**SAUL:** *(Fearful.)* Who are You, Lord?

**VOICE:** I am Jesus, whom you are persecuting. Now get up and go into the city and you will be told what you must do.

*(Flashlight turns off.* SAUL *looks around blankly.)*

**NABAL:** *(Impressed.)* Oooo! That's very good!

**SAUL:** *(Dazed.)* What?

**NABAL:** Your ventriloquism act. I didn't even see your lips move.

**SAUL:** That wasn't me.

**NABAL:** It wasn't?

**SAUL:** No, Nabal. It...it...sounded like the voice of God. We must go to Damascus at once! *(Looks around blankly.)* But where is it?

**NABAL:** *(Pointing with one arm outstretched.)* It's that way.

**SAUL:** Nabal, I can't see anything! I'm blind! You'll have to guide me to the city.

**NABAL:** Cool! I've always wanted to be a guide. Where shall we go first? There's the museum. And the outdoor market. The library, the synagogue, and city hall...

**SAUL:** Why do I feel this is a classic case of the blind leading the blind? (NABAL *takes* SAUL *by the hand and leads him offstage.*)

**Scene Two:** ANANIAS' *House.*

(WIFE *pretends to straighten the house.* ANANIAS *enters.*)

**WIFE:** Oh, there you are. Have you been praying all this time?

**ANANIAS:** Yes, and it was a little disturbing.

**WIFE:** Don't know what to pray about? It happens to the best of us. Well, sit down. I've fixed you a lovely lunch.

**ANANIAS:** Sorry. I've got to go out.

**WIFE:** Well, you could have told me you were planning to eat out.

**ANANIAS:** I didn't know. Not until God spoke to me while I was praying.

**WIFE:** God told you not to eat my cooking?

**ANANIAS:** No. God told me I'm supposed to meet a man named Saul who is staying in a house on Straight Street.

**WIFE:** What a coincidence! I heard today that Saul of Tarsus is coming to Damascus to persecute the Church. (*Shrugs.*) Oh, well. It is a common name.

**ANANIAS:** It isn't a coincidence. It's the same man.

**WIFE:** (*Alarmed.*) And you're going to see him?!

**ANANIAS:** Yes. The Lord told me that he's blind. And I'm supposed to restore his sight.

**WIFE:** What? Are you crazy? Are you nuts? Did you just escape from a fruitcake?

**ANANIAS:** God told me, "Go to the house on Straight Street and ask for a man from Tarsus named Saul, for he is praying."

**WIFE:** Oh! I should have known! Your hearing is getting bad. God didn't say "praying" with an *a.* He said "preying" with an *e.* Saul is preying upon followers of Jesus, like a lion stalks his prey.

**ANANIAS:** No, because God also said, "In a vision he has seen a man named Ananias come and place his hands on him to restore his sight."

**WIFE:** Oh, it's definitely your hearing. I'm sure God said you were to "lay hands on Saul." You know. Beat him up. Teach him a lesson.

**ANANIAS:** I considered that! I told God what I heard about Saul—that he came to Damascus with authority from the chief priests to arrest everyone who follows Jesus.

**WIFE:** I still say it's some kind of mistake.

**ANANIAS:** There's no mistake. God said, "Go! This man is My chosen instrument to carry My name before the Gentiles and their kings and before the people of Israel. I will show him how much he must suffer for My name."

**WIFE:** AHA! I told you! You were supposed to make him suffer.

**ANANIAS:** No, I think God meant he will be persecuted for his new faith in our Lord Jesus. I'm going to obey God's word and restore Saul's sight. (*Exits.*)

**WIFE:** (*Calling after him.*) Wait! I'll wrap up your lunch for you! If he arrests you and drags you off to Jerusalem, you'll need your strength!

For the **real story** read Acts 8:26-40

# The Miracle Play

**Characters: BRUSHWORTH,** a master painter; **MICHAEL,** Brushworth's apprentice; **ANGELO,** Brushworth's apprentice; **BROTHER QUILLEN,** a scribe from neighboring monastery; **ANGEL; PHILIP; ETHIOPIAN**

**Props:** Characters may wish to pantomime the use of props.

**Scene One:** *English Castle in the Middle Ages.* BRUSHWORTH, MICHAEL *and* ANGELO *are preparing to paint a picture on the walls of the castle chapel. They are joined by* BROTHER QUILLEN *and some actors who are rehearsing their play for the village faire.*

**BRUSHWORTH:** Michael! Angelo! I can't find my drawing!

**MICHAEL:** Angelo's looking at it again, sir.

**ANGELO:** *(Hands drawings to* BRUSHWORTH.*)* Master Brushworth? I thought we were painting the story of Philip and the Ethiopian. What are these other drawings?

**MICHAEL:** Angelo, Angelo. Your mind is as thick as the plastic on these walls!

**ANGELO:** Thick, schmick! I just want to understand what I'm painting.

**BRUSHWORTH:** If you know so much, Michael, why don't YOU want to tell us what these drawings are about?

**MICHAEL:** Well, I think they're about...uh, words from a prophet named Mariah...or Josiah...

*(*BROTHER QUILLEN *enters.)*

**QUILLEN:** ISAIAH, my dear boy, the prophet ISAIAH. But please, no talk about Isaiah right now!

**BRUSHWORTH:** Why not, Brother Quillen?

**QUILLEN:** I have to copy the entire manuscript of Isaiah! My back is breaking, my fingers are cramping and my mind is spinning! I need a break!

**Scene Two:** *Actors playing* PHILIP, ANGEL *and* ETHIOPIAN *enter to rehearse for the village faire.* ETHIOPIAN *has Bible.*

**ANGEL:** Philip! I've got a message from the Lord. Go down to the desert road to Gaza.

**PHILIP:** Gaza?!!? OK. I'll guess I'll be off to Gaza. *(*ANGEL *escorts* PHILIP *to* ETHIOPIAN *and then exits.)* Good day, sir. What are you reading?

**ETHIOPIAN:** I'm reading the words of the prophet Isaiah, but I find them most perplexing—

**ANGELO:** *(Interrupting.)* Yeah, him and everyone else.

**MICHAEL:** Sh!

**PHILIP:** Which words are those?

**ETHIOPIAN:** *(Reads Acts 8:32-33.)*

**PHILIP:** Ah, yes! I know that passage well!

**ETHIOPIAN:** This is BAD news! Who is this

Lamb who was killed and did not defend Himself?

**PHILIP:** These words describe Jesus, the Son of God!

**ETHIOPIAN:** I heard stories about this Jesus when I was in Jerusalem. I heard He was killed by men who hated Him. How could He be the Son of God if people treated Him so badly?

**PHILIP:** Jesus LET them kill Him. He took the punishment for all the wrong things we've ever done when He died on the cross. Because He died, we can be forgiven and live with God forever!

**ETHIOPIAN:** So this is really GOOD news?

**PHILIP:** There's even more good news! Three days later Jesus came back to life! More than 500 people saw Him eating and drinking and talking!

**ETHIOPIAN:** Now that IS good news! Are you a follower of this Jesus?

**PHILIP:** Yes! You can become a follower of Jesus, too.

**ETHIOPIAN:** What must I do?

**PHILIP:** Admit that you have done wrong things and need to be forgiven—

**ANGELO:** (*Interrupting.*) Oh. I get it now.

**MICHAEL:** Sh!

**ETHIOPIAN:** Yes, I know I have done wrong. And I am sorry that my wrongs made it necessary for Jesus to die on the cross.

**PHILIP:** Then tell God you're sorry and ask to become a part of His family.

**ETHIOPIAN:** That's ALL I have to do?

**PHILIP:** That's what makes it such GOOD news!

**ETHIOPIAN:** Is there something I can do to show I have become a part of God's family like you?

**PHILIP:** Yes. Jesus' followers are baptized with water. Then to show we are His followers, we try to love each other as God loves us.

**ETHIOPIAN:** Stop the chariot! There's some water! I can be baptized now!

(*PHILIP and ETHIOPIAN exit.*)

**ANGELO:** (*Pointing to drawings.*) I get it, Master Brushworth! Here is Philip talking to the Ethiopian. And these drawings explain Isaiah's words about Jesus!

**MICHAEL:** It's a masterful design, Master Brushworth! Well done!

**QUILLEN:** This whole chapel helps people understand the Bible. You can see the stories told in the beautiful art, like your picture about Philip, or in the stained-glass windows. Or you can watch the story acted out, like in the miracle play.

**BRUSHWORTH:** And when we understand the good news for ourselves, then we can use our talents and abilities to help others understand it, too!

**MICHAEL:** Master Brushworth, when we finish the walls, can we start on the ceiling?

**ANGELO:** Yes! I've always wanted to see what it was like to paint lying down!

**BRUSHWORTH:** The CEILING? Good news painted on the ceiling...hmm, it has possibilities.

For the **real story** read Acts 9:1-22

# What Happened to Saul?

**Characters: MATTHIAS; ALEXANDER; JETHRO; NICOLAS**

**Scene:** *The Temple in Jerusalem.*

**MATTHIAS:** He should be returning soon.

**ALEXANDER:** Who? Who should be returning soon?

**MATTHIAS:** Saul! Soon we will wipe out all this foolishness!

**ALEXANDER:** Foolishness? What foolishness?

**MATTHIAS:** The followers of the Way!

**ALEXANDER:** Way? Which Way?

**MATTHIAS:** The Way of Jesus!

**ALEXANDER:** Oh, that Way. But what's Saul got to do with it?

**MATTHIAS:** Saul went to Damascus to arrest the followers of Jesus. As soon as he brings them here, we'll have a quick trial and then we'll rid ourselves of the problem.

**ALEXANDER:** How? How are we going to rid ourselves...

**MATTHIAS:** Alexander, exactly where have you been these past few months?

**ALEXANDER:** Well, um...my sister got sick, and then we had that wonderful trip to Jericho, and then...

**MATTHIAS:** Listen! Saul, one of our most promising young Pharisees, has gone to Damascus to arrest the followers of Jesus to bring them back here so that we can put an end to all this foolishness about Jesus being the Son of God and rising from the dead and forgiving people's sins.

**ALEXANDER:** Aha!

**JETHRO:** Good morning, friends.

**MATTHIAS:** Jethro! You've returned from your trip!

**ALEXANDER:** Where did YOU go?

**JETHRO:** I've been up north, and I have the most distressing news.

**MATTHIAS:** More distressing than these followers of Jesus?

**JETHRO:** There's a new follower. His name is Paul and he's a powerful preacher!

**ALEXANDER:** Powerful? How is he powerful? Does he have magic powers?

**JETHRO:** No! When he talks, people listen. And get this, he's not only been talking to the Jewish people, but I understand he's planning on telling the Gentiles about Jesus, too!

**MATTHIAS:** Blasphemy! Everyone knows that the Messiah was promised to the Jewish people!

**ALEXANDER:** I thought we didn't believe Jesus is the Messiah.

**MATTHIAS:** That's not the point! Whoever this Paul person is, he certainly doesn't know his Scriptures.

**JETHRO:** They say Paul was trained by Gamaliel himself.

**MATTHIAS:** Gamaliel? But he's the wisest and most knowledgeable Pharisee we've got!

**ALEXANDER:** Wasn't Saul educated by Gamaliel?

**MATTHIAS:** Precisely. And look how phenomenally he turned out. Saul knows the Law. He knows our ways! This Paul mustn't have been a very good student.

**JETHRO:** They say Paul was once a well respected Pharisee.

**MATTHIAS:** Nonsense! I've never heard of him! How respected could he be?

**ALEXANDER:** Paul. Saul. Their names are almost the same.

**MATTHIAS:** We don't have time to deal with trivia. What's the news about Saul? Certainly he's shaking up the place. He'll take care of this Paul person.

**JETHRO:** I didn't hear anything about Saul.

**MATTHIAS:** What?!? Hasn't he been arresting Christians?

**JETHRO:** Not that I heard of. The only talk in Damascus is about this Paul and his amazing conversion.

**ALEXANDER:** Con-what?

**JETHRO:** Conversion. That means he changed from being a Pharisee and became a follower of Jesus.

**MATTHIAS:** I don't understand what happened to Saul.

**ALEXANDER:** You know, this Paul and Saul could be the same person.

**MATTHIAS:** Don't be foolish! Saul would have to be struck blind before he'd leave the true way of the Pharisees!

**NICOLAS:** *(Entering.)* Have you heard the news about Saul?

**MATTHIAS:** No, what news?

**NICOLAS:** It seems he's become a follower of Jesus! He's even changed his name.

**MATTHIAS:** No! But why? What happened?

**NICOLAS:** I'm not sure. But he's become a powerful preacher for the Way.

**MATTHIAS:** I don't believe it! Not Saul!

**NICOLAS:** I found it hard to believe, too. But it's true.

**MATTHIAS:** *(Exiting with* NICOLAS.*)* This is awful! Just awful!

**ALEXANDER:** *(To* JETHRO.*)* Hm, I wonder what happened to Saul?

**For the real deal read Acts 9:1-22**

# He's Back!

## Characters: DOUG; JOE; BARNEY; TONY

**DOUG:** Did you hear the news about Tough Tony?

**JOE:** What about him? He moved away. We don't have to worry about him.

**DOUG:** Oh, yeah? He's back.

**JOE:** He CAN'T be back!

**DOUG:** Well, he's back anyway.

**JOE:** And just when things were getting better. I can't believe he's back.

**DOUG:** He'll be stealing everything we have.

**JOE:** Maybe we can avoid him.

**DOUG:** Yeah, right.

*(BARNEY enters with TONY.)*

**BARNEY:** Hi, guys.

**JOE:** Hi, Barn—

**DOUG:** Barney! What are you doing with him?

**BARNEY:** Guys, meet my friend, Tony.

**TONY:** Hi, guys.

**JOE:** Barney! Are you crazy? Why'd you bring Tough Tony here?

**BARNEY:** His name's not Tough Tony.

**TONY:** It's just Tony, now.

**DOUG:** Right. Well, we don't want him here. You know what he did to us before.

**BARNEY:** But that was before. He's different now.

**JOE:** Oh, yeah! How? Is he only going to beat us up every OTHER day instead of EVERY day?

**BARNEY:** Listen, guys. Tony has changed. And he wants to be friends with us.

**DOUG:** Well, we don't want to be friends with him.

**JOE:** Yeah. How do we know he's changed?

**TONY:** Honest, guys—I really have changed.

**JOE:** No way. Once a bully, always a bully.

**BARNEY:** But he has changed. When he moved to the other side of town, he met some new friends. And they invited him to church with them. Now, he's different.

**DOUG:** Come off it, Barney! Church doesn't change people.

**BARNEY:** Sure it does.

**TONY:** No, he's right, Barney. Church doesn't change people.

**BARNEY:** What?

**JOE:** See, I told you. He's just pretending.

**TONY:** Church doesn't change people. But Jesus does.

**DOUG:** What are you talking about?

**TONY:** I met Jesus.

**JOE:** Right! Jesus died a long time ago. He's history.

**BARNEY:** Joe, I thought you were a Christian.

**DOUG:** Sure he is. We both are.

**BARNEY:** Well, you don't talk like you are.

**JOE:** What do you mean?

**BARNEY:** Jesus is alive.

**DOUG:** Well, yeah. But you don't meet Him.

**BARNEY:** Maybe you don't. But you can talk to Him.

**DOUG:** Maybe. But Jesus doesn't talk to people today.

**TONY:** You're wrong, Doug. Jesus spoke to me.

**JOE:** Prove it. How did Jesus speak to you?

**TONY:** He used a teacher at the church—a man who used to be a gang leader.

**BARNEY:** And now, Tony knows Jesus. And he's changed.

**TONY:** Please, guys. I'm sorry for all the stuff I did before. Please forgive me and let me be your friend.

**JOE:** We'll think about it.

**DOUG:** But don't hold your breath.

**JOE:** Yeah! We're not sure about you. (JOE and DOUG exit.)

**TONY:** How can I make them believe me?

**BARNEY:** It may take a while, but together, we'll convince them. I'll tell them what you've done. You'll have to show them by the way you live. Hey! I'll ask Mom if you can come for supper tonight.

**TONY:** Great!

**BARNEY:** And Tony, I'm glad you're back.

For the **real story** read Acts 9:20-30

# It's a Trap!

**Characters: AMOS; ZACHARIAS; SAUL; BARNABAS; PETER; OTHER APOSTLES**

**Scene:** *A street in Jerusalem.*

**AMOS:** *(Pointing toward the distance.)* Hey, look! Isn't that Saul?

**ZACHARIAS:** Oh, no! Quick, HIDE!

**AMOS:** Too late. He's walking this way. But isn't he a follower of Jesus now, just like us?

**ZACHARIAS:** It's a TRAP! He's just pretending to be one of us so we'll trust him—

**AMOS:** My cousin Thaddeus in Damascus says Saul's been telling everyone that Jesus is the Son of God.

**ZACHARIAS:** *(Ignoring AMOS.)* And then he'll JUMP through the air and SLAM us to the ground!

**AMOS:** I don't know, Zacharias. He doesn't look that strong.

**ZACHARIAS:** He'll TIE us up with heavy chains and blindfold us!

**AMOS:** *(Beginning to worry.)* Do you think so? I'm afraid of the dark!

**ZACHARIAS:** Then he'll DRAG us before the judge, and—

**SAUL:** *(Entering cheerily.)* Hello, fellow followers! My name is Saul. I'd like to team up with you and tell others about Jesus.

**ZACHARIAS:** Hold it right there mister! We know who you are and why you're REALLY here! *(Backing away.)* We're just going to back away slowly and—

**AMOS:** RUN!!! *(ZACHARIAS and AMOS run away.)*

**SAUL:** Hey guys! Wait for me! *(To himself.)* Well, I guess I can't blame them. I just have to pray that God will send someone who will trust me.

**BARNABAS:** *(Walking by. Stops abruptly.)* Hey! Aren't you Saul of Tarsus?

**SAUL:** Yes, I'm Saul. Who are you?

**BARNABAS:** I'm Barnabas, one of Jesus' disciples.

**SAUL:** Really! And you're still talking to me?

**BARNABAS:** Actually I'd like to hear about your experience. I've heard that you believe Jesus is God's Son—and that Jesus actually spoke to you. Everyone's talking about it, but not many people believe it's true. So tell me—what happened? *(SAUL and BARNABAS exit.)*

*(Later, in PETER's house. PETER is talking with the OTHER APOSTLES and ZACHARIAS.)*

**PETER:** We've all heard stories about Saul—

**ZACHARIAS:** Did you hear the one about Saul almost catching me? Amos and I escaped just before he jumped in the air and—

**PETER:** I MEANT the stories about his becoming a follower of Jesus.

**ZACHARIAS:** You can't believe Saul! It's a TRAP!

**PETER:** It might be a trap. Or it might be true. I wish I knew what to think. *(Knock on the door. PETER opens the door. BARNABAS and SAUL enter.)*

**BARNABAS:** Hi, Peter! Hi guys! I'd like you to meet Saul of Tarsus.

**ZACHARIAS:** It's him! It's a TRAP! We're doomed!

**PETER:** Calm down, Zacharias! I don't know if we can trust Saul, but we know that we can trust Barnabas.

**BARNABAS:** I do trust Saul. He WAS going to Damascus to arrest our friends. But on the way, Jesus spoke to him. Jesus told him to stop causing trouble. I'm convinced that Saul is telling the truth. In Damascus, he's been preaching about Jesus. And he really knows what he's talking about!

**PETER:** *(Thoughtfully.)* Hmm. You make a good case. *(To OTHER APOSTLES.)* What do you think? Should we trust him?

**OTHER APOSTLES and ZACHARIAS:** *(Mumbling negative responses among themselves.)* No way! I don't know. I don't trust him. He looks suspicious to me. Nah!

**SAUL:** *(Desperate.)* Wait! Please—won't you forgive me? Jesus forgave me for all the wrong things I did. Now I want everyone to know that He'll forgive them, too, if they ask.

**BARNABAS:** *(Persuading apostles.)* I believe that Saul loves Jesus, just like we do. I vote we give him a chance to prove himself!

**OTHER APOSTLES:** *(Mumbling among themselves, and then, all together)* Yes!

**PETER:** Well, it's agreed then! Any friend of Jesus is a friend of ours!

For the **real story** read Acts 9:32-43

# Good News, Bad News

**Characters: SIMON,** a Bible-times man; **HIRAM,** a Bible-times man

**Scene:** *A port city near the town of Lydda. HIRAM and SIMON pass each other on the street.*

**HIRAM:** Simon! Simon! I've got news from Lydda!

**SIMON:** *(Groans.)* How long will this take? I don't have all day for one of your LONG stories.

**HIRAM:** Oh no, this is a quick story. I have good news and bad news.

**SIMON:** OK. What's the news?

**HIRAM:** Well, you know the difficulties the widows and orphans have.

**SIMON:** Yes. It's a terrible shame. They are left with no one to take care of them. It's just awful. Is that your news?

**HIRAM:** Oh no. See, there's a woman there; her name is Dorcas. She's been making clothing for the poor and the widows.

**SIMON:** Well, that is wonderful news. Thanks for sharing. *(Turns to go.)*

**HIRAM:** Oh no, there's more. You see, she's a follower of Jesus. Dorcas lives just the way Jesus wants people to—loving their neighbors and stuff.

**SIMON:** Sounds like a wonderful person. I'd like to meet her sometime.

**HIRAM:** She died.

**SIMON:** Well, that's terrible news! I'm sure there were many mourners at her funeral.

**HIRAM:** Oh yes, there would have been, but she didn't have a funeral.

**SIMON:** No funeral? What did they do?

**HIRAM:** The women dressed her in clean clothes and put her in an upper room of the house. And then they sent for Peter.

**SIMON:** Peter? Peter who?

**HIRAM:** He was one of Jesus' disciples, able to heal people.

**SIMON:** By his own power?

**HIRAM:** Oh no. It's God's power.

**SIMON:** But how does—? Wait! Never mind. You say this Peter was in town when Dorcas died?

**HIRAM:** Oh no. Peter was in the town of Joppa, about 12 miles away.

**SIMON:** Ah. So I suppose that's why Dorcas died. Peter couldn't get there in time.

**HIRAM:** Oh no. They didn't even send for Peter until after Dorcas had died.

**SIMON:** But that was too late.

**HIRAM:** Oh no. Peter got there before the burial.

**SIMON:** I thought you said there wasn't a burial.

**HIRAM:** There wasn't. You see, when Peter got to Lydda, the widows showed Peter all the wonderful clothes Dorcas had made for them.

**SIMON:** Why?

**HIRAM:** They wanted Peter to know what a wonderful person Dorcas was, and how much they needed her, I guess.

**SIMON:** Then they decided not to bury her? I don't understand.

**HIRAM:** Well, Peter made everyone leave the room where Dorcas was.

**SIMON:** THAT I can understand. Not to be insensitive, but dead bodies do begin to smell, you know. I never have understood how mourners can stand being in the same room.

**HIRAM:** Me neither. Anyway, Peter knelt down by Dorcas's bed and prayed. Then he said, "Tabitha, get up."

**SIMON:** Why'd he call her Tabitha?

**HIRAM:** That's her other name. It means the same as "Dorcas."

**SIMON:** OK. So what did Peter expect would happen when he told Dorcas to get up?

**HIRAM:** I don't know what he expected, but Dorcas sat up.

**SIMON:** I thought you said she was dead.

**HIRAM:** Yeah, well, she was, but she isn't any more.

**SIMON:** She's alive again?

**HIRAM:** Yep!

**SIMON:** Hiram! This is incredible news! Who did you say she was a follower of?

**HIRAM:** Jesus.

**SIMON:** I've got to find out more about Him. I mean, teaching people to care about each other, and then raising them from the dead! Wow! Why didn't you tell me all this in the first place?

**HIRAM:** Didn't want to ruin the rest of the story by telling the ending first.

**For the real story read Acts 10:1—11:18**

# Tough Case

**Characters: JUDGE; PETER; BAILIFF; PROSECUTOR; LAWYER; CORNELIUS**

**Props:** Characters may wish to pantomime the use of props.

**Scene:** *Bailiff stands to one side of the room.*

**BAILIFF:** Criminal court now in session. The honorable Judge Hangemhigh presiding. All rise.

*(Have class stand as JUDGE enters with gavel and sits in chair.)*

**JUDGE:** Be seated, *(Bangs gavel on table.)* I love that. Call the first case.

**BAILIFF:** The people versus Peter. Attempting to bribe a Roman official.

*(PETER, DEFENSE LAWYER and PROSECUTOR enter and stand before the JUDGE.)*

**JUDGE:** How do you plead?

**LAWYER:** Not guilty, Your Honor.

**JUDGE:** Mr. Prosecutor, you may begin.

**PROSECUTOR:** Yes, Your Honor. At ten o'clock A.M. on the 15th of the month, the defendant was seen entering the prem-

ises of Cornelius, a Roman centurion. Since Cornelius is a Roman officer and the defendant is Jewish, bribery is the obvious conclusion.

**LAWYER:** My client was there on a social visit, Your Honor, at Cornelius's request.

**PROSECUTOR:** *(Sarcastically.)* Oh, right! Like a Jew would pay a social visit to a Gentile!

**JUDGE:** Very good point, counselor. The Jews are well known for their rules against associating with Gentiles. What about it, Pete?

**PETER:** It's true I was taught that God only loved the Jews. But I learned that is wrong.

**JUDGE:** Continue.

**PETER:** I was in Joppa visiting my friend Simon the tanner. About noon, I was on the roof, praying. I was hungry, but lunch wasn't ready. While I was waiting, I saw a vision. A large sheet containing various animals, birds and reptiles came down from heaven. A voice said, "Take. Kill and eat."

**JUDGE:** I bet they all looked good, since lunch was late.

**PETER:** NO, Your Honor. They were all unclean.

**JUDGE:** Well, haven't you heard of water? You could have washed them.

**LAWYER:** My client refers to the well-known Jewish custom of designating some animals clean and others unclean. They are forbidden to eat unclean animals.

**JUDGE:** I knew that. Continue.

**PETER:** I protested. I said, "I would never eat anything unclean." Then the voice said, "Don't call unclean the things I have made clean." This happened three times.

**JUDGE:** You take a lot of convincing. So you ate something?

**PETER:** No, it was just a vision. While I was trying to understand it, God told me there were men waiting for me downstairs and to go with them.

**JUDGE:** And these men were?

**PETER:** Servants of Cornelius. They told me Cornelius wanted to speak with me. Suddenly, I understood the vision. God was telling me the Gentiles are not unclean. So the next day, I went with them to Caesarea.

**JUDGE:** And that's when and where you tried to bribe Cornelius?

**PETER:** I never tried to bribe him. I went to speak to him about Jesus, because now I know God's love is for everyone—even Gentiles like Cornelius.

**LAWYER:** Your Honor, we submit there is no evidence of bribery and ask for dismissal of all charges.

**PROSECUTOR:** No evidence? A Jew in a Gentile's home and you say no evidence?

**JUDGE:** Yes, that does seem suspicious.

**LAWYER:** Then the defense calls Cornelius.

(CORNELIUS *approaches* JUDGE's *table.*)

**BAILIFF:** Do you swear that the testimony you are about to give is true, so help you Caesar?

**CORNELIUS:** I do.

**LAWYER:** Please state your name and occupation for the record.

**CORNELIUS:** My name is Cornelius. I am a centurion in the Roman Army.

**LAWYER:** Cornelius, would you please tell us what happened on the days in question.

**CORNELIUS:** I was in my house praying to the God of Israel. I have been stationed in Caesarea many years and I know that Israel's God is the only true God.

**PROSECUTOR:** Throw the book at him! He can't say that!

**JUDGE:** Actually, he can. According to Roman law he can believe in any god. Continue.

**CORNELIUS:** I had a vision. In my vision, an angel told me God had heard my prayers and seen my gifts to the poor. Then he told me to send men to the house of Simon the tanner in Joppa and ask for a man named Peter.

**PROSECUTOR:** (*Sarcastically.*) Oh, please!

**JUDGE:** No more outbursts, Mr. Prosecutor! (*Bangs gavel.*) I love that! Continue.

**CORNELIUS:** Peter came to my house and told me about a man named Jesus, who was sent by God. His enemies killed Him, but God brought him back to life to forgive our sins. When we heard this good news, we believed Jesus was God's Son and were baptized and became followers of Jesus.

**LAWYER:** No further questions.

**JUDGE:** Mr. Prosecutor?

**PROSECUTOR:** (*Meekly.*) No questions.

**LAWYER:** We submit there is no evidence of bribery and ask for dismissal of all charges.

**JUDGE:** I have to agree with the defense. Case dismissed. (*Bangs gavel.*) Love it.

**PETER:** (*To* LAWYER.) Thank you for your brilliant defense.

**LAWYER:** This was easy, convincing a Roman court. Now for the hard part—convincing your friends that God's plan includes the Gentiles. Tough case!

For the **real story** read Acts 12:1-17

# Look Up!

**Characters: MARY; BELIEVER 1; BELIEVER 2; BELIEVER 3; RHODA; PETER**

**Props:** Characters may wish to pantomime the use of props.

**Scene:** MARY, BELIEVERS and RHODA are on their knees, praying.

**MARY:** Oh, Lord, we beg You to keep watch over Peter in prison. We pray that You will take charge of this awful problem.

**BELIEVER 1:** We beg that You will not allow Herod to do to Peter what he did to James.

**BELIEVER 2:** Yes, Lord. Do not allow Herod to execute Peter.

**BELIEVER 3:** But if he does, let it be quick and painless.

**MARY:** But mostly keep him safe and comfortable. Don't let his shackles hurt him.

**BELIEVER 1:** And don't let the guards keep him awake all night.

**BELIEVER 2:** And don't let other prisoners' groans of agony keep him awake all night.

**BELIEVER 3:** And don't let him brood on the sorry fate that will befall him in the morning.

*(Loud knocking.)*

**MARY:** Who's knocking at the door? We're trying to pray. Rhoda, get the door!

*(RHODA exits.)*

**MARY:** Now then, let's continue. Oh Lord, we know You are all powerful and are in control of all things, so please keep Peter safe. Rescue him from evil King Herod.

*(RHODA screams in surprise offstage.)*

**MARY:** Now what in the world—

*(RHODA enters, running.)*

**RHODA:** Mary! Mary! Mary!

**MARY:** What is the matter with you, girl? Can't you se we're praying? Quiet down!

**RHODA:** But...but...but...

**MARY:** Stop stuttering and go about your chores if you're not going to pray with us.

**RHODA:** But...it's Peter!

**MARY:** Yes. We're all sad about Peter. But we'll keep praying.

**BELIEVER 1:** We will continue to ask God to protect Peter.

**BELIEVER 2:** We will ask that no evil befall him.

**BELIEVER 3:** Or, if it does, that it ends quickly.

**RHODA:** No! No! Peter's at the door!

**MARY:** What are you talking about? Peter's in prison. We're praying for his safety right now.

**RHODA:** No, he's not! He spoke to me. I recognized his voice.

**MARY:** Nonsense! You're just a silly girl. If he were here, he would come in.

**RHODA:** Oh! I forgot to let him in! *(Runs out.)*

**MARY:** I don't know why I put up with that girl. She's always imagining things.

**PETER:** Friends!

**MARY:** Peter! You're here! But you're in prison! I mean, you're supposed to be in prison. No, no. I don't mean you're supposed to be there. I mean...Herod arrested you!

**PETER:** Be of good cheer. God heard your prayers and answered them.

**MARY:** But how? I mean—

**BELIEVER 1:** Who? That is—

**BELIEVER 2:** Where? Or rather—

**BELIEVER 3:** What? Or should I say—

**RHODA:** How did you get away? Who saved you? Where are you going? What happened?

**PETER:** I'll tell you all about it. Of course, you know Herod had me arrested.

**BELIEVER 1:** It was terrible news!

**BELIEVER 2:** We heard that you were to be executed tomorrow.

**BELIEVER 3:** But I guess that's not true, because Herod released you tonight.

**PETER:** Herod didn't let me go. I've escaped!

**MARY:** But, how?

**BELIEVER 1:** Who?

**BELIEVER 2:** Where?

**BELIEVER 3:** What?

**RHODA:** How did you get away? Who saved you? Where are you going? What happened?

**PETER:** There I was in prison, chained between two soldiers, bound with two chains. And two guards stood at the entrance.

**BELIEVER 2:** They weren't taking any chances, were they?

**PETER:** Even in those uncomfortable circumstances, I was able to sleep! I'm sure your prayers helped me.

**BELIEVER 3:** Always happy to do our part.

**PETER:** Suddenly, there was a bright light in the cell and a stranger appeared.

**MARY:** Another prisoner?

**PETER:** He said, "Quick, get up."

**RHODA:** But you were in chains. How could you get up?

**PETER:** The locks opened and the chains fell away!

**MARY:** It must have been a kind jailer who unlocked you. But how did you get past the Roman guard?

**PETER:** How? I thought I was dreaming, because I wrapped my cloak around me and we walked right past the guards—both of them.

**BELIEVER 3:** What about the gate leading to the city? Wasn't it locked?

**PETER:** It was. But as we approached it, it opened by itself! We walked down one street and suddenly, I was alone. Then I realized— I wasn't dreaming!

**MARY:** But who was this stranger?

**PETER:** Now I know that it was an angel. There's no other explanation. God heard your prayers and sent His angel to rescue me. Now I must go. You're not safe if I'm here. After I've gone, send someone to tell the other believers. (PETER *exits.*)

**MARY:** Rhoda! Do as Peter says. Hurry and tell the others that he's free. (RHODA *exits.*)

**BELIEVER 1:** Our prayers worked.

**BELIEVER 2:** God answered.

**BELIEVER 3:** Of course, we knew He would. No question about it.

# Visitors to Lystra

**Characters: HERMIA,** a Greek woman, wife of Homer; **HOMER,** a Greek man, husband of Hermia; **JULIUS,** a friend of Homer and Hermia; **ABNER,** a Jewish merchant recently from Antioch

**Scene:** *A street in Lystra. HOMER enters, running. HERMIA slowly follows him.*

**HERMIA:** *(Out of breath.)* Whoa! Stop! *(Sits down.)* Explain to me again why we are running off to the temple.

**HOMER:** To get the priests of Zeus! You saw what happened! Hermes healed that crippled man!

**HERMIA:** Yeah, but that guy you call Hermes said his name was Paul.

**HOMER:** Don't you remember the story of how the gods Hermes and Zeus came to our town once before disguised as humans? They killed everyone who didn't recognize them!

**HERMIA:** Well, all I'm saying is that before I

run all over town announcing the arrival of Hermes and Zeus, I want to make sure I'm not going to look like a fool later!

**JULIUS:** *(Entering.)* What's all the excitement in town?

**HOMER:** Hermes and Zeus have come to visit!

**JULIUS:** Who?

**HOMER:** Zeus, the greatest of the gods, and his messenger, Hermes!

**JULIUS:** How do you know it's Zeus?

**HOMER:** We saw Hermes heal a crippled man!

**JULIUS:** Really? So you say there were two men?

**HOMER:** Yes, but only one of them did all the talking.

**HERMIA:** And HE said his name was PAUL.

**HOMER:** But it's really Hermes in disguise.

**JULIUS:** Have the priests been told?

**HOMER:** We were on our way there right now.

**HERMIA:** I still think that before we all make fools of ourselves, we should KNOW what we're talking about. That Paul didn't say anything about Zeus. He was talking about someone named Jesus.

**HOMER:** Probably just poor pronunciation. "Jesus," "Zeus"—they're similar sounding.

**HERMIA:** They are NOT similar sounding at all. And why would Hermes, the god of communication, not speak clearly?

**HOMER:** To make a better disguise!

**HERMIA:** Augh! *(HERMIA gets up to stomp away and bumps into ABNER.)*

**ABNER:** Whoa! Where are you going in such a huff?

**HERMIA:** These fools believe that the two men who just arrived in the town are Zeus and Hermes.

**ABNER:** What two men?

**HERMIA:** Some guy named Paul, and I think the other guy's name was Barnabas.

**JULIUS:** I thought you said his name was Jesus.

**HERMIA:** No, no. I said Paul was talking about Jesus.

**ABNER:** I know of this Paul. He's a dangerous man!

**JULIUS:** Dangerous?

**HOMER:** I told you! See, they ARE Zeus and Hermes! And they kill those who don't recognize them, right?

**ABNER:** No. These men aren't gods. But they ARE dangerous! They spread lies about this Jesus—a man who was executed as a CRIMINAL. They say He's raised from the dead and is the Son of the ONLY God. Trouble follows them wherever they go!

**JULIUS:** Really? What kind of trouble?

**HOMER:** Trouble is trouble! These men must be stopped!

**HERMIA:** Now hold everything. How can talking about someone be dangerous? And why would dangerous men take the time to heal someone?

**ABNER:** Do you want your children to hear these lies? What if they believed these men?

**HOMER:** Yes, we must protect our children!

**HERMIA:** We don't have any children.

**HOMER:** *(Ignores HERMIA.)* Our children might not recognize Zeus and Hermes when they visit! That would be awful!

**HERMIA:** YOU don't even seem to be able to recognize when it's NOT Zeus and Hermes!

**ABNER:** *(To HOMER.)* And what about your wives?

**HOMER:** Yes! Yes! We must protect our wives!

**HERMIA:** From what? A man's speeches? Or maybe you're worried we might be healed!

**ABNER:** Their teachings will anger the leaders of Rome—then what will happen to your families and town?

**HOMER:** Yes! We must protect our families! We must protect our town!

**JULIUS:** These men ARE dangerous! We must rid our town of them immediately!

**HOMER:** We must warn everyone! Come on, Hermia! Hurry! *(Exits running with JULIUS and ABNER.)*

**HERMIA:** Oh! That man NEVER listens to me! I just know we're going to look like fools! *(Runs after HOMER.)* Wait for me! Why does everything have to be done in such a hurry?

For the **real story** read Acts 16—18:11

# News Night

## Characters: NICO; TABITHA; MYRNA; MARCUS

**Props:** Characters may wish to pantomime the use of props.

**Scene:** *News Night Broadcasting Studio.*

**NICO:** *(Speaking as if to a camera.)* Good evening! This is NewsNight and I'm your host, Nico. It's time for Tabitha's Top-Ten Teens. That's the part of our show when our reporter Tabitha interviews today's most talented teenagers. Take it away, Tabitha!

**TABITHA:** Thanks, Nico! I'm in Lystra to interview Timothy, today's Top-Ten Teen, but apparently he's left town! We've learned that Tim took off with two troublemakers. This is a terrible, terrible turn!

**NICO:** Two troublemakers?

**TABITHA:** Paul and Silas. You'll remember Paul, formerly known as Saul, from our feature stories "Danger in Damascus" and "Jumpin' Jerusalem." Recently, Paul and his friend Silas have been traveling from town to town, talking about Jesus.

**NICO:** And what does that have to do with Top-Ten Timothy?

**TABITHA:** It turns out Timothy's a follower of Jesus, too! Now Tim travels with them, helping them teach and tell total strangers that Jesus is the Son of God. *(Sadly.)* And now my touching tribute to terrific teenagers is totally trashed!

**NICO:** *(Shaking his head.)* Tragic. *(To camera, cheerfully.)* And now let's hear what's happening in the Macedonian music scene. Our music reporter, Myrna, is in Philippi with news of an exciting new band known as the Jailbirds. Myrna?

**MYRNA:** Well, Nico, there's a bit of a snag. The band was really just a couple of guys who were in jail.

**NICO:** So who's their lead singer?

**MYRNA:** There are two guys, Paul and Silas. They say God sent Paul a dream to tell them to come to Macedonia. So they came here and started telling people that God loves them and that He sent His Son, Jesus, so they could be forgiven.

**NICO:** So how did they end up in jail?

**MYRNA:** Some people got angry with Paul and Silas and had them beaten up and thrown in jail, even though they did nothing wrong. That's when the singing started.

**NICO:** I hear their music really brought the house down!

**MYRNA:** Um...sort of. They were singing songs to praise God. Then around midnight, a big earthquake shook apart the whole jail!

**NICO:** So did the band take off to start their world tour?

**MYRNA:** No. Paul and Silas told the jailer about Jesus. The jailer was so interested; he brought them to his home. Now he and his whole family are followers of Jesus.

**NICO:** So where does the band play next?

**MYRNA:** They go wherever God tells them. Amphipolis, Apollonia, Thessolonica. They were in Berea for a couple of days, until some men from another town tried to start a riot. I lost track of them after that. But it's not really a band, Nico.

**NICO:** *(To camera, seriously.)* You heard it here first, folks: It's not really a band. *(Cheerfully.)* Now let's go live to our reporter, Marcus, at the scene of breaking news in Athens, Greece. Marcus?

**MARCUS:** Nico, it all started when two strangers, Paul and Silas, saw the statues of our dozens and dozens of gods. I'm here at the statue of an unknown god. That's the statue we made just in case there was some god that we had forgotten about.

**NICO:** Astonishing, Marcus! And what does Paul say this one true God is made out of? Bronze? Silver? Gold?

**MARCUS:** Nico, I think he's saying that the one true God can't be made out of any kind of metal.

**NICO:** So this God is made of stone.

**MARCUS:** No! We can't make Him out of anything. The one true God made the whole world—and all of us, too. He made us—we don't make Him.

**NICO:** So how are people reacting to these amazing developments?

**MARCUS:** It's mixed. Some people are hassling Paul. But some are asking to know more about this one true God.

**NICO:** *(To camera.)* Well, we're about out of time. But to recap tonight's startling events: Top-Ten Teen Tim left town with Paul and Silas, Macedonian music makes a mess, and Athenian altars aren't adequate for the one true God. Good news, and good night!

For the **real deal** read Acts 17:16-34

# Speaking the Language

### Characters: KEITH; KIM

**Props:** Characters may wish to pantomime the use of props.

**KEITH:** *(Standing in front of a mirror, practicing different ways of speaking.)* "Howdy, pard! Been cuttin' cattle for long?"

**KIM:** Keith, what on earth are you doing?

**KEITH:** Practicing.

**KIM:** Practicing what?

**KEITH:** Speaking the language! "Saddle yer paint!" You gotta know the lingo.

**KIM:** Why?

**KEITH:** So I can tell them barrel ridin' muscaleros about the Big Pardner in the Sky!

**KIM:** Keith, you don't make any sense.

**KEITH:** Look, I want to talk about Jesus to rodeo cowboys.

**KIM:** And you think making fun of the way they speak is going to help you?

**KEITH:** No! We learned at church that you've got to RESPECT the ways of other people in order to talk to them about Jesus.

**KIM:** And imitating them is showing respect? You might just make them mad!

**KEITH:** Yeah, but look! I have the right clothes, too. Check out this bolo tie!

**KIM:** You DON'T look like a cowboy. You look ridiculous! Be yourself!

**KEITH:** Not on your saddle horn! Then they wouldn't pay ANY attention to me!

**KIM:** Look, Keith, people who ride the rodeo or work ranches for a living are really no different from you and me. They just have different problems.

**KEITH:** So spit it out. What's the burr under your saddle, pardner?

**KIM:** Maybe you should find out what they believe, first. Get to know them!

**KEITH:** Why? We're talkin' about a dangerous bunch here!

**KIM:** What? For example?

**KEITH:** Well, they shoot people and chase down innocent natives and...

**KIM:** Whoa, pardner! How many cowboys do you know very well?

**KEITH:** Listen, Kim! I've watched every cowboy movie ever made!

**KIM:** So maybe you only know the MOVIE version of who cowboys are. You need to know real people!

**KEITH:** How can hanging around with a bunch of gunslingers help me?

**KIM:** Get real, Keith. Why do you think people carry guns, anyway?

**KEITH:** To feel safe! It's dangerous on the range! Shoot or be shot!

**KIM:** So why not tell them that they don't have to be afraid?!

**KEITH:** Like they're going to believe that from a greenhorn city slicker!

**KIM:** They might, if they KNEW you! Then maybe they'd listen if you tell them that God is always on the side of the ones who ride with Him.

**KEITH:** Watch your talk, there! People won't like you saying God has a horse!

**KIM:** Keith, LISTEN! It's just a figure of speech. When Paul talked to the Greeks, he told them about Jesus in a way they could UNDERSTAND.

**KEITH:** I don't see any connection between Greeks and cowpunchers.

**KIM:** My point exactly! Until you KNOW them, you can't make ANY connection! Look, let's start at the beginning. You want to tell people about Jesus...

**KEITH:** Absolutely!

**KIM:** ...and how He died to take the punishment for our sins...

**KEITH:** You got that right!

**KIM:** ...and how He wants us to be members of His family.

**KEITH:** Yup, that's what I want to do! Pass me that lariat, will ya?

**KIM:** But you've got to tell them in a way they'll understand, speak their language!

**KEITH:** That's what I was trying to DO!

**KIM:** No, no! It's more than words! First, you've got to understand what's important to them.

**KEITH:** So like saying being a part of God's family is like riding with God as the trail boss because there's always Someone there to help you?

**KIM:** That's right, buckaroo.

**KEITH:** And saying that you don't HAVE to get even with others because Jesus took EVERYONE'S punishment?

**KIM:** NOW you're talking!

**KEITH:** Awright! Hey! How about if I just wear this hat? Ten gallons! Too cool, huh? Yee-haaa!

**KIM:** *(Groans.)*

For the **real story** read Acts 27

# Stormy Seas

**Characters: JULIUS,** a Roman in charge of prisoners headed for Rome; **CAPTAIN,** a sailor of the seas most of his life; **PAUL,** an apostle of Christ and a prisoner

**Scene One:** *The deck of a Bible-times ship docked in Fair Havens and headed for Rome.*

**JULIUS:** Will we soon be ready to sail, Captain?

**CAPTAIN:** Aye, soon enough. Ship's nearly loaded.

**PAUL:** Julius, I think it would be best to wait.

**CAPTAIN:** Oh? And would you be a sailor?

**PAUL:** No, I am a tentmaker. But I have traveled a lot.

**CAPTAIN:** No doubt you have great wisdom of the ways of the sea. Forbid it that I, a mere sea captain, should know as much as yourself.

**JULIUS:** Why do you think it unwise to sail, Paul?

**PAUL:** This voyage will be perilous. I think there will be danger and damage, not only to the ship and cargo, but also to everyone aboard.

**CAPTAIN:** Late in the season it might be, but I've sailed worse seas and am alive to tell my adventures. Of course, I can understand how one having to face trial in Rome might want to put off his arrival!

**PAUL:** I am not afraid of what might await me in Rome. But this voyage is ill-advised.

**CAPTAIN:** The poor tentmaker isn't afraid of Rome? Then he's a fool. But, sail we must. This is no place to winter a ship. If you're afraid to sail for Rome, then we will sail by way of Phoenix.

**JULIUS:** Paul, you know I respect your opinion. But I must believe that the captain knows his business. We'll sail to Phoenix and from there we'll decide whether or not to continue to Rome.

**CAPTAIN:** There's a man who knows how to be a leader. That's why he's a centurion. Tentmakers! Pah!

**JULIUS:** All right, men! Load the prisoners on board!

**Scene Two:** *The deck of the same ship, now at sea.*

**CAPTAIN:** *(Sees* PAUL *walking on deck.)* Oh, they let prisoners have their free roam of the ship, do they?

**PAUL:** Julius knows I have no intention of escaping.

**CAPTAIN:** Oh, you haven't noticed the gentle south breeze under which we're sailing, have you? Makes you fear for your life, don't it? A few more days, and we'll be in Phoenix, safe and sound.

**PAUL:** I don't want to alarm you, but hasn't the wind shifted direction? And isn't it blowing stronger?

**CAPTAIN:** Oh, I'm SO frightened. Ha! Haven't you seen the wind change before? Sometimes it swirls a bit. Sometimes it changes speed. But then, being a tentmaker, you must live all your life indoors. Wouldn't know about the wind, would you?

**PAUL:** I know you don't believe me. But the wind is considerably stronger and has shifted direction.

**CAPTAIN:** Hmph! C'mon sailors. Look alive! Let's show these landlubbers how real men face the weather.

**Scene Three:** *The deck of the same ship two weeks later.*

**JULIUS:** Captain, we've been tossed about in this storm for days without seeing the sun or the stars. Have you any idea where we are?

**CAPTAIN:** Aye. We're in the middle of the Great Sea in a tempest. And we're headed for destruction, every man of us. Make your peace with your god.

**PAUL:** Gentlemen, I hate to say I told you so...

**JULIUS:** But you told us so. Paul, before we all perish, let me say it has truly been a pleasure to know you.

**PAUL:** Thank you, Julius. But do not fear. All is not lost. True, the ship and its cargo have been damaged, but no man aboard shall lose his life.

**CAPTAIN:** So you're a fortune-teller now?

**PAUL:** No. But this very night, an angel of the God I serve stood before me and told me not to be afraid. He told me that God will spare everyone on this ship. I believe God. However, before we're through, we'll be cast ashore on an island.

**CAPTAIN:** Well, excuse me for livin', but I'll believe the wisdom of the sea. Not your angels.

**JULIUS:** Paul, you've shown much wisdom in the past. I believe you. Can we make it to the island?

**CAPTAIN:** Ha! There's rocks all about and it's the middle of the night. Throw four anchors from the stern! We'll sail tomorrow in daylight! And we'll want to be setting anchors in the fore. Let down the boat!

**PAUL:** *(Whispers to JULIUS.)* Julius, the captain is not planning to use the small boat to set anchors in the fore of the ship. He and the crew are planning to abandon the ship. If they do not stay with the ship, we'll all perish.

**JULIUS:** Paul, I failed to listen to you in the past and I regretted it. Soldiers, cut the ropes and let that boat fall into the sea.

**CAPTAIN:** Think you're smart, don't you, tentmaker! Now we will all die!

**PAUL:** Not likely, Captain. Not likely. Men! All of you—soldiers, sailors, prisoners—for 14 days we've battled the storm, and we haven't had time or the stomach to eat. Take food now and eat. You'll need all your strength in the morning.

**CAPTAIN:** Now that's the first decent idea you've had this trip!

**PAUL:** But first, let's give thanks to God.

**JULIUS:** Would you lead us in prayer to your God, Paul?

For the **real story** read Acts 28

# Homework

### Characters: LUCAS; DOMINIC; ALTHEA; CECILIA; BENEDICTUS

**Props:** Characters may wish to pantomime the use of props.

**Scene:** DOMINIC, ALTHEA *and* CECILIA *are sitting around a campfire.*

**LUCAS:** *(Entering.)* Mr. Dominic! Quick! Can you please tell me everything you know about Paul?

**DOMINIC:** So you have Mr. Benedictus's history class, do you? When's the report due?

**LUCAS:** *(Embarrassed.)* In the morning.

**ALTHEA:** TOMORROW morning? *(Scolding LUCAS.)* Back in my day, we started our homework much sooner.

**CECILIA:** You've come to the right place, Lucas. We remember Paul very well.

**DOMINIC:** Paul was here a long time ago, son. Before your father was even born. I was a boy not much older than you are now. And Paul was a prisoner aboard a ship that got blown here by a terrible storm.

**CECILIA:** We saw the ship go down off the coast. We were sure they'd all drown.

**ALTHEA:** Then they started coming to shore. One...two...three...Every last one of them survived—276 soggy sailors, soldiers, prisoners and passengers!

**DOMINIC:** They said that God—the God Paul served—had rescued them. I didn't know much about Paul's God at the time, but I would have been grateful, too, if God had rescued me from THAT storm!

**LUCAS:** So what did you do?

**DOMINIC:** Only thing we could do with 276 wet castaways on a cold night. We made a campfire. Paul helped put some wood on the fire. That's when it happened! All of a sudden, a poisonous snake jumped out! It bit right into Paul's hand and wouldn't let go.

**ALTHEA:** I was sure Paul had to be a murderer! I told everyone, "Only someone who had done terrible things would have so much trouble!" The sea didn't kill him, but the snakebite surely would!

**CECILIA:** Now, Althea. You know Paul wasn't a murderer.

**ALTHEA:** Well, he could have been!

**LUCAS:** What happened next? Did Paul die? Did he swell up and turn purple and go like this? *(Making gagging sounds.)*

**DOMINIC:** Paul calmly shook the snake into the fire. We waited. And we waited. But he didn't die. He didn't even get sick! People started saying Paul must be a god.

**CECILIA:** Later on, we learned there's only one true God. He's the One who protected Paul from that snake.

**DOMINIC:** Paul became quite a celebrity! Publius, the chief official of the whole island, invited Paul and his friends to stay in his home.

**ALTHEA:** I've lived on this island for 86 years, and not ONCE have I been invited to the chief official's house!

**DOMINIC:** Publius treated Paul as an honored guest. Good food. Entertainment. Everyone had a great time. Everyone except one person.

**ALTHEA:** I guess you mean me. I wasn't invited.

**CECILIA:** No, Althea. I believe he means Publius's father. *(To LUCAS.)* The poor man was so sick, he couldn't get out of bed.

**DOMINIC:** Paul went in to see him. He prayed that God would heal him. Then Paul placed his hands on him. Suddenly, Publius's father felt better. He was healed!

**CECILIA:** After that, sick people came from all over the island. You might expect Paul to have gotten sick of sick people! But he prayed, and every one of them was healed.

**ALTHEA:** Well, he sure didn't heal me!

**CECILIA:** But you weren't sick, Althea.

**ALTHEA:** Well, I could have been! *(To LUCAS.)* I thought those castaways would never leave! I always say, houseguests are like fish: After three days, they start to stink!

**CECILIA:** Everyone was happy to have them here. *(Looking at ALTHEA.)* ALMOST everyone.

**ALTHEA:** I figured Paul wanted to stay on the island instead of going to Rome to face a trial in front of Caesar, the ruler of the whole Roman empire!

**DOMINIC:** But Paul seemed excited to go to Rome. He said he'd been trying to go to Rome for years. He felt badly that most people there didn't know about Jesus.

**CECILIA:** Then one day the weather was better for sailing. It was time for Paul to leave. We gave him and his friends all the supplies they'd need, wished them a safe trip and—

**BENEDICTUS:** *(Entering.)* Good evening, folks! Out kind of late, aren't you, Lucas?

**LUCAS:** Mr. Benedictus! I was just, um...

**BENEDICTUS:** Have you finished your report on Barnabas?

**LUCAS:** Barnabas? I thought it was on Paul!

**BENEDICTUS:** That was last week. I'll see you—and your Barnabas report—in the morning!

*(BENEDICTUS leaves.)*

**LUCAS:** Mr. Dominic! Quick! Tell me everything you know about Barnabas!

**For the real story read 1 Corinthians 13:4**

# You've Got to Be Kidding!

**Characters: ANDY,** a sixth-grade student; **FRIENDS 1-4,** friends of Andy; **KATIE,** a first-grade student, and Andy's sister; **MOM; AUDIENCE**

**Props:** Characters may wish to pantomime the use of props.

**Scene:** ANDY's room. ANDY is sitting on bed, reading Bible.

**ANDY:** (Looks up at AUDIENCE.) There's one thing I can tell you: Whoever wrote 1 Corinthians 13:4 didn't have a sister like Katie. Let me show you what I mean. (ANDY gets up and walks over to FRIENDS 1 and 2.) Take the first day of school. Where we live, the elementary school and middle school are at the same place.

**FRIEND 1:** Hey, Andy! Isn't this great?! We're finally middle-school students!

**FRIEND 2:** Yeah, no more hanging out with the little elementary kids! And we've got the same first class together! Let's go check it out!

**ANDY:** (Looking over his shoulder.) Yeah, great.

**FRIEND 1:** Is something wrong?

**ANDY:** I'm looking for Katie. Mom told me to make sure she got to her class OK.

**FRIEND 2:** Where is she?

**ANDY:** I don't know. We got off the bus together and I told her we were going over to meet you guys. She NEVER listens to me.

**FRIEND 1:** Isn't that her over there crying?

**ANDY:** Oh, great! She'll go home and tell Mom it's all my fault. She's such a pain. I'd better go get her. (ANDY turns back to AUDIENCE.) See what I mean? The biggest day of my life, and Katie messes it up. "Love is patient." How can you be patient with THAT? (Walks over to FRIENDS 3 and 4.) It's even worse at church.

**FRIEND 3:** I'm on my way to try out for the church play. How about you, Andy?

**ANDY:** Absolutely! Think I could get the main role?

**FRIEND 4:** Not if I have anything to say about it.

**ANDY:** Oh yeah? We'll just see about that.

**KATIE:** (Entering.) Andy, can you help me tie my shoe?

**ANDY:** Katie, why can't you tie your own shoe?

**KATIE:** I try, but it keeps coming untied.

**FRIEND 3:** Come on, Andy. Mrs. Matters doesn't take ANY excuses for not being on time.

**FRIEND 4:** Yeah. You won't even have a chance at the lead. That will leave it to ME! (FRIENDS 3 and 4 exit.)

**ANDY:** Katie, this is really important to me. Can't you ask someone else to tie your shoe?

**KATIE:** *(Crying.)* Everyone makes fun of me when I can't tie my shoe.

**ANDY:** OK, Katie. Come with me. I'll tie it at rehearsal.

**KATIE:** *(In a loud wail.)* NO! I want it tied now!

**ANDY:** *(Looks at watch.)* Great! It's too late now anyway. *(Turns to tie KATIE's shoe. KATIE giggles and runs away.)* KATIE!!! *(Turns to AUDIENCE.)* Now I ask you, could you be KIND in a situation like that? *(Walks over to MOM.)* And then today I got asked to go to this great new skate park. But we needed my mom to pick us up.

**ANDY:** So, may I go?

**MOM:** Sorry, dear. Katie's going on a zoo field trip today, and I promised I'd drive.

**ANDY:** But she went to the zoo last month, too.

**MOM:** Last month was with the after-school program. This is her Fly-Up Girls group.

**ANDY:** But it's not fair!

**MOM:** Sorry, honey. Maybe tomorrow. Oh, dear. That won't work, either. Katie's got that birthday party to go to. Well, I'm sure we'll get it in sometime. *(Exits.)*

**ANDY:** Groan! *(Turns to AUDIENCE.)* Wouldn't you be envious, too? *(Goes back and sits on bed.)* So here I am, trying to catch up on my Bible reading. "Love is patient, love is kind." Not with Katie!

**KATIE:** *(Enters with a rubber snake.)* Andy! Andy! Look at this great rubber snake I got at the zoo!

**ANDY:** *(To AUDIENCE.)* Now she's pestering me with a rubber snake!

**AUDIENCE:** "Love is patient."

**ANDY:** Patient. *(Turns to KATIE.)* That's great, Katie. Let me see it.

**KATIE:** Doesn't it look real? Isn't it cool?

**ANDY:** *(Looks at snake and then looks at AUDIENCE.)* How come she didn't buy me a souvenir?

**AUDIENCE:** "Love is kind. It does not envy."

**ANDY:** Kind. Doesn't envy. Great. *(Turns to KATIE.)* Yes, Katie, it's a very nice rubber snake.

**KATIE:** It's better than any of the zoo souvenirs you've got, isn't it? *(ANDY turns and looks helplessly at the AUDIENCE.)*

**AUDIENCE:** Love does "not boast, it is not proud."

**ANDY:** Great. *(Turns to KATIE.)* Yes, I think it's a great souvenir!

**KATIE:** *(KATIE hands snake to ANDY.)* That's why I wanted to get it for you.

**ANDY:** For me? Why?

**KATIE:** Because I love you.

**ANDY:** *(Turns to AUDIENCE.)* Well, maybe the writer of 1 Corinthians 13:4 DID have a sister like Katie.

For the **real story** read Ephesians 2:6-10

# Fringe Benefits

**Characters: DAYZ,** a representative of the Know-It-All Insurance Company; **WRIGHT,** the Membership Director of Heaven

**Scene:** WRIGHT's *office in the Corporate Headquarters for Heaven.*

**DAYZ:** *(Entering.)* You wanted to meet with me?

**WRIGHT:** Yes, I've received a request from our Boss to draw up a benefits plan for those who become members of our corporation.

**DAYZ:** Certainly. I'm an expert in all types of benefits*. Will you be including life insurance? People are very attracted by a good life insurance policy**.

**WRIGHT:** Yes.

**DAYZ:** Great! Now will you be offering a $50,000 policy or a $25,000 policy?

**WRIGHT:** What are you talking about?

**DAYZ:** Life insurance. When the person dies, how much will be paid to the deceased's relatives?

**WRIGHT:** *(Sighs.)* Not THAT kind of life insurance.

**DAYZ:** What kind of life insurance ARE you offering?

**WRIGHT:** Eternal life insurance. Members of our corporation will live forever.

**DAYZ:** They won't die? Great! Then we NEVER have to pay life insurance benefits!

**WRIGHT:** Oh no! Their bodies will wear out, but their spirits won't die.

**DAYZ:** I don't get it. What's a spirit?

**WRIGHT:** It's the part of us that doesn't need a physical body. It can exist forever.

**DAYZ:** But I should point out that if your members live forever, you're going to rack up huge costs in other benefits.

**WRIGHT:** Our Boss is willing to pay the price.

**DAYZ:** Uh-huh. So NO life insurance. But you're offering eternal life. Anything else?

**WRIGHT:** Yes, forgiveness for sins.

**DAYZ:** Excuse me?

**WRIGHT:** The Boss will forgive them for all the times they do wrong things and all the times they forget to do what He wants them to.

**DAYZ:** You can't attract good members with a policy like that! Why, ANYONE could apply!

**WRIGHT:** These benefits ARE for anyone. All they have to do is join the corporation.

*Benefits: Extras that businesses offer employees—vacation time, health insurance, dental plan, discounts to amusement parks and free parking. **Life Insurance: When a person dies, the insurance company gives his or her family a certain amount of money.

And the Boss wants EVERYONE to join His corporation.

**DAYZ:** EVERYONE? That's nuts! Can you imagine the problems? Who wants the riffraff?

**WRIGHT:** We do. Now, the Boss will always be available to listen to whatever the members want to talk to Him about.

**DAYZ:** How far in advance should they make an appointment?

**WRIGHT:** They don't need an appointment. Anytime, anyplace, He'll listen.

**DAYZ:** You're kidding! They'll all know His e-mail address? Have His home phone number?

**WRIGHT:** Something like that.

**DAYZ:** *(Whistles.)* He's going to be busy! Anything else?

**WRIGHT:** He will offer them assistance and support when they are in trouble.

**DAYZ:** Support? How? Are you talking about disability insurance***?

**WRIGHT:** You don't understand. When the members are in trouble, the Boss will be there for them. He'll give them comfort and help them know what to do.

**DAYZ:** Even if they're in trouble because of things they've done?

**WRIGHT:** Sure. It doesn't mean they'll never have to face the consequences for things they do, but He promises to be there to encourage them and help them do better. He'll take care of all their needs!

**DAYZ:** Food, clothing, stuff like that?

**WRIGHT:** Hm. Well, yes. But also their needs to be loved, to have a friend—

**DAYZ:** He's going to be their friend? *(WRIGHT nods head.)* I've NEVER heard of a benefit plan like this! But—He's the Boss! So how long is the waiting period before they can start receiving these benefits?

**WRIGHT:** No waiting period.

**DAYZ:** They join the corporation and they receive all these benefits, *(Snaps fingers.)* just like that?

**WRIGHT:** Absolutely!

**DAYZ:** That's crazy! There's no incentive to work hard.

**WRIGHT:** They don't have to work hard. They just need to love Him. They'll do what He wants them to do because they love Him.

**DAYZ:** Because they love Him. Yeah, right. Look, have you had your Boss checked out for, um, mental stability? I mean, these are weird benefits.

**WRIGHT:** Wouldn't you like to receive them?

**DAYZ:** Well, sure. Who wouldn't? But no one can offer eternal life, complete forgiveness for sins and help for everyone! It just isn't possible!

**WRIGHT:** It's possible for our Boss!

**DAYZ:** If you say so. I'll get this written up for you. But you'd better be prepared! When people hear about these benefits, they'll be joining by the millions!

---

***Disability Insurance: If you get injured and can't work, the insurance company pays you part of your salary.

For the **real deal** read Ephesians 4:29—5:1

# Rumors

**Characters: DIRECTOR; SARAH; MANNY; ANNE; BRIT; JASON; HEATHER; NITA**

**Scene:** *Rehearsal for a play.* SARAH, MANNY, ANNE, BRIT, JASON *and* HEATHER s*tand in order in a line.*

## ACT ONE

**DIRECTOR:** Okay, okay! Quiet everybody! Let's take it from the top!

**SARAH:** *(To* MANNY.*)* Did you hear that Nita stepped in a shell at the beach? It got stuck on her toe. They had to break it to get her toe out.

**MANNY:** Really? *(Turns to* ANNE.*)* Did you hear how Nita broke her toe at the beach?

**ANNE:** Broke her toe?

**MANNY:** Yeah, her foot got caught in this HUGE conch shell! They had to break it off to get her toe out.

**ANNE:** Oh, that must have hurt. *(Turns to* BRIT.*)* Have you heard about Nita's toe? Her leg got caught in something at the beach and they had to break it off to get her out. Now she sits around on a couch all day.

**BRIT:** How awful! *(Turns to* JASON.*)* Did you hear the awful news about Nita? She lost her leg at the beach the other day.

**JASON:** How?

**BRIT:** I'm not sure, but something at the beach caught hold of it and broke it off.

**JASON:** A shark?

**BRIT:** That's what I'm thinking.

**JASON:** She's lucky to be alive!

**HEATHER:** Who's lucky to be alive?

**JASON:** Nita. She was attacked by a shark!

**HEATHER:** Oh no! Is she okay?

**JASON:** She lost her leg. She's in the hospital fighting for her life, right now.

**HEATHER:** How awful!

**DIRECTOR:** I thought I asked for quiet! Nita's late, so Heather will you read her part?

**HEATHER:** Late? Haven't you heard? Nita was attacked by sharks. She's in the hospital right now, and she may die any second!

**NITA:** Hi guys, sorry I'm late.

**HEATHER:** Nita! Oh, I'm so thankful you're all right!

**NITA:** Why shouldn't I be?

**JASON:** Because you lost your leg.

**BRIT:** No, no, she lost her toe.

**DIRECTOR:** Weren't you attacked by sharks?

**NITA:** No! Where did everyone get these

strange ideas? (*Everyone points to* SARAH.)

## ACT TWO

**DIRECTOR:** All right, everyone's here. We can start our rehearsal now.

**NITA:** (*To* HEATHER.) I can't believe Sarah made up such a story about me. She's my best friend!

**HEATHER:** I don't blame you for being mad.

**NITA:** It's not that I'm mad....

**JASON:** Who's mad?

**HEATHER:** (*Turns to* JASON.) Nita's mad at Sarah for making up stories about her.

**JASON:** I don't blame her.

**BRIT:** You don't blame who for what?

**JASON:** (*Turns to* BRIT.) Nita for being furious with her former best friend, Sarah.

**BRIT:** Why?

**JASON:** Sarah's been telling stories about Nita everywhere.

**BRIT:** Oh, well I don't blame her either.

**ANNE:** You don't blame who for what?

**BRIT:** (*Turns to* ANNE.) I don't blame Nita for not wanting to be friends with Sarah anymore because Sarah's been telling lies about Nita.

**ANNE:** Really? Sarah always seemed so nice to me.

**MANNY:** What's this about Sarah?

**ANNE:** She's been telling horrible lies about Nita. Now Nita doesn't want to be her friend anymore.

**MANNY:** She doesn't want to be her friend anymore? Does Sarah know?

**SARAH:** Does Sarah know what?

**MANNY:** Well, I probably shouldn't be telling you this, but Nita said she's not your friend anymore because you tell lies.

**SARAH:** Tell lies! I don't tell lies! I'm glad she doesn't want to be my friend.

**DIRECTOR:** What is going on here? Sarah, what's wrong?

**SARAH:** Nita said I was a liar and that she didn't want to be my friend.

**NITA:** I never said that! I just didn't understand why Sarah told people I'd been attacked by a shark!

**SARAH:** I never said you were attacked by a shark. I was just telling Manny about how you got your toe stuck in a shell the other day.

**MANNY:** I thought you said she had to break her toe to get the shell off.

**SARAH:** No! I said they had to break the SHELL to get her TOE out!

**HEATHER:** But Nita, you sounded angry with Sarah.

**DIRECTOR:** Aha! It seems to me that if you people had been rehearsing instead of gossiping, this problem wouldn't have occurred. Now, CAN WE GET TO WORK?

**EVERYONE:** OKAY!

**JASON:** (*To* BRIT.) I've heard that all Directors are kind of cranky.

**DIRECTOR:** (*Throws hands up in air.*) AUGH!

For the **real story** read Philemon

# Story of Onesimus

**Characters: NARRATOR; ONESIMUS** (oh-NEHS-eh-muhs), our main character and, hopefully, a hero; **SERIUS,** a slave; **PAUL,** a famous follower of Jesus and writer of letters

**Props:** Characters may wish to pantomime the use of props.

**NARRATOR:** This is the story of the slave Onesimus. The story begins at the home of Philemon, the owner of Onesimus.

**ONESIMUS:** *(Enters with sack.)* These should bring enough money to get me to Rome.

**SERIUS:** *(Enters and sees* ONESIMUS.*)* Hey, Onesimus, where you going with that sack?

**ONESIMUS:** None of your business! *(Turns to go and drops a silver necklace from sack.)*

**SERIUS:** *(Stoops to pick up necklace.)* Wait a minute—this belongs to our master's wife. I know what you're doing—you're running away, and stealing on top of it.

**ONESIMUS:** So what if I am? That's not your problem. You just keep your mouth shut.

**SERIUS:** No skin off my back if you run away, but it'll be skin off your back, I'm sure!

**ONESIMUS:** I'll risk anything to get out of slavery! Out of my way! *(Exits.)*

**NARRATOR:** Onesimus ran all the way to Rome and into a man who was about to change his life.

**ONESIMUS:** *(Bumps into* PAUL.*)* Watch where you're going!

**PAUL:** Are you injured?

**ONESIMUS:** No. But why should you care? What's it to you?

**PAUL:** The One I serve asks me to care about others.

**ONESIMUS:** You're a slave?

**PAUL:** In a way, I am! I am a servant of my Lord Jesus Christ.

**ONESIMUS:** Why are you wearing chains?

**PAUL:** *(Laughs.)* You are very observant, my friend. I am happy to tell you that for the sake of my Lord, I am a prisoner of Rome.

**ONESIMUS:** And you're HAPPY? You must be nuts! I'd NEVER serve anyone who'd ask ME to be a prisoner!

**PAUL:** Perhaps if you knew more about Him, you would. Come, let's talk. *(Both exit.)*

**NARRATOR:** When Onesimus heard the good news about Jesus, he realized that Jesus was the Master he wanted to serve. Onesimus worked hard to serve his new Master,

Jesus, and in the process he was a great help to Paul. But one thing really bothered Onesimus. *(PAUL enters.)*

**ONESIMUS:** *(Enters.)* Paul, there's something I must tell you. You're not going to like it.

**PAUL:** Onesimus, you are like a son to me. Do not be afraid to tell me anything.

**ONESIMUS:** *(Ashamed.)* Paul, I am not a free man. I'm a runaway slave. Not only that, but I stole from my master before I left.

**PAUL:** Onesimus, this IS serious news. Who was your master?

**ONESIMUS:** A man named Philemon in Colosse.

**PAUL:** Philemon? Why, I know him well. He has a church meeting in his house! I've been there.

**ONESIMUS:** Well, I want to go home, but I'm afraid!

**PAUL:** Onesimus, I don't know how I will get along without you, but you must return to your master. Do you understand why?

**ONESIMUS:** *(Sadly.)* Yes, I must be honest about what I have done. I know that.

**PAUL:** Cheer up, son. I will write Philemon a letter on your behalf. *(PAUL hands ONESIMUS a letter and exits.)*

**NARRATOR:** So Onesimus returned to his master not knowing what fate awaited him. All that stood between him and horrible punishment was Paul's letter.

**SERIUS:** *(Enters.)* Onesimus! What are YOU doing here?

**ONESIMUS:** I have returned to set things right with our master, Philemon.

**SERIUS:** You've done WHAT? You know the punishment for runaway slaves!

**ONESIMUS:** Yes, but I have a letter.

**SERIUS:** A letter? Who's it from? The emperor? That's what you'll need to save you!

**ONESIMUS:** I've already been saved, in a way. I may have to take the punishment our master may give me. But it's all in this letter from Paul.

**SERIUS:** You know Paul? The apostle? Then you're now a follower of Jesus! Well, brother, I'll tell our master you've come home!

For the **real deal** read James 3:2-12

# Central Control

**Characters: DIRECTOR,** supervisor; **TRAINEE,** new employee; **No. 14,** worker

**Scene:** Joan's Brain, Central Control.

**DIRECTOR:** I think you're going to like working here at Central Control. In this part of the brain, we oversee all communication. We're the most important part of Brain Control.

**TRAINEE:** When I was at Heart Pumping, they said THAT was the most important part of Brain Control!

**DIRECTOR:** Heart Pumping! What do they know? It's just in and out over there. Here we sort, we analyze, we decide.

**TRAINEE:** Ah, yes, sir!

**DIRECTOR:** Now, over here we have the Sensory Input station. All the information from the five senses comes to this station. And what are those senses, trainee?

**TRAINEE:** HEARING, SEEING, TOUCHING, SMELLING, and, ah..., TASTING, SIR!

**DIRECTOR:** Very good. I see you've read the manual. Now, the information is passed along the conveyor belt to the Knowledge Deposit. Here, specially trained workers analyze the information and develop a Knowledge Packet to go with it.

**TRAINEE:** What's in a Knowledge Packet, sir?

**DIRECTOR:** Everything Joan has already learned about the information.

**TRAINEE:** Everything?

**DIRECTOR:** Everything!!

**TRAINEE:** Wow!

**DIRECTOR:** Now, the whole bundle is sent to the Choices Department and then the Logic Stop. This is our quality control checkpoint. Logic workers double check everyone's work. They throw out any misunderstandings, and senseless and uncaring remarks. Finally, it's taken to the Response Center, where a recommended remark is decided upon and sent to Joan.

**TRAINEE:** But all that must take a long time, sir.

**DIRECTOR:** That's why we always have Joan on a "Think-Before-You-Speak" status.

**TRAINEE:** I see, sir.

**DIRECTOR:** Hm, there seems to be a lot of activity in the Sensory area. Is there a problem, Number 14?

**NO. 14:** She's sending this stuff out too fast, sir. We're ready to blow!

**DIRECTOR:** Send the "Count-to-Ten" alert!

**NO. 14:** Yes, sir! Oh no, look at these angry

words. They're coming one after another! They're aimed at her Mom!

**DIRECTOR:** Catch them! Don't let them out!

**NO. 14:** They're going too fast, sir! They're gone!!

**DIRECTOR:** No! What are the damages?

**NO. 14:** It's not good, sir. All stations have crashed. It's going to take a while to clear this one up.

**DIRECTOR:** How's our Spiritual Connection holding?

**NO. 14:** Sorry, sir. With all this commotion, the connection was lost.

**DIRECTOR:** But we can't get this damage fixed without it! See if you can get her to open it up again.

**NO. 14:** Yes, sir.

**TRAINEE:** What happened, sir?

**DIRECTOR:** Joan said something pretty bad to her mother before giving us time to work on it. And just look at the damage!

**TRAINEE:** What's the Spiritual Connection, sir?

**DIRECTOR:** Surely they told you about the Spiritual Connection in Heart Pumping?

**TRAINEE:** No, sir. It's like you said, sir—it's mostly just in and out.

**DIRECTOR:** Well, the Spiritual Connection is our connection to the Creator. The One who designed this place. Without His help, repair is impossible. We need that connection open so we can run according to His plan.

**TRAINEE:** But why would Joan do something that would cause a disconnection?

**DIRECTOR:** She forgets, I guess. Oh look, the "I-Made-a-Mistake" message got through. She's requesting forgiveness from the Creator. Okay, the Spiritual Connection is coming back on-line. Now we can get somewhere.

**NO. 14:** Should we send the "I'd-Better-Apologize-to-Mom" message?

**DIRECTOR:** Of course! We can't keep the Spiritual connection on line until Joan makes things right with her mother. So, what do you think, trainee?

**TRAINEE:** I hope there aren't too many days like this.

**DIRECTOR:** So do I, trainee, so do I.

*Note: James 3:2-12 tells about the damage that can be caused by unkind words.*

# Bible Index

## BIBLE INDEX CONTINUED

## New Testament

## BIBLE INDEX CONTINUED

# Character Index

## CHARACTER INDEX CONTINUED

# CHARACTER INDEX CONTINUED

## CHARACTER INDEX CONTINUED

# CHARACTER INDEX CONTINUED

# Topical Index

## How to Use the CD-ROM

### Getting Started:

- Insert the CD-ROM into the CD-ROM drive.

- Double-click on *The Big Book of Captivating Skits* pdf icon located on the CD-ROM.

- Once the file is opened you can manually scroll through the pages (using the scroll bar on the right of the Acrobat window), or you can access any skit by clicking on the skit title in the table of contents. At the bottom of each page the Return to Main Menu link will take you back to the table of contents.

- You can print single or multiple pages. In the Adobe Acrobat Reader print dialogue box select the appropriate button in the print range field. (Before printing please read "How to Make Clean Copies from This Book" on page 2.)

### Problems?

- If you have any problems that you can't solve by reading the printed or online manuals that came with your software, please contact the technical support department for the software manufacturer. (Sorry, but Gospel Light cannot provide software support.)

# More Great Resources from Gospel Light

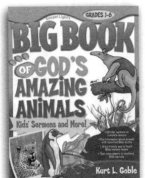

### The Big Book of God's Amazing Animals
This book includes 52 lessons about a variety of animals that will intrigue kids, such as dolphins, penguins, koala bears, whales and condors. Each lesson relates facts about the featured animal to a particular Bible verse. As kids learn about fascinating animals that God created, they'll also learn about Him and how He wants them to live.
**ISBN 08307.37146**

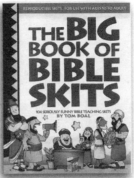

### The Big Book of Bible Skits
*Tom Boal*
104 seriously funny Bible-teaching skits. Each skit comes with Bible background, performance tips, prop suggestions, discussion questions and more. Ages 10 to adult. Reproducible.
**ISBN 08307.19164**

### The Really Big Book of Kids' Sermons and Object Talks with CD-ROM
This reproducible resource for children's pastors is packed with 156 sermons (one a week for three years) that are organized by topics such as friendship, prayer, salvation and more. Each sermon includes an object talk using a household object, discussion questions, prayer and optional information for older children. Reproducible.
**ISBN 08307.36573**

### The Big Book of Volunteer Appreciation Ideas
*Joyce Tepfer*
This reproducible book is packed with 100 great thank-you ideas for teachers, volunteers and helpers in any children's ministry program. An invaluable resource for showing your gratitude!
**ISBN 08307.33094**

### The Big Book of Christian Growth
Discipling made easy! 306 discussion cards based on Bible passages, and 75 games and activities for preteens. Reproducible.
**ISBN 08307.25865**

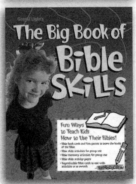

### The Big Book of Bible Skills
Active games that teach a variety of Bible skills (book order, major divisions of the Bible, location references, key themes). Ages 8 to 12. Reproducible.
**ISBN 08307.23463**

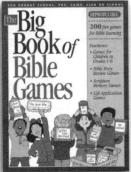

### The Big Book of Bible Games
200 fun, active games to review Bible stories and verses and to apply Bible truths to everyday life. For ages 6 to 12. Reproducible.
**ISBN 08307.18214**

### The Big Book of Bible Games #2
150 active games—balloon games, creative team relays, human bowling, and more—that combine physical activity with Bible learning. Games are arranged by Bible theme and include discussion questions. For grades 1 to 6. Reproducible.
**ISBN 08307.30532**

**To order, visit your local Christian bookstore or www.gospellight.com**

**Gospel Light**
God's Word for a Kid's World!

# Honor Your
# Sunday School Teachers

**SUNDAY SCHOOL**
**TEACHER**
APPRECIATION DAY
Third Sunday in October

## On Sunday School Teacher Appreciation Day
## the Third Sunday in October

Churches across America are invited to set aside the third Sunday in October as a day to honor Sunday School teachers for their dedication, hard work and life-changing impact on their students. That's why Gospel Light launched **Sunday School Teacher Appreciation Day** in 1993, with the goal of honoring the 15 million Sunday School teachers nationwide who dedicate themselves to teaching the Word of God to children, youth and adults.

Visit **www.mysundayschoolteacher.com** to learn great ways to honor your teachers on Sunday School Teacher Appreciation Day and throughout the year.

NOMINATE YOUR TEACHERS FOR SUNDAY SCHOOL TEACHER OF THE YEAR!

**Winner Receives a Dream Vacation to Hawaii!**

**An integral part of Sunday School Teacher Appreciation Day** is the national search for the **Sunday School Teacher of the Year.** This award was established in honor of Dr. Henrietta Mears— a famous Christian educator who influenced the lives of such well-known and respected Christian leaders as Dr. Billy Graham, Bill and Vonette Bright, Dr. Richard Halverson, and many more.

You can honor your Sunday School teachers by nominating them for this award. If one of your teachers is selected, he or she will receive **a dream vacation for two to Hawaii,** plus free curriculum, resources and more for your church!

Nominate your teachers online at **www.mysundayschoolteacher.com.**

Sponsored by

**Gospel Light**

*Helping you honor Sunday School teachers,*
*the unsung heroes of the faith.*

In Partnership With